IN MEMORY OF

Helen Lovitt

from

Allen and Georgia Ruff

THE DWIGHT PUBLIC LIBRARY

MOTHERS

*A celebration
in prose, poetry,
and photographs
of mothers
and motherhood*

Edited by
ALEXANDRA TOWLE

SIMON AND SCHUSTER

NEW YORK • LONDON • TORONTO • SYDNEY • TOKYO

Copyright © 1988 by The Watermark Press
All rights reserved
including the right of reproduction
in whole or in part in any form.
Published by Simon and Schuster
A Division of Simon & Schuster Inc.
Simon & Schuster Building
Rockefeller Center
1230 Avenue of the Americas
New York, NY 10020
SIMON AND SCHUSTER and colophon are
registered trademarks of Simon & Schuster Inc.
Designed by Edith Fowler
Picture Editor: Cheryl Moch

10   9   8   7   6   5   4   3   2   1

Library of Congress Cataloging in Publication Data
ISBN 0-671-66056-X

CONTENTS

THE
MATERNAL INSTINCT

Nancy Friday

MY MOTHER/MY SELF

We are raised to believe that mother love is different from other kinds of love. It is not open to error, doubt, or to the ambivalence of ordinary affections. This is an illusion.

Mothers may love their children, but they sometimes do not like them. The same woman who may be willing to put her body between her child and a runaway truck will often resent the day-by-day sacrifice the child unknowingly demands of her time, sexuality, and self-development.

Theodor Reik

OF LOVE AND LUST

Romance fails us—and so do friendships—but the relationship of— Mother and Child—remains indelible and indestructible—the strongest bond upon this earth.

Macaulay

In after life you may have friends fond, dear friends, but never will you have again the inexpressible love and gentleness lavished upon you which none but a Mother bestows.

Euripides

> Oh what a power is motherhood, possessing
> A potent spell
> All women alike
> Fight fiercely for a child.

Priscilla Kincaid-Smith

No woman who has not experienced the mixed blessings of mother-hood, could possibly imagine the strength of the tie between a mother and her children. Any working mother who wishes to continue working when she has children needs a serious dedication to her work, if she is to resist the temptation of spending all day with her children.

Barbara Trapido

BROTHER OF
THE MORE FAMOUS JACK

The house, as it presents itself from the road, is like a house one might see on a jigsaw puzzle box, seasonally infested with tall hollyhocks. The kind one put together on a tea tray while recovering from the measles.

We are in the Sussex countryside, not far from Glyndebourne. We are in Virginia Woolf country. Mrs. Goldman is in her vegetable garden, but leaves it and comes over when she sees us. She puts down a gardener's sieve containing potatoes and a lettuce and takes John's hands warmly in her own.

"Darling John," she says. "How truly lovely to see you. You're as handsome as ever, but I have to tell you you are going grey." Her voice is a stylish combination of upper-class vowels and tongue-tied sibilants.

"You're pregnant," John says reproachfully, still holding her hands. "You were pregnant when I left." She smiles at him.

"But not quite as pregnant as this, was I?" she says. Jane Goldman has that indiscreet full-term bulge women get when the foetal head engages. She stands hugely in strong farmer's wellingtons into which she has tucked some very old corduroy trousers. She has these tied together under a man's shirt with pyjama cords because the zip won't come together over the bulge. Bits of hair are falling out of her dark brown plait. She has a face like a madonna. She wears a contained, ironic smile which makes dimples in her cheeks and is blessed with the bluest of eyes. A neglected Burne-Jones, she is, in wellingtons.

"New babies have such lovely legs," she says in her own defence. "That's an awfully nice pullover thing you're wearing, John. What elegance you always bring to our establishment." John Millet has clad his torso in an impeccable sky-blue velour article with sleeves that blouse into ribbed wristbands.

"This is Katherine," he says. Jane Goldman peers at me with her myopic blue eyes in the bright sunlight.

"Hello there," she says, taking my hand and bestowing her smile upon me.

"Why have you grown your hair?" John says possessively. "This heavy Teutonic hairstyle. I don't like it."

Jane laughs. "It's not a hairstyle. It's neglect," she says. "Go and admire my daughter. Rosie is over there. Isn't she nice?" She gestures to where her leggy, dark nine-year-old and friend are making a tent with a garden bench and a collection of dusty Persian rugs.

"Your children are dragging your heirlooms in the mud," John says. Jane surveys her wordly goods with marvellous indifference.

"If you want the truth, John," she says, "you won't get it from Jake. I'm pregnant because it seemed a delightful idea to him and me after we'd blown all the twins' birthday money last winter on an extravagant drunken lunch. I'm afraid it impaired our judgement. We made eyes at each other over grilled lobsters and resolved to jettison our humble rubber goods. I agree with Jake about the pills and the other things. You may not, but then you haven't been on the slab in the Family Planning Clinic. Anyway, the point is that any day now we'll suffer for it. My darling Jake will hold bowls for me half the night, while I vomit in labour and botch the breathing exercises, which I always do. Then he'll spend the next three years suffering his insomniac's agony after being woken at night. And he'll put up with us having our bed peed on and his manuscripts scribbled over. Jonathan woke him up nearly every night for four years. He and Roger are violently allergic to each other. Rosie caused him to slip a disc last summer. He had to spend all his income tax rebate on what Sammy here calls his fizzy old therapist. Oh, if only they weren't always so lovely, John, it wouldn't be half so tempting." John smiles at her.

Nora Ephron

CRAZY SALAD

It's about this mother-of-us-all business.

It is Sunday morning in Miami Beach, the day before the Democratic Convention is to begin, and the National Women's Political Caucus is holding a press conference. The cameras are clicking at Gloria, and Bella has swept in trailed by a vortex of television crews, and there is Betty, off to the side, just slightly out of frame. The cameras will occasionally catch a shoulder of her flowered granny dress or a stray wisp of her chaotic graying hair or one of her hands churning up the air; but it will be accidental, background in a photograph of Gloria and Bella. Betty's eyes are darting back and forth trying to catch someone's attention, anyone's attention. No use, Gloria is speaking, and then Bella, and then Sissy Farenthold from Texas. And finally . . . Betty's lips tighten as she hears the inevitable introduction coming: "Betty Friedan, the mother of us all." That does it. "I'm getting sick and tired of this mother-of-us-all thing," she says. She is absolutely right, of course: in the women's movement, to be called the mother of anything is rarely a compliment. And what it means in this context, make no mistake, is that Betty, having in fact given birth, ought to cut the cord. Bug off. Shut up. At the very least, retire gracefully to the role of senior citizen, professor emeritus. Betty Friedan has no intention of doing anything of the kind. It's her baby, damn it. Her movement.

ON DOROTHY L. SAYERS

By the end of May at the latest Dorothy must have been sure that she was pregnant, and the future had to be faced. Everything in her rebelled against the thought of an abortion—her religious beliefs, her upbringing, and the sense of physical outrage which is common to many women, but which seems to have been particularly strong in Dorothy, given her feeling for physical "wholesomeness."

On the other hand, the pregnancy was unquestionably a disaster. Though she had wanted a child by John Cournos, she had never much cared for children in general; and to be encumbered by a baby now could be seen only as a most unwelcome interruption of the career which she had so recently, and with such effort, got under way. Nor was it only the job that was in danger. Her relationship with Bill was also threatened, for he had no inclination whatever for fatherhood.

So whatever physical fulfillment her condition afforded her, Dorothy enjoyed none of the psychological satisfactions of a woman happily with child. She could talk about it to no one. To her lover it was a nuisance, and to her parents, with whom she had shared other problems so openly and blithely, it would have been a shock which they could not endure—or so she believed. That being the case, she decided that she could confide in nobody, for fear that the news might get back to them.

The arrangement with Ivy was that Dorothy should pay her three pounds per month—which she dutifully did, increasing the sum as the cost of living rose, as John Anthony's requirements increased, and as her own financial situation made her more able.

At first she went to Oxford as frequently as she possibly could to see the baby; but after eight or nine months the visits grew gradually less frequent and the excuses for not managing to get to Oxford at that particular weekend more numerous. Dorothy was a lady with a positive turn of mind, and though she would never abandon her responsibilities, she would certainly not dwell on her failures or waste time on something in which she had perforce only an unsatisfactory and intermittent role. The bringing up of the boy had been entrusted to Ivy; Dorothy could only drop in from time to time, and coo and comment. There is nothing so frustrating as being half in, half out of an enterprise, having an interest but no responsibility; she had enough sense to know that there could be only one person who stood in the role of mother to the boy, and she was not the one.

Dorothy's attitude towards John Anthony was as brisk and businesslike as her attitude to everything else. When he broke a collar bone, at the age of two and a half, she wrote: "I am glad the kid has pluck anyhow —maternal affection is by no means my strong point, I must say, but if there must be children, it is preferable they should have some guts."

Dorothy came back from her trip with several things settled: she was not going to make the break with Mac—she would stand by him till death did them part; she had given up hope of bringing Anthony into the home, Mac being the way he was; and she had gone as far towards acknowledging Anthony as she possibly could in the circumstances, without actually letting the cat out of the bag. Personal matters thus being tied up, she was ready to write the book that would say, clearly and decisively, that in her opinion no trust could be placed in personal matters; that the only salvation came through work, through craftsmanship, through the creations of mind and of hand and through the intellectual passion that controlled those creations.

John Nicholson

MEN AND WOMEN

Where human beings are concerned, the evidence for a maternal instinct is rather flimsy. The argument in favour of it, like so many of the

arguments we have examined, begins in the mists of time. Some biolo-
gists maintain that caring for children must have been bred into women,
and bred out of men, for the species to have survived for so long. They
argue that since primitive children would have been entirely dependent
on their mothers' milk, only those with the most nurturant mothers
could have survived, so that the genes of non-nurturant mothers must
have died out. Men, on the other hand, would have been most likely to
pass on their genes by impregnating as many women as they could lay
their bodies on. So it would have been the genes of the nurturant, stay-
at-home men which would have died out, and those of the hit-and-run
Don Juans which would have been most likely to be perpetuated.

It is impossible to prove that this story is fiction. But we could
write it very differently, and no less plausibly. We might for example
argue that it would have been counter-productive for a primitive man to
sire large numbers of children, because he would have been unable to
provide food and protection for all their mothers. As a result, many of
them would have died. Prolific fathers would also not have been available to stand in for their children's mothers when they became ill, so we
could make a perfectly respectable case for saying that it would actually
have been the stay-at-home man who had the best chance of being
survived by children carrying his genes. This implies that evolutionary
considerations would have favoured the development of an instinct to
produce and rear children in both sexes, and . . . that there is very little
about the way in which mothers and fathers treat their babies—or the
way in which babies respond to their parents—which suggests that any
instinct we may have to bring up children is the prerogative of one sex
rather than the other.

Perhaps the most frequently heard argument in favour of a maternal
instinct stems from the fact that there have been very few societies in
which women have not been responsible for child care. This has led to
the assumption that they are uniquely well equipped for the role. In fact
it proves nothing of the sort. People who argue in this way are merely
putting themselves in the position of the disc-jockey who says, "A million people have bought this record so it must be good," and you have
only to listen to some of the records which sell a million to see how
shaky this proposition is! They are also guilty of a logical error known
as the naturalistic fallacy—the belief that the way things are is the way
they ought to be—which commits them to the view that any change
must be for the worse. It only requires one instance of a historical change
which has been for the good of mankind—the abolition of slavery, for
example—to prove them wrong.

While we are looking at history, it is important to record the fact that although women have always looked after children, they have also been responsible for most of the violence which children have suffered. In societies which permitted infanticide, it was often women who performed the grisly task. Even when it was not sanctioned—in Victorian England, for example—women have been prepared to murder their illegitimate children rather than face social ostracism. No doubt they felt remorseful and deprived as a result of their action. But an "instinct" which is subordinate to economic and social pressures looks increasingly suspect, especially in the light of baby-battering. The factors which cause parents to inflict deliberate physical damage on their children are still something of a mystery. But we know that mothers are far more often involved than fathers (unsurprisingly perhaps, given the relative amounts of time the two sexes spend in their children's company), and that the phenomenon has reached disturbing proportions in recent years.

According to popular wisdom, however, motherhood comes naturally to women. On becoming pregnant, a woman is gripped by a primeval instinct which ensures that she will love, cherish and instinctively recognize the needs of her child after it is born. It may seem churlish to question so attractive a picture, but several lines of evidence suggest that it reflects at least a degree of wishful thinking. For a start, recent surveys have shown that only about half of all women feel an immediate sense of love for their babies. Four out of ten first-time mothers recall that their predominant emotion on holding their baby for the first time was indifference. In the huge majority of cases, however, this is replaced by love and affection within a week of delivery, and it should be said that an early lack of affection is often linked to some understandable cause such as difficult labour, unusually large doses of pain-killers, or depression which existed before the child was born.

The condition of post-natal depression, which affects a significant number of new mothers, is less well understood. Contrary to what many doctors believe, it does not seem to be caused by hormonal irregularities, and is not confined to the weeks after giving birth. It is unknown in most non-industrial societies, especially in those where long-established custom removes the need for parents to make decisions about how to rear their children. Post-natal depression may well be the price of individual freedom and responsibility in this aspect of living. But it is another phenomenon which suggests that we should reexamine one of the two most important implications of the maternal instinct hypothesis: the notion that all women take to motherhood as easily as ducks take to water.

Its second implication—that all normal women must want to become mothers—has led to a great deal of misery, not only among women who have been unable to have children, but also for those mothers—and their children—who had babies as the result of social pressures rather than from a positive desire to do so. Since there is no convincing evidence that women are governed by an instinct to have children, I think we should abandon the notion of a maternal instinct, while acknowledging that the experience of being a mother is one which the great majority of women still prefer not to miss.

But I see no reason to be apprehensive about the well-being of those who decide not to have children. Indeed, the results of a survey carried out recently in Holland suggest that both men and women can be just as happy without children as with them. A large and representative sample of men and women between the ages of twenty-five and sixty-five answered questions about their satisfactions and fears, and their replies offered no support whatever for the view that having children is a recipe for happiness in either sex. Parents in the sample were no happier than non-parents—if anything, the reverse was true—and older people without children were found to be no more anxious about old age or death than those who had children, nor were they more doubtful about the purpose of life. All these findings applied equally to men and women, so if either sex has an innate need to produce children, it seems that a significant proportion of the Dutch population is frustrating it without suffering any obvious ill-effects!

These results are surprising. We might have expected to find that at least the older members of the sample were regretting that they had never had children. But they tie in with the findings of surveys carried out in several countries on the attitudes of parents approaching the time when their children leave home to begin independent lives. It is commonly believed that parents become depressed at this point. There is even a name for the malaise which is supposed to afflict them—the Empty Nest syndrome. But this is the opposite of what researchers have actually found. Most of the couples they have talked to seem to be positively looking foward to life without their children (many of them spontaneously describe it as a bonus for reaching middle age!). If we take these results in conjunction with the finding that 42 percent of British working-class mothers who are confined to their homes with young children suffer from clinical depression, and the fact that up to the age of thirty-five women without children are less prone to neurotic disorders than those who have them, the conclusion seems inevitable: it is impossible to maintain that a woman who decides not to have children must necessarily be less happy than one who makes the opposite decision.

Theodore Zeldin

THE FRENCH

Probably the leading figure in the popularization of women's new hopes, unknown outside France, but to whom virtually every French woman has listened at some time, is Menie Grégoire. She started the first women's problem radio programme in 1967, which instantly won a mass audience, and which created a new public consciousness of shared worries and animosities. Menie Grégoire has, however, deliberately opposed women's liberation as preached both by Simone de Beauvoir and by the Americans, and she has sought to build a distinctive French form of feminism. Menie Grégoire was inspired to get a job by reading Beauvoir, but she says work is not enough. She had married after finishing her history degree and when she was just embarking on research in Egyptology. "I sought, met and snatched love in two months." For ten years she dropped all her intellectual pursuits like a worn-out dress, and had three children. She insists that motherhood has been the most important and best part of her life, more than any career, "more than happiness and love"; and she predicts that her grandchildren will return to the worship of motherhood.

Marilyn French

THE WOMEN'S ROOM

But there were pleasures in Mira's life: the children themselves. They were a deep pleasure, especially when she was alone with them and wasn't anxious about preparing Norm's dinner, or about their making noise. Holding their tiny bodies, bathing them as they gurgled with pleasure, oiling and powdering them while they poked at her face or at their own, trying to figure out what eyes and noses were, she would smile endlessly, unconsciously. She had seen their birth and the birth of her love for them as miraculous, but it was just as miraculous when they first smiled, first sat up, first babbled a sound that resembled, of course, mama. The tedious days were filled with miracles. When a baby first looks at you; when it gets excited at seeing a ray of light and like a dog pawing a gleam, tries to capture it in his hand; or when it laughs that deep, unselfconscious gurgle; or when it cries and you pick it up and it clings sobbing to you, saved from some terrible shadow moving across the room, or a loud clang in the street, or perhaps, already, a bad dream: then you are—happy is not the precise word—filled. Mira still felt as she had the first time she held Normie in the hospital, that the child and her feeling for it were somehow absolute, truer and more binding than any other experience life had to offer: she felt she lived at the blind true core of life.

Robert Graves

I, CLAUDIUS

It will be supposed that my mother Antonia, a beautiful and noble woman brought up to the strictest virtue by her mother Octavia, and

the one passion of my father's life, would have taken the most loving care of me, her youngest child, and even made a particular favourite of me in pity for my misfortunes. But such was not the case. She did all for me that could be expected of her as a duty, but no more. She did not love me. No, she had a great aversion to me, not only because of my sickliness but also because she had had a most difficult pregnancy of me, and then a most painful delivery from which she barely escaped with her life and which left her more or less an invalid for years. My premature birth was due to a shock that she got at the feast given in honour of Augustus when he visited my father at Lyons to inaugurate the "Altar of Roma and Augustus" there: my father was Governor of the Three Provinces of France, and Lyons was his headquarters. A crazy Sicilian slave who was acting as waiter at the feast suddenly drew a dagger and flourished it in the air behind my father's neck. Only my mother saw this happening. She caught the slave's eye and had presence of mind enough to smile at him and shake her head in deprecation, signing to him to put the dagger back. While he hesitated two other waiters followed her glance and were in time to overpower and disarm him. Then she fainted and immediately her pains began. It may well be because of this that I have always had a morbid fear of assassination; for they say that a pre-natal shock can be inherited. But of course there is no real reason for any pre-natal influences to be mentioned. How many of the Imperial family have died a natural death?

Since I was an affectionate child my mother's attitude caused me much misery. I heard from my sister Livilla, a beautiful girl but cruel, vain and ambitious—in a word a typical Claudian of the bad variety— that my mother had called me "a human portent" and said that when I was born the Sibylline books should have been consulted. Also that Nature had begun but never finished me, throwing me aside in disgust as a hopeless start. Also that the ancients were wiser and nobler than ourselves: they exposed all weakly infants on a bare hillside for the good of the race. These may have been embroideries by Livilla on less severe remarks—for seven-months' children are very horrible objects—but I know that once when my mother grew angry on hearing that some senator had introduced a foolish motion in the House she burst out: "That man ought to be put out of the way! He's as stupid as a donkey —what am I saying? Donkeys are sensible beings by comparison—he's as stupid as . . . as . . . Heavens, he's as stupid as my son Claudius!"

G. K. Chesterton

SONGS OF EDUCATION:
III. FOR THE CRÈCHE

(Form 8277059, Sub-Section K)

I remember my mother, the day that we met,
A thing I shall never entirely forget;
And I toy with the fancy that, young as I am,
I should know her again if we met in a tram.
    But mother is happy in turning a crank
    That increases the balance at somebody's bank;
    And I feel satisfaction that mother is free
    From the sinister task of attending to me.

They have brightened our room, that is spacious and cool,
With diagrams used in the Idiot School,
And Books for the Blind that will teach us to see;
But mother is happy, for mother is free.
    For mother is dancing up forty-eight floors,
    For love of the Leeds International Stores,
    And the flame of that faith might perhaps have grown cold,
    With the care of a baby of seven weeks old.

For mother is happy in greasing a wheel
For somebody else, who is cornering Steel;
And though our one meeting was not very long,
She took the occasion to sing me this song:
    "O, hush thee, my baby, the time will soon come
    When thy sleep will be broken with hooting and hum;
    There are handles want turning and turning all day,
    And knobs to be pressed in the usual way;
O, hush thee, my baby, take rest while I croon,
For Progress comes early, and Freedom too soon."

ON GEORGE BERNARD SHAW

In this shabby-genteel home (Synge St., Dublin) her dreams of freedom and splendour with the pensioned cousin of a wealthy banker-baronet were all dispelled; and here, in four years, her three children were born —Lucinda Frances Carr, commonly called Lucy; Elinor Agnes, sometimes called Yuppy, . . . and George Bernard, known as Sonny, though his father, when he was a baby, had called him Bob. It was a graceless house, ill-managed and impecunious. "The adult who has been poor as a child," GBS remarked late in life, "will never get the chill of poverty out of his bones." But he and his sisters had a sharper chill than poverty to bear: a home in which there was no love and little affection. It was ruled by a disillusioned young woman who had neither taste nor talent for domesticity and was married to a furtive drunk whom she despised. "Technically speaking," her son wrote, "I should say she was the worst mother conceivable, always, however, within the limits of the fact that she was incapable of unkindness to any child, animal or flower, or, indeed, to any person or thing whatsoever": a statement which seems to suggest that neglect and incompetence and a total lack of love and affection are not culpable and need not be denounced.

GBS letter to Mrs. Patrick Campbell, after his mother's cremation. "The undertaker approached me in the character of a man shattered with grief; and I, hard as nails and in loyally high spirits (rejoicing irrepressibly in my mother's memory) tried to convey to him that this professional chicanery, as I took it to be, was quite unnecessary. And lo! it wasn't professional chicanery at all. He had done all sorts of work for her for years, and was actually and really in a state about losing her, not merely as a customer, but as a person he liked and was accustomed to. And the coffin was covered with violet cloth, not black."

Sarah Bernhardt

MEMOIRS

My mother was fond of travelling: she would go from Spain to England, from London to Paris, from Paris to Berlin, and from there to Christiania; then she would come back, embrace me, and set out again for Holland, her native country. She used to send my nurse clothing for herself and cakes for me. To one of my aunts she would write: "Look after little Sarah; I shall return in a month's time." A month later she would write another of her sisters: "Go and see the child at her nurse's; I shall be back in a couple of weeks."

One day my mother took me on her knees and said to me, "You are a big girl now, and you must learn to read and write." I was then seven years old and could neither read, write, nor count, as I had been five years with the old nurse and two years ill. "You must go to school," continued my mother, playing with my curly hair, "like a big girl." I did not know what all this meant, and I asked what a school was.

"It's a place where there are many little girls," replied my mother.

"Are they ill?" I asked.

"Oh, no. They are quite well, like you are now, and they play together, and are very gay and happy."

I jumped about in delight and gave free vent to my joy, but on seeing tears in my mother's eyes I flung myself in her arms.

"But what about you, mamma?" I asked. "You will be all alone and you won't have any little girl."

She bent down to me and said, "God has told me that he will send me some flowers and a little baby."

My delight was more and more boisterous.

"Then I shall have a little brother!" I exclaimed, "or else a little sister! Oh, no, I don't want that; I don't like little sisters!"

Mamma kissed me very affectionately, and then I was dressed, I remember, in a blue corded velvet frock, of which I was very proud. Arrayed thus in all my splendour, I waited impatiently for Aunt Rosine's carriage, which was to take us to Auteuil.

It was about three o'clock when she arrived. The housemaid had gone on about an hour before, and I had watched with delight my little trunk and my toys being packed into the carriage. The maid climbed up and took the seat by the driver, in spite of my mother protesting at first against this. When my aunt's magnificent equipage arrived, mamma was the first to get in, slowly and calmly. I got in slowly too, giving myself airs because the concierge and some of the shopkeepers were watching. My aunt then sprang in lightly, but by no means calmly, after giving her orders in English to the stiff, ridiculous-looking coachman, and handing him a paper on which the address was written. Another carriage followed ours, in which three men were seated: Regis L——, a friend of my father's, General de P——, and an artist named Fleury, I think, whose pictures of horses and sporting subjects were very much in vogue just then.

I heard on the way that these gentlemen were going to arrange about a little dinner near Auteuil to console mamma for her great trouble in being separated from me. Some other guests were to be there to meet them. I did not pay very much attention to what mother and my aunt said to each other. Sometimes when they spoke of me they talked either English or German, and smiled at me affectionately. The long drive was greatly appreciated by me, for, with my face pressed against the window and my eyes wide open, I gazed out eagerly at the grey, muddy road, with its ugly houses on each side and its bare trees. I thought it was all very beautiful—because it kept changing.

The carriage stopped at 18, Rue Boileau, Auteuil. On the iron gate was a long, dark signboard, with gold letters. I looked up at it, and mamma said: "You will be able to read that soon, I hope." My aunt whispered to me, "Boarding School. Madame Fressard," and, very promptly, I said to mamma, "It says, 'Boarding School. Madame Fressard.' "

Mamma, my aunt, and the three gentlemen laughed heartily at my assurance, and we entered the house. Mme. Fressard came forward to meet us, and I liked her at once. She was of medium height, rather stout, with a small waist, and her hair turning grey " 'en Sevigné." She had beautiful, large eyes, rather like George Sand's; very white teeth, which showed up all the more as her complexion was rather tawny. She looked healthy, spoke kindly; her hands were plump and her fingers long. She took my hand gently in hers and, half-kneeling, so that her face was level with mine, she said, in a musical voice, "You won't be afraid of me, will you, little girl?" I did not answer, but my face flushed as red as a coxcomb. She asked me several questions, but I refused to reply. They all gathered round me. "Speak, child!" "Come, Sarah, be a good girl!" "Oh, the naughty little child!"

It was all in vain. I remained perfectly mute. The customary round was then made of the bedrooms, the dining-hall, the classrooms, and the usual exaggerated compliments were paid. "How beautifully it is all kept! How spotlessly clean everything is!" and a hundred stupidities of this kind about the comfort of these prisons for children. My mother went aside with Mme. Fressard, and I clung to her knees so that she could not walk. "This is the doctor's prescription," she said, and then followed a long list of things that were to be done for me.

Mme. Fressard smiled rather ironically. "You know, madame," she said to my mother, "we shall not be able to curl her hair like that." "And you certainly will not be able to uncurl it," replied my mother, stroking my head with her gloved hands. "It's a regular wig, and they must never attempt to comb it until it has been well brushed. They could not possibly get the knots out otherwise, and it would hurt her too much. What do you give the children at four o'clock?" she asked, changing the subject. "Oh, a slice of bread and just what the parents leave for them."

"There are twelve pots of different kinds of jam," said my mother, "but she must have jam one day and chocolate another, as she has not a good appetite, and requires change of food. I have brought six pounds of chocolate." Mme. Fressard smiled in a good-natured but rather ironical way. She picked up a packet of the chocolate and looked at the mark.

"Ah, from Marquis? What a spoilt little girl it is!" She patted my cheek with her white fingers, and then, as her eyes fell on a large jar, she looked surprised. "That's cold cream," said my mother. "I make it myself, and I should like my little girl's face and hands to be rubbed with it every night when she goes to bed."

"But—" began Mme. Fressard.

"Oh, I'll pay double laundry expenses for the sheets," interrupted my mother, impatiently. (Ah! my poor mother, I remember quite well that my sheets were changed once a month, like those of the other pupils.)

The farewell moment came at last, and everyone gathered round mamma, and finally carried her off, after a great deal of kissing, and with all kinds of consoling words. "It will be so good for her." "It is just what she needs." "You'll find her quite changed when you see her again," etc., etc.

The General, who was very fond of me, picked me up in his arms and tossed me in the air.

"You little chit," he said; "they are putting you to the barracks, and you'll have to mind your pace."

I pulled his long moustache, and he said, winking, and looking in the direction of Mme. Fressard, who had a slight moustache, "You mustn't do that to the lady, you know!"

My aunt laughed heartily, and my mother gave a little stifled laugh, and the whole troop went off in a regular whirlwind of rustling skirts and farewells, whilst I was taken away to the cage where I was to be imprisoned.

Gloria Vanderbilt

WOMAN TO WOMAN

I've gained a great feeling of peace from being a parent. I'm deeply fulfilled that Stan, for instance, is able to relate to women in a positive way. Because he is able, it's possible for me to let go. His ability to relate to women naturally gives me a sense of achievement, and it's something I want for all my sons. The ability to love is the heart of the matter. That is how we must measure our success or failure at being parents.

The actual experience of being a mother is one of the most fulfilling I've ever had. Pregnancy was the most continuous happiness I've known. Each time I've experienced birth there's been an overbearing feeling of loss, in the hospital right after the baby's birth, when the baby would be taken into the nursery. And then the greatest flooding of joy when the baby would be brought back to me.

My only regret is that I haven't had a daughter. That experience must be extraordinary—for a woman to have a daughter and really see another woman, part image of herself. I often look at my children and think I was once that height—exactly—or read that book, or perhaps dreamed that dream.

It's very hard for me to imagine that a woman would not want to have a child. However, personal feelings aside, I feel we have taken a

giant step forward, in knowing that in today's society a woman can decide she does not want to have children and do so without censure. I believe there are women who should not have children because to do so is against the inner fiber of their beings. Their involvements and interests are concentrated elsewhere. Having a child will only distract and therefore the child will always feel a sense of not belonging and of alienation. A woman must extend herself a great deal to raise a child successfully. Every mother knows this, every woman senses it. I respect enormously a woman who knows herself well enough to come to the decision that she is not meant to be a mother. I know of many women who have been pressured by their parents or husbands into having a child because it was "unnatural" not to. It takes courage to stand fast by one's inner truth under these circumstances.

William Shakespeare

MACBETH

Lady Macbeth comments on her husband's failure to murder the King.

LADY M: What beast was it, then,
That made you break this enterprise to me?
When you durst do it, then you were a man;
And, to be more than what you were, you would
Be so much more the man . . . I have given suck, and know
How tender 'tis to love the babe that milks me:
I would, while it was smiling in my face,
Have pluck'd my nipple from his boneless gums,
And dash'd the brains out, had I so sworn as you
Have done to this.

MACBETH: Bring forth men-children only!
For thy undaunted mettle should compose
Nothing but males.

Ira Levin

ROSEMARY'S BABY

The thing to do was kill it. Obviously. Wait till they were all sitting at the other end, then run over, push away Laura-Louise, and grab it and throw it out the window. And jump out after it. *Mother Slays Baby and Self at Bramford*.

Save the world from God-knows-what. From Satan-knows-what.

A tail! The buds of his horns!

She wanted to scream, to die.

She would do it, throw it out and jump.

They were all milling around now. Pleasant cocktail party. The Japanese was taking pictures; of Guy, of Stavropoulos, of Laura-Louise holding the baby.

She turned away, not wanting to see.

Those eyes! Like an animal's, a tiger's, not like a human being's!

He *wasn't* a human being, of course. He was—some kind of a half-breed.

And how dear and sweet he had looked before he had opened those yellow eyes! The tiny chin, a bit like Brian's; the sweet mouth; all that lovely orange-red hair . . . It would be nice to look at him again, if only he wouldn't open those yellow animal-eyes.

She tasted the tea. It was tea.

No, she *couldn't* throw him out the window. He was her baby, no matter who the father was. What she had to do was go to someone who would understand. Like a priest. Yes, that was the answer; a priest. It was a problem for the Church to handle. For the Pope and all the cardinals to deal with, not stupid Rosemary Reilly from Omaha.

Killing was wrong, no matter what.

She drank more tea.

He began whimpering because Laura-Louise was rocking the bassinet too fast, so of course the idiot began rocking it faster.

She stood it as long as she could and then got up and went over.

"Get away from here," Laura-Louise said. "Don't you come near Him. Roman!"

"You're rocking him too fast," she said.

"Sit down!" Laura-Louise said, and to Roman, "Get her out of here. Put her back where she belongs."

Rosemary said, "She's rocking him too fast; that's why he's whimpering."

"Mind your own business!" Laura-Louise said.

"Let Rosemary rock Him," Roman said.

Laura-Louise stared at him.

"Go on," he said, standing behind the bassinet's hood. "Sit down with the others. Let Rosemary rock Him."

"She's liable—"

"*Sit down with the others, Laura-Louise.*"

She huffed, and marched away.

"Rock Him," Roman said to Rosemary, smiling. He moved the bassinet back and forth toward her, holding it by the hood.

She stood still and looked at him. "You're trying to—get me to be his mother," she said.

"*Aren't* you His mother?" Roman said. "Go on. Just rock Him till He stops complaining."

She let the black-covered handle come into her hand, and closed her fingers around it. For a few moments they rocked the bassinet between them, then Roman let go and she rocked it alone, nice and slowly. She glanced at the baby, saw his yellow eyes, and looked to the window. "You should oil the wheels," she said. "That could bother him too."

"I will," Roman said. "You see? He's stopped complaining. He knows who you are."

"Don't be silly," Rosemary said, and looked at the baby again. He was watching her. His eyes weren't that bad really, now that she was prepared for them. It was the surprise that had upset her. They were pretty in a way. "What are his hands like?" she asked, rocking him.

"They're very nice," Roman said. "He has claws, but they're very tiny and pearly. The mitts are only so He doesn't scratch Himself, not because His hands aren't attractive."

"He looks worried," she said.

Dr. Sapirstein came over. "A night of surprises," he said.

"Go away," she said, "or I'm going to spit in your face."

"Go away, Abe," Roman said, and Dr. Sapirstein nodded and went away.

"Not you," Rosemary said to the baby. "It's not *your* fault. I'm angry at *them,* because they tricked me and lied to me. Don't look so worried; I'm not going to hurt you."

"He knows that," Roman said.

"Then what does he look so worried for?" Rosemary said. "The poor little thing. Look at him."

"In a minute," Roman said. "I have to attend to my guests. I'll be right back." He backed away, leaving her alone.

"Word of honor I'm not going to hurt you," she said to the baby. She bent over and untied the neck of his gown. "Laura-Louise made this too tight, didn't she. I'll make it a little looser and then you'll be more comfortable. You have a very cute chin; are you aware of the fact? You have strange yellow eyes, but you have a very cute chin."

She tied the gown more comfortably for him.

Poor little creature.

He couldn't be *all* bad, he just *couldn't*. Even if he was half Satan, wasn't he half *her* as well, half decent, ordinary, sensible, human being? If she worked *against* them, exerted a good influence to counteract their bad one . . .

"You have a room of your own, do you know that?" she said, undoing the blanket around him, which was also too tight. "It has white-and-yellow wallpaper and a white crib with yellow bumpers, and there isn't one drop of witchy old black in the whole place. We'll show it to you when you're ready for your next feeding. In case you're curious, *I* happen to be the lady who's been supplying all that milk you've been drinking. I'll bet you thought it comes in bottles, didn't you. Well it doesn't; it comes in *mothers,* and I'm yours. That's right, Mr. Worryface. You seem to greet the idea with no enthusiasm whatsoever."

Silence made her look up. They were gathering around to watch her, stopping at a respectful distance.

She felt herself blushing and turned back to tucking the blanket around the baby. "*Let* them watch," she said; "we don't care, do we? We just want to be all cosy and comfortable, like so. There. Better?"

"Hail Rosemary," Helen Wees said.

The others took it up. "Hail Rosemary. Hail Rosemary." Minnie and Stavropoulos and Dr. Sapirstein. "Hail Rosemary." Guy said it too. "Hail Rosemary." Laura-Louise moved her lips but made no sound. "Hail Rosemary, mother of Adrian!" Roman said. She looked up from the bassinet. "It's Andrew," she said. "Andrew John Woodhouse." "Adrian Steven," Roman said.

Guy said, "Roman, look," and Stavropoulos, at Roman's other side, touched his arm and said, "Is the name of so great an importance?"

"It is. Yes. It is," Roman said. "His name is Adrian Steven."

Rosemary said, "I understand why you'd like to call him that, but I'm sorry; you can't. His name is Andrew John. He's my child, not yours, and this is one point that I'm not even going to argue about. This and the clothes. He can't wear black all the time."

Roman opened his mouth but Minnie said, "Hail Andrew" in a loud voice, looking right at him.

Everyone else said "Hail Andrew" and "Hail Rosemary, mother of Andrew" and "Hail Satan."

Rosemary tickled the baby's tummy. "You didn't like Adrian, did you?" she asked him. "I should think not. Adrian Steven! Will you *please* stop looking so worried?" She poked the tip of his nose. "Do you know how to smile yet, Andy? Do you? Come on, little funny-eyes Andy, can you smile? Can you smile for Mommy?" She tapped the silver ornament and set it swinging. "Come on, Andy," she said. "One little smile. Come on, Andy-candy."

The Japanese slipped forward with his camera, crouched, and took two three four pictures in quick succession.

Nicholas Mosely

RULES OF THE GAME

My mother seems to have tried, in a way beyond what was usual at the time and for her class, to be a "good" mother: she was certainly seen as such: but it would have been almost impossible for her to take much of her allegiance away from Tom. Tom himself tried (for the sake of *Ganzheit?*) to be a good father: but it was his theory that the upbringing of children should be left to "professionals": this was the same sort of theory that had led him to believe that the maintenance of aeroplanes should be left to professionals when he had crashed in 1915. The conventions of the time were that upper-class children should visit their mother in her bedroom after breakfast, and that they should go down to be on show in the drawing room after tea; but for the rest of the time their place was in the nursery, which was in relation to their parents' world as real life is to a stage.

In the afternoons we would go down to our mother in the drawing room when she and my father were there. I remember nothing of these times. One of my sister's few memories (she was at Smith Square on and off till she was ten) is of our mother reading a story to us in the drawing room and then having to break off and rush away to vote in the House of Commons—a bell which had been installed in the house having gone off like a burglar alarm.

Children find it difficult to be aware of their parents' sicknesses: parents are like the natural course of events: what happens when a course of events gets out of joint? I remember getting on badly with my sister at this time: we had ferocious fights: after one which went up and down the corridors of the huge hotel like one of our father's street-fights my mother came out of her room and admonished both of us equally. I was outraged at this: I thought I was in the right: but anyway, where was justice in a world that did not even enquire into rights? I rushed into our bedroom and locked myself in the lavatory. I thought I would stay there until I died; then the grown-ups would be sorry. My mother and sister did come to the door from time to time and ask me to come out: they even pushed food under the door for me: I pushed this back. It seemed that I was in there for a vast stretch of time: I suppose in fact it was no more than most of a day. I became aware after a time that although I seemed to be winning there was in fact no such thing as winning: I would lose face if I came out but if I stayed in I would die: this might be some sort of victory, but I would not be there to see it. This perhaps is a common romantic predicament. Eventually I emerged tentatively at night and my mother appeared at the bedroom door and held out her arms to me and I ran into them and cried. I remember this well: it is almost the only time I remember my mother holding me.

At Abinger Hill, in my dormitory, I remember the headmaster coming in and saying Nanny was downstairs and would I go to her; and I was so pleased, so pleased; I had been back at school for about a week; I had been told my mother was ill, but children do not quite believe their parents' illnesses. (I had written to her two days before. "How are you feeling? And is your tummy still aching?") I ran down to the headmaster's drawing-room and there was Nanny on the sofa and she told me my mother was dead and there was the feeling of the bottom falling out of the world, space and time going, and a terrible fear that this might not be bearable. I cried. Perhaps it is true that I remember so little about my mother because of what was not bearable.

Nancy Mitford

THE PURSUIT OF LOVE

Linda's child, a girl, was born in May. She was ill for a long time before, and very ill indeed at her confinement. The doctors told her that she must never have another child, as it would almost certainly kill her if she did. This was a blow to the Kroesigs, as bankers, it seems, like kings, require many sons, but Linda did not appear to mind at all. She took no interest whatever in the baby she had got. I went to see her as soon as I was allowed to. She lay in a bower of blossom and pink roses, and looked like a corpse. I was expecting a baby myself, and naturally took a great interest in Linda's.

"What are you going to call her—where is she, anyway?"

"In Sister's room—it shrieks. Moira, I believe."

"Not Moira, darling, you can't. I never heard such an awful name."

"Tony likes it, he had a sister called Moira who died. . . ."

"All the same, I don't see how you can saddle the poor little thing with a name like Moira, it's too unkind."

"Not really, if you think. It'll have to grow up a Moira if the Kroesigs are to like it (people always grow up to their names I've noticed) and they might as well like it because frankly, I don't."

"Linda, how can you be so naughty, and, anyway, you can't possibly tell whether you like her or not, yet."

"Oh, yes I can. I can always tell if I like people from the start, and I don't like Moira, that's all . . . wait till you see her."

At this point the Sister came in, and Linda introduced us.

"Oh, you are the cousin I hear so much about," she said. "You'll want to see the baby."

She went away and presently returned carrying a Moses basket full of wails.

"Poor thing," said Linda indifferently. "It's really kinder not to look."

"Don't pay any attention to her," said the Sister. "She pretends to be a wicked woman, but it's all put on."

I did look, and, deep down among the frills and lace, there was the usual horrid sight of a howling orange in a fine black wig.

"Isn't she sweet," said the Sister. "Look at her little hands."

I shuddered slightly, and said:

"Well, I know it's dreadful of me, but I don't much like them as small as that; I'm sure she'll be divine in a year or two."

The wails now entered on a crescendo, and the whole room was filled with hideous noise.

"Poor soul," said Linda. "I think it must have caught sight of itself in a glass. Do take it away, Sister."

Aunt Emily said at once, when I told her about Linda and poor Moira:

"She's too young. I don't believe very young mothers ever get wrapped up in their babies. It's when women are older that they so adore their children, and maybe it's better for the children to have young unadoring mothers and to lead more detached lives."

"But Linda seems to loathe her."

"That's so like Linda," said Davey. "She has to do things by extremes."

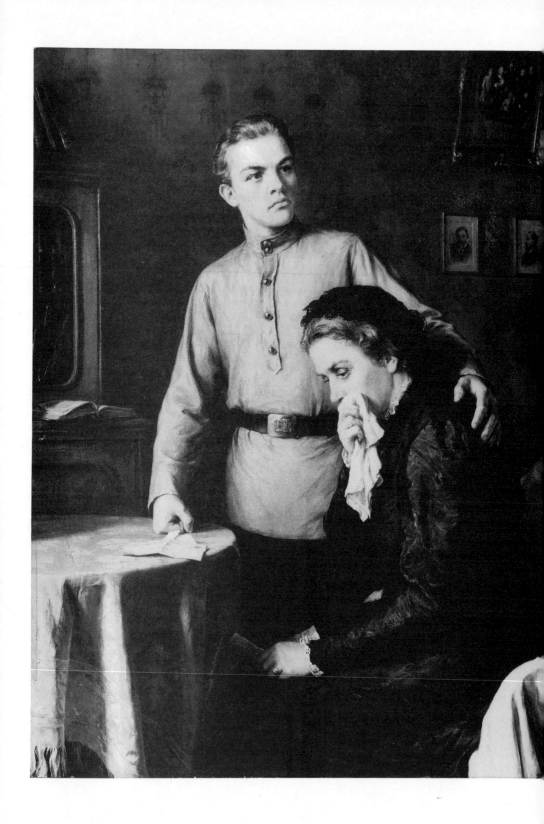

MOTHERS AND SONS

Sigmund Freud

A man who has been the indisputable favourite of his mother keeps for life the feeling of a conqueror, that confidence of success that often induces real success.

Anonymous

Clean-limbed American boys are not like any others.
Only clean-limbed American boys have mothers.

Quentin Crisp

THE NAKED CIVIL SERVANT

My mother protected me from the world and my father threatened me with it.

Gabriel Fielding

THE BIRTHDAY KING

It's not what men fight for. They fight in the last resort to impress their mothers.

Joseph L. Mankiewicz

The best friend of a boy is his mother, of a man his horse; only it's not clear when the transition takes place.

W. Somerset Maugham

THE CONSTANT WIFE

I was brought up by a very strict mother to believe that men were naturally wicked.

George Bernard Shaw

MAN AND SUPERMAN

Of all human struggles there is none so treacherous and remorseless as that between the artist man and the mother woman.

Oscar Wilde

THE IMPORTANCE
OF BEING EARNEST

All women become like their mothers. That is their tragedy. No man does. That's his.

Dame Enid Lyons

In his mother's heart no baby ever grows up completely and in some mysterious fashion a part of every man remains a child, peculiarly his mother's, even though they are estranged. In that case there is sorrow for them both but whatever sense of hurt or injustice a man may har-bour, he knows, in the depth of his soul, that his mother is waiting always for his return.

Alfred, Lord Tennyson

THE PRINCESS

Happy he
With such a mother!
Faith in womankind
Beats with his blood.

Noël Coward

PRESENT INDICATIVE

Nobody seemed to be interested in my plays. Nobody seemed anxious to offer me parts at even reasonable salaries. Every now and then I managed to sell a short story or a song, and once I got a hundred pounds for grinding out an adaption of a French play for Dennis Eadie. Altogether it was a gloomy and depressing period.

In former days, of course, I could probably have gone out on tour or procured a small job in London, but now, having played two or three leading parts, and actually appeared in my own play in the West End, I was in the awkward situation of being too well known to be able to accept little jobs, and not well known enough to be able to command big ones.

Every morning Mother used to come and sit on my bed while I had my breakfast. This was the one hour in the day that she allowed herself to relax, and I could always tell by her face, the moment it appeared round the door, if anything had happened. There was a certain artificial chirpiness about her on bad days, manufactured out of a determination not to let me see that she was worried, which generally broke down before I had finished my first cup of coffee.

We were getting more and more deeply into debt, and even with the house full, which it wasn't, the income from it was not sufficient to meet the quarterly instalments, the rent, the taxes, the electric light bills, and the living expenses of Father, Mother, Auntie Vida, Eric, and me.

What worried me most was the dread that Mother would suddenly break completely and become seriously ill. Her heart was not strong, and the strain of the last few years had been appalling. This I was determined to avert at all costs, even if the brokers took possession of the house and we were all flung into the street.

I went to see Ned Lathom, knowing how kind and generous he was, and also knowing how many hundreds of people had already sponged upon him, and asked him flatly, without preliminaries, to lend me two hundred pounds. He refused almost sharply, and he added that he would willingly give me two hundred pounds, but that never, in any circumstances, would he lend money to anybody ever again, it was too dangerous a commodity, he said, to pass between friends.

I have a lot of gratitude in my heart, towards many people, but it is too special and private an emotion to spill into print. There are hundreds of ways of describing unkindness and meanness and little cruelties. A sly dig at the right moment can work wonders. But just try to write of generosity. Try to frame in words an unrelated, motiveless gesture of sheer kindness and you are lost. The warmth behind the phrases dissipates before they reach the paper, and there they lie, under your hand, sneering up at you, coldly effusive and dead as mutton.

At any rate, with Ned's cheque in my pocket, the sun shone, temporarily, with all its might. About a hundred and fifty of the two hundred pounds went immediately to various creditors. The remaining fifty I held on to, because I had a plan in mind which, after a discussion with Gladys Calthrop, I sprang on Mother, suddenly, and clinched before she had time to argue.

The plan was that Father was to take charge of the house, and that I was to find a little cottage in the country somewhere, where she could rest completely, for several months, and where I could come for weekends, and write. She at once made a pyramid of small difficulties which I swept grandly away. There wasn't much conviction behind them anyhow, and a few days later Gladys and I went to Dymchurch, where Athene Seyler had lent me her cottage for a fortnight, and from this we set forth daily in search of a small, inexpensive house for Mother.

Dymchurch in March was bleak, windy, cold and full of charm.

We bicycled and walked for days over the marshes, with Fred, Gladys's brown spaniel, padding along behind us, and plunging in and out of the dykes. We zigzagged backwards and forwards between Ham Street and Ivychurch, Appledore and New Romney. We climbed up on to Aldington Knoll and looked at the cliffs of France glinting in the sun across the steely grey channel. We found some early primroses and a lame sea-gull, which bit us fiercely, and messed, with the utmost abandon, all over the cottage. We went systematically through every available habitation within a radius of twenty-five miles, and finally found a small and tender one, nestling up against a public-house in the village of St. Mary in the Marsh. It had four rooms, outside sanitation, a rental of ten shillings a week, and a superb view from the upper windows of unlimited sheep.

Mother seemed to be quite pleased with it, and so we moved in, and very soon the sea and the sky and the marshes began to work a little homely Kentish magic. There was nothing to do but read and write, and make expeditions into Dymchurch or New Romney to get provisions, and a lot of the tiredness was smoothed away from Mother's face within the first few weeks.

I bought a black mongrel at the Battersea Dogs' Home, and conveyed him, radiant in a new collar, to New Romney Station, where Mother met us and fell in love with him at once. He was very young and spindly in the legs, and he promptly had a violent attack of distemper, which kept him hovering between life and death for seven weeks. However, nursing him provided an occupation for Mother during the days I had to spend in London.

There were a few neighbours for her to talk to: Mrs. Hinds, the owner of the inn next door, Mr. and Mrs. Cook, the Vicar and his wife, Miss Hammond, the local school teacher. There were also the Bodys, who owned much of the property round about, and, not very far off, at Jesson, none other than E. Nesbit, who lived with her husband, and a gentle friend, in a series of spacious huts.

I called on her very soon, and found her as firm, as nice, and as humorous as her books had led me to expect. The skipper, her husband, was a grand old man, who loved her and guarded her devotedly through her last, rather sad years.

The friend, Miss Hill, was a wispy creature, with an air of vague detachment, which inspired Athene Seyler to christen her irreverently, "The Green Hill Far Away."

During that spring, I spent most of my time at St. Mary's. The churchyard just across the road was a peaceful place in which to work, and it was there, propped up against a family tombstone, that I wrote *The Queen Was in the Parlour*. Nothing could be further removed from that play than the surroundings in which I wrote it. Its passionate love-scenes and Rurtanian splendours emerged from my mind to the gentle cawing of rooks and the bleating of new-born lambs. When I raised my eyes from a Palace courtyard, lit by the flare of torches and brimming with revolutionaries, I saw the marshes stretching to the dark line of the sea wall, broken every now and then by dumpy little Martello towers, and slightly inland on the right, a cluster of trees and houses and a square church tower—the village of New Romney.

On long summer evenings, Mother and I used to ride up to Aldington Knoll on our bicycles, and wait there in the growing dusk until the thin line of sea, four miles away, faded and disappeared in the white mist rising from the dykes, and then looking down over the darkening country spreading all the way from Folkestone to Hastings, we would see lamps twinkling in cottage windows, bats swooping down from the high trees, and the lighthouses flashing all along the coast.

It would have been cheering had we known, then, that the land just below us would belong to us one day. That the farmhouse, the five poplars, the thick woods and lush fields stretching down to the Military Canal, would be ours to do with as we liked. But even as it was, without clairvoyance and future certainties, those evenings were lovely enough, and we pedalled home happily through the dark, our bicycle lamps making wobbling shadows across the roads, feeling that, after all, money troubles, rate collectors, and brokers' men didn't matter so very much as long as we had a water-tight ten-shilling-a-week roof over our heads.

Gerald Durrell

MY FAMILY AND OTHER ANIMALS

"Excuse me a moment," he would say. "I must go and see Mother."

At first this rather puzzled me, for I was convinced that Kralefsky [his tutor] was far too old to have a mother still living. After considerable thought, I came to the conclusion that this was merely his polite way of saying that he wished to retire to the lavatory, for I realized that not everyone shared my family's lack of embarrassment when discussing this topic. It never occurred to me that, if this was so, Kralefsky closeted himself more often than any other human being I had met. One morning I had consumed for breakfast a large quantity of loquats, and they had distressing effects on me when we were in the middle of a history lesson. Since Kralefsky was so finicky about the subject of lavatories I decided that I would have to phrase my request politely, so I thought it best to adopt his own curious term. I looked him firmly in the eye and said that I would like to pay a visit to his mother.

"My mother?" he repeated in astonishment. "Visit my mother? Now?"

I could not see what the fuss was about, so I merely nodded.

"Well," he said doubtfully, "I'm sure she'll be delighted to see you, of course, but I'd better just go and see if it's convenient."

He left the room, still looking a trifle puzzled, and returned after a few minutes.

"Mother would be delighted to see you," he announced, "but she says will you please excuse her being a little untidy?"

I thought it was carrying politeness to an extreme to talk about the lavatory as if it were a human being, but, since Kralefsky was obviously a bit eccentric on the subject, I felt I had better humour him. I said I did not mind a bit if his mother was in a mess, as ours frequently was as well.

"Ah . . . er . . . yes, yes, I expect so," he murmured, giving me rather a startled glance. He led me down the corridor, opened a door, and, to my complete surprise, ushered me into a large shadowy bedroom. The room was a forest of flowers; vases, bowls, and pots were perched everywhere, and each contained a mass of beautiful blooms that shone in the gloom, like walls of jewels in a green-shadowed cave. At one end of the room was an enormous bed, and in it, propped up on a heap of pillows, lay a tiny figure not much bigger than a child. She must have been very old, I decided as we drew nearer, for her fine, delicate features were covered with a network of wrinkles that grooved a skin as soft and velvety-looking as a baby mushroom's. But the astonishing thing about her was her hair. It fell over her shoulders in a thick cascade, and then spread half way down the bed. It was the richest and most beautiful auburn colour imaginable, glinting and shining as though on fire, making me think of autumn leaves and the brilliant winter coat of a fox.

"Mother dear," Kralefsky called softly, bobbing across the room and seating himself on a chair by the bed, "Mother dear, here's Gerry come to see you."

ON TOLSTOY

The harder little Leo tried to remember his mother, the more she eluded him. He tried to identify her by questioning those who had known her, but in vain. They told him she was good, gentle, upright, proud, intelligent, and an excellent storyteller, but he could not attach a face to this assortment of qualities, and as though to deepen the mystery, there was not a single portrait of her in the house. Only a silhouette cut out of black paper, showing her at the age of ten or twelve, with a round forehead and a round chin, her hair in a veil at the nape of her neck. His whole life long Leo Tolstoy tried to instill life into this frustrating profile. He grew older, but his mother remained a little girl. Driven by his need for love, he finally came to think of her as a mythical being to whom he had recourse in times of distress and upon whom he relied for supernatural assistance. Only a few years before his death he wrote, ". . . I walk in the garden and I think of my mother, of Maman; I do not remember her, but she has always been an ideal of saintliness for me. I have never heard a single disparaging remark about her." And also, "Felt dull and sad all day. Toward evening the mood changed into a desire for caresses, for tenderness. I wanted, as when I was a child, to nestle against some tender and compassionate being and weep with love and be consoled . . . become a tiny boy, close to my mother, the way I imagine her. Yes, yes, my Maman, whom I was never able to call that because I did not know how to talk when she died. She is my highest image of love—not cold, divine love, but warm, earthly love, maternal . . . Maman, hold me, baby me! . . . All that is madness, but it is all true."

A. A. Milne

DISOBEDIENCE

James James
Morrison Morrison
Weatherby George Dupree
Took great
Care of his Mother,
Though he was only three.
James James
Said to his Mother,
"Mother," he said, said he;
"You must never go down to the end of town, if you don't go
    down with me."

James James
Morrison's Mother
Put on a golden gown,
James James
Morrison's Mother
Drove to the end of the town.
James James
Morrison's Mother
Said to herself, said she:
"I can get right down to the end of the town and be back in time
    for tea."

King John
Put up a notice,
"LOST OR STOLEN OR STRAYED!
JAMES JAMES
MORRISON'S MOTHER
SEEMS TO HAVE BEEN MISLAID.
LAST SEEN

WANDERING VAGUELY:
QUITE OF HER OWN ACCORD,
SHE TRIED TO GET DOWN TO THE END OF THE TOWN—FORTY SHILLINGS
REWARD!"

James James
Morrison Morrison
(Commonly known as Jim)
Told his
Other relations
Not to go blaming *him.*
James James
Said to his mother,
"Mother," he said, said he;
"You must *never* go down to the end of the town without consult-
ing me."

James James
Morrison's mother
Hasn't been heard of since.
King John
Said he was sorry,
So did the Queen and Prince.
King John
(Somebody told me)
Said to a man he knew:
"If people go down to the end of the town, well, what can *anyone*
do?"

ON MONTGOMERY CLIFT

Mr. McCloud also remembers something much more ominous for the
future of Montgomery Clift. "Mrs. Clift was a lovely lady but a nervous
person who had a penchant for things happening to her. Once she

claimed that the maid had set fire to a clothes closet and the house almost went up in flames. She was timorous about staying alone at night when Bill traveled, and, I think because she asked him to, he used to recruit young men from the office to stay with her overnight in his house while he was out of town. Mrs. Clift was afraid of everything. One night while I was staying over, I was awakened in the middle of the night by having a flashlight and a gun pointed at my face, and I saw that it was she. She said that she thought there was somebody in the house. I said: 'For God's sake, put the gun away and let's go see.' I think the truth of the matter is that she had a vivid imagination." These indications of instability were not to be the last.

Perhaps Ethel's extravagant fears abated, or, more likely, whatever was disturbing her intensified, for when the twins were hardly a year old, she left Omaha, and Bill, and began to take frequent extended trips with the three children. During a recent interview for this book, Ethel recalled the reasons for these trips as having to do with the extreme heat of the summertime in Omaha, but soon these excursions to the Berkshires, to Switzerland, to Great Barrington, Massachusetts, began to take place at all times of the year.

Monty hated to talk about what happened back then, undoubtedly because he never fully understood it himself. The closest he ever came to it was to say, in a mid-fifties interview, "Traveling is a hobgoblin existence for children. Why weren't roots established? My brother has been married three times now." Privately, Monty would lash out at his mother and attack her character to his friends—but this would not happen until he was a grown man.

Years later, Monty's friend and physician, Dr. Rex Kennamer, would say, "I'm sure it can all be traced back to the mother."

But the boy still had to deal with his mother's smothering ways. Monty was irritated. He wanted to be left alone with his new theater friends, to express himself freely—to have fun. Ethel wouldn't permit it. As Monty, in adulthood, complained to a friend, "She was always with me. She never wanted me to socialize with the other members of the company."

Geraldine Kay, who played one of the other children, remembers something similar. "Mrs. Clift was a small, slender, rather unobtrusive little lady. But you always knew she was there. You felt her presence and her influence on Monty, because when she was not there he seemed to blossom and be himself, and the moment she appeared he would withdraw."

What was it with Monty? He was obviously strong-willed, but around Ethel he would submit totally to *her* will. He was annoyed by her oppressive presence, yet never once did he ever show a sign of rebellion toward her—strange, in view of the fact that Monty was not a submissive boy. What is even stranger is that Monty was at an age when most children go through a kind of identity crisis, in which they often pout and complain about always being told what to do. Why wasn't Monty going through the same kind of overt adolescent rebellion? His obviously repressed resentment would bear violent fruit later on.

The best agents in town were now competing wildly for Monty. Just to be glanced at by agent Maynard Morris was, to the young actor of the day, like being touched by the Pope, and here was Maynard Morris waiting patiently for Monty backstage on many nights, along with another top agent, William Levine. Monty was becoming quite a prize. Maynard Morris wound up handling Monty, though not exclusively.

All this time, Monty still lived in the Clift apartment. He certainly didn't have to. He was making good money on Broadway and could have left his parents and his mother's strictures anytime he wished. But he still needed her, for a role model, for her dominating support. So there he stayed.

Lehman Engel, another friend of Monty's, sheds more light on the relationship. Engel was fast gaining a reputation as a talented musical conductor when he first met Monty, and happened to make a reference to a lecture he was scheduled to give at a Stamford, Connecticut, YMCA.

Two weeks later, Engel walked out onto the Stamford platform and there in the very first row was Montgomery Clift. Lehman was surprised; he and the young man hadn't exchanged a word since that first meeting in New York. Later, Monty deliberately waited until everyone had left before quietly approaching Engel and asked, "How are you going back to New York?" "By train," Lehman said. "Then," said Monty, "would you mind if I rode back with you?"

Of course Lehman Engel did not mind at all. One cannot help but notice how calculatingly Monty had planned the situation. He had known for weeks how he was going to flatter the twenty-eight-year-old musician by making a painstaking two-hour trip to attend a relatively unimportant talk. It was Ethel all over again, making a special trip with Monty up to Rhode Island just to betroth him to a friend.

Practically the first thing Monty did was to introduce him to his mother and father. It was as if Ethel and Bill came packaged with Monty as a single social entity. By now there was every indication that Ethel had become Monty's "other self," his alter ego. In order to truly make a friend, Monty was compelled to have the new friend become involved with those "other parts" of his personality—his coterminous existence with Ethel.

Another time, Monty and his mother planned a special trip to Philadelphia for days and sprang it on Engel only hours before the departure. Monty was just like a little child going to the circus. It was an extravagant expedition involving theater tickets, museum visits and a suite at the most expensive hotel in Philadelphia, and Ethel had organized it all for Monty and Lehman Engel. Monty just thought she was being very kind and generous, but, at twenty-eight, Lehman could sense a disturbing reality that Monty, at eighteen, could not. "Mrs. Clift thought that my relationship with Monty was the greatest thing in the world, and I think I know the reason for that. He would occasionally date Fortune Ryan, one of the big Ryan millionaires, and she was wild. He would see Diana Barrymore, who was already a big lush. Mrs. Clift would make catty remarks about them, and I think she felt that he was safe when he was with me because then he wasn't about to run off and get married to one of those girls. Mrs. Clift was Monty's girl friend, his mother, his everything. She would skip down the street with Monty. She never had this kind of relationship with her daughter or with her other son. They would skip down the street because that's the way Monty was, and the way he was, she was; she followed him. Monty was on top of the world in those days. He didn't know what sadness was."

Nevertheless, the first signs of ambivalence toward his mother began to appear. As Lehman notes: "There was something very strange about Mrs. Clift which Monty and I often discussed. Apparently, she didn't have a bank account. Instead, she walked around with her handbag filled with rolls of hundred dollar bills, and paid the light and telephone bills by hand. I knew that his father wasn't successful and that Mrs. Clift wasn't wealthy, but neither Monty nor I could figure out where she got all this money. Monty had been taking piano lessons and Ethel asked me, 'What kind of piano do you think Monty should have?' I told her that it depended, but that the best pianos were made by Steinway. And she went out and bought a Steinway grand, the most expensive. She went to Jensen's and bought a set of silver flatware to put on the table—it cost a fortune. It was very mysterious, where she could have gotten this money. Once upon a time she told me—with Monty there—that she frequently went up to Boston, because there was a very kind man there who owned a large factory or mill of some sort, and she was ghosting his biography. Now, anyone who's talked with Mrs. Clift knows that she doesn't use the King's English; she doesn't know a verb from a pronoun. She couldn't write an English sentence. Both Monty and I wondered if there wasn't something between them."

For the first time, Monty's resentment of his mother's presence came out into the open. Everyone around Monty became painfully aware of the tension building up in him toward his mother's unwelcome visits. "When Mrs. Clift came up to see him," says Janet Cohn, "Monty just blew up. He would come over to my place to get away from her and growl about her being there. Ordinarily, Monty was very exuberant and expressive but whenever his mother came up, he withdrew. He would try to get her to go back to the city, but I don't think she took his objections too seriously. When he would talk to her brusquely, she would just go on as if nothing had happened. She would fix things up around the barn for him, but the more she tried to have Monty depend on her, the more he would resent it. Once she came up from New York with a lot of expensive lilies, and planted them in his garden. As soon as she went back to New York, he tore up every single one of them and threw them in the lake. It just broke my heart."

Ethel made the grievous tactical error of not taking Monty's rebellion seriously. In her eyes, he still needed her now as much as he had during Jubilee. In reality, Monty did not need her then as much as she needed him. But he did need her now. The fact that he was still willing, as an adult, to remain so unnaturally a part of her domain proves that he had to cling to her. Ethel's mistake was in not giving her grown son more breathing space, as a result, she pushed the truth of their relationship into his face. The mistake would cause her boundless grief.

The problem for Monty now was that although he resisted his mother's strong ego, he had little else to take its place. His sense of self was so hazy and incomplete that one minute he would be full of great ambition, the next he couldn't care less what happened to him.

In early 1943, Kazan drew Monty aside for a private discussion. It is doubtful he said anything as cruel as "You better leave home because half of Broadway already thinks you're a fairy," but Monty could not fail to understand Kazan's meaning.

Monty said very little during the conversation, except to agree.

Almost immediately, he moved out of his parents' apartment. But Monty didn't move far. He took a little sublet walk-up above a laundromat at 127 East 55th Street, between Park and Lexington, about a minute's walk away. Ethel and Bill were dumbstruck. Why did he want to desert them? Monty did come home all the time for dinner, and would sometimes move back for a week or so when he got tired of taking care of himself, but his manner with the Clifts wasn't as before; the seed was planted, the blame already placed. After a week with Bill and Ethel, Monty would get thoroughly disgusted and run out on them. He began to use the term "my Goddamned mother" when speaking of the woman whose hospitality he continued to accept.

Just because he left his mother, however, doesn't mean he lost his need for a mother. Immediately after leaving home, Monty became thickly entangled in relationships with two older women, relationships that lasted the rest of his life. If he couldn't have Mrs. Clift, he would have substitutes for her.

Rick, a male lover of the bisexual Monty, recalls:
"He was still living in two places—at his parents' and in his own apartment, the one-room walk-up off Lexington Avenue. His mother couldn't understand why he had to do that. But Monty used to tell her that he needed his privacy. My mother and father had a place in Kennebunkport, Maine, and he'd come up there with me for days at a time. We went boating a lot. We'd have sex in the boat, in the woods in the moonlight. Monty was always good sexually for me . . . He got to love my mother. He'd say to me, 'She's my real mother!' I told him he shouldn't say things like that. Monty's mother was a thoroughly possessive woman, peculiar in some ways. When she was alone with me, she'd say things like, 'I'm glad you and Monty are such good friends. I don't really like theater people.' It was a funny thing to say to the friend of a man who had been in the theater since he was fourteen."

Laurence Olivier

CONFESSIONS OF AN ACTOR

The slight disgust that he [his father] felt at his first viewing of me seemed to me and, I feel sure, to my mother, to last all my boyhood until my heaven, my hope, my entire world, my own worshipped Mummy died when I was twelve. From this I learnt that great suffering could sometimes implant in some mysterious way an unexpected strength. I have managed to cling to that belief throughout my life, and in any really appalling circumstances it has given me a small, narrow shelf that could afford me a moment's rest, a borrowed moment of strength like the loan of oxygen that we feel on taking a deep breath.

From the age of five until I was nine my Mummy had, more often than it pleases me to remember, to quell the natural anguish which she suffered at what was to her the dreaded prospect of spanking me for one inveterate and seemingly irresistible sin, that of lying, it was apparently impossible for me to resist this temptation. It was a compulsion in me to invent a story and tell it so convincingly that it was believed at first without doubt or suspicion.

After three or four years of the monotonous exchange of sin and punishment, it eventually pierced my sluggish little brain that this operation really did hurt her more than it hurt me. I noticed at last while I was removing the necessary garments that she was in a state of high distress. She caught me staring at her and said, "How I wish you wouldn't persist in making this hateful business necessary. I do detest it so." I resolved that on this occasion I would grit my teeth and not cry out until I could stifle my cries no longer. She stopped after the fourth stroke; I was surprised as I was expecting six. She said, "Yes, it should have been six really but you were so brave I couldn't go on." This amazed me; I had always assumed that if a person did not cry out the punisher would continue, unsatisfied until the expected reaction was brought forth.

I thereupon resolved that she should never again be made to suffer in this way and that I would forever remove the cause of it all. And so my habit of lying ceased . . . for a time, anyway.

If my wonderful Mums had lived to watch me at work, at times more glowingly fortunate than I would have dared to imagine, I have sometimes wondered whether she might not have come to the conclusion that those years of habitual lying were due to an instinct for some intitial practice in what was to become my trade. Let it not be thought that I am attempting to find any excuse whatever for my early wicked tendencies, but it might, as is said west of the Atlantic, it might well figure.

Russell Baker

GROWING UP

My mother's efforts to turn poor specimens of manhood into glittering prizes began long before she became my mother. As the older daughter in a family of nine children, she had tried it on her younger brothers without much success. When she married she had tried it on my father with no success at all.

Her attitudes toward men were a strange blend of twentieth-century feminism and Victorian romance. The feminism filled her with anger against men and a rage against the unfair advantages that came with the right to wear trousers. "Just because you wear pants doesn't mean you're God's gift to creation, sonny boy," she shouted at me one day when I said something about the helplessness of women. Of a man vain about his charm with women: "Just because he wears pants he thinks he can get through life with half a brain."

The unfair advantage bestowed by pants was a lifelong grievance. As a girl of sixteen she denounced it while arguing the case for women's suffrage in her 1913 high school debate. "Women do not ask to be placed on a throne as goddess or queen," she said. "They are content to be equal. At present they are only half-citizens. Is the right to vote to be not a matter of right or justice, but a mere matter of pantaloons?"

She was so pleased with the phrase that she underlined "pantaloons" twice on her script before concluding: "A noted man once said to a young man starting out to practice law, 'Young man, espouse some righteous unpopular cause.' That is just what I have been called upon to do, and whether I win or lose, 'I had rather be right than President'—and perhaps, when women shall have won the ballot, some one of the Lancaster High School girls will be both right *and* President."

The flaw in my character which [my mother] had already spotted was lack of "gumption." My idea of a perfect afternoon was lying in front of the radio rereading my favorite Big Little Book, *Dick Tracy Meets Stooge Viller*. My mother despised inactivity. Seeing me having a good time in repose, she was powerless to hide her disgust. "You've got no more gumption than a bump on a log," she said. "Get out in the kitchen and help Doris do those dirty dishes."

My sister Doris, though two years younger than I, had enough gumption for a dozen people. She positively enjoyed washing dishes, making beds, and cleaning the house. . . . Doris could have made something of herself if she hadn't been a girl. Because of this defect, however, the best she could hope for was a career as a nurse or schoolteacher, the only work that capable females were considered up to in those days.

This must have saddened my mother, this twist of fate that had allocated all the gumption to the daughter and left her with a son who was content with Dick Tracy and Stooge Viller. If disappointed, though, she wasted no energy on self-pity. She would make me make something of myself whether I wanted to or not. "The Lord helps those who help themselves," she said. That was the way her mind worked.

She was realistic about the difficulty. Having sized up the material the Lord had given her to mould, she didn't overestimate what she could do with it. She didn't insist that I grow up to be President of the United States.

Fifty years ago parents still asked boys if they wanted to grow up to be President, and asked it not jokingly but seriously. . . . I was asked many times myself. No, I would say, I didn't want to grow up to be President. My mother was present during one of these interrogations. An elderly uncle, having posed the usual question and exposed my lack of interest in the Presidency, asked, "Well, what do you want to be when you grow up?"

I loved to pick through trash piles and collect empty bottles, tin cans with pretty labels, and discarded magazines. The most desirable job on earth sprang instantly to mind. "I want to be a garbage man," I said.

My uncle smiled, but my mother had seen the first distressing evidence of a bump budding on a log. "Have a little gumption, Russell," she said.

ON JANE AUSTEN

The fortunes of Edward, the second son [of George and Jane Austen], were different. Mr. and Mrs. Thomas Knight, the son and daughter-in-law of George Austen's patron, a childless couple, took a fancy to him as a boy. They had him to stay for longer and longer visits till his father began to be worried. Edward, he said, was getting shockingly behind-hand with his Latin grammar; should he not be more at home? Mrs. Austen did not agree; she had a shrewder sense of priorities. "I think," she said, "you had better oblige your cousins and let the child go." Since Edward was not a particularly promising Latin scholar, George Austen let himself be persuaded. Edward began to spend more and more time each year with the Knights; in due course of time, Thomas Knight adopted him and made him his heir, the fortunate and future owner of two fine country houses and a great deal of money. The story is evidence of Mrs. Austen's realistic good sense. She was rewarded by the fact that Edward remained extremely fond of her—as much so as if they had not been separated.

ON NOËL COWARD

Noël's childhood had on the whole been a most happy one: his only unhappinesses seem to have been caused by separations from his mother, as for instance when she decided to let the flat in Battersea and that the family should stay with his Grannie and two of his numerous aunts at Southsea. His education had been sporadic to say the least, which from time to time caused Mrs. Coward pangs of conscience, and from Southsea she suddenly packed Noël off alone to London to stay with yet another aunt and continue his schooling.

"Dear darling old Mother, I am still very unhappy and I shan't get over it till I see you again . . . oh Mother do send me some money to come down to you please do I am not very happy here without you . . . good bye now darling old mother from your loveing son Noel, please do do do do send back for me." This was written at the age of ten. Two years later, while Noël was appearing for the second time in *Where The Rainbow Ends,* she not only suffered further pangs of guilt but writes that she was "a good deal pestered by relations and friends about letting Noël be on the stage instead of at school, and had doubts in my mind as to what was the wisest thing to do.

An end was put to her indecision once and for all in a startling manner: a friend asked Mrs. Coward to accompany her to a variety performance at the Coliseum, where a thought-reader, Anna Eva Fay, was topping the bill.

She had created a tremendous sensation in America and the Coliseum was packed. A man came round with slips of paper for you to write your question on. "I was not going to ask anything but my friend persuaded me to. . . . 'Do you advise me to keep my son Noel Coward on the stage? Violet Coward.' Then there was a hush and Miss Fay came on to the stage, with her male assistant. She spoke a few words, then sat on a chair and the man put a sheet over her. She held out her arms like a ghost, answered one or two questions and then called out, 'Mrs. Coward, Mrs. Coward'—my friend prodded me in the side and I had to stand up and she shouted, 'You ask me about your son. Keep him where he is, keep him where he is, he has great talent and will have a wonderful career!' I was entirely flabbergasted . . . my feelings were beyond words, how could she know and why should she have answered me amongst so many people! When I mentioned my experience [to the relatives] I was met with pitying smiles! So I did not say any more about it but I knew perfectly well that Anna Eva Fay was right."

ON D. H. LAWRENCE

Having nursed him through the crisis, his mother transferred to him all the intense love and all the ambitions she had had for Ernest [his brother]. Thus, at sixteen, at that very moment in his life when he left school, started work, met his first serious girlfriend, and should have been given his first push towards independence by his mother, she tightened her emotional grip on him almost to strangulation. On him alone rested the responsibility for making up to her for the failure of her marriage and for all her suffering.

Young Bert was not only tied to his mother's apron strings, he would frequently wear the apron, making bread or potato cakes. He would help his mother with such jobs as blackleading or scrubbing the floor, establishing early an aptitude for and enjoyment of traditionally feminine tasks which was to last a lifetime. He was loath to begin shaving, because that would be to admit that his boyhood was over, and he did not feel ready to assume the independence of a young man.

ON RUPERT BROOKE

Mrs. Brooke, who was often shrewd in assessing character but pitifully ignorant of psychology, allowed Rupert to know how deeply she had hoped for another daughter before his birth. He was to write later:

> I am here because at Fettes, in the seventies, Willie Brooke and May Cotterill got thrown together. And then they had a son and a daughter, and the daughter died, and while the mother was thinking of her daughter another child was born, and it was a son, but in consequence of all this very female in parts— *sehr dichterisch*—me.

As Hassall comments, there was nothing effeminate about him; but the fascination that there might be, and the fear that others might suppose there was, made him concerned both to convince himself and to persuade others of his virility.

Christopher Milne
(Son of A. A. Milne)

THE ENCHANTED PLACES

Mallord Street was my mother's work: hers alone. My father paid the bills but it was she who planned it all—who chose the furniture and the carpets and the curtains and the colour of the walls—she who decided what (and indeed who) would go where. But if there was no collaboration, there was also no argument. It was agreed that the house was her domain, and that, provided she didn't spend money that wasn't there, she could rule as she pleased. And this she did. She was a firm ruler. If there were any obstacles in the way she would ignore them. If any unwelcome facts upset her hopes, she would treat them as if they didn't exist. I suggested earlier that one of the unwelcome facts that faced her soon after my arrival was that I was clearly a boy, and that for nine years she tried to ignore this by dressing me as a girl. I am not entirely sure how seriously I take this theory, but at least it is not out of character. Fortunately, in this particular instance, mind failed to triumph over matter and I remained a boy. But only just; and I was one of her few failures.

Marilyn French

THE WOMEN'S ROOM

She was sick during the entire pregnancy, with constant nausea and stomach pain. It never occurred to her that this might be other than physically caused. Her small body swelled up enormously with the child, and by the seventh month she was miserably uncomfortable. She ate constantly to calm her stomach, and gained thirty-five pounds. During the last two months, after she had stopped working, she was so off balance that even walking was an effort and lying down was not much better. Mostly she sat in the darkened living-bedroom, her great belly propped by cushions on either side of her, her feet propped on a footstool, and read *Remembrance of Things Past*. She shopped, and cleaned the apartment, and cooked, and took the laundry to the laundromat (little dreaming that after the baby was born this would become one of her great pleasures—the chance to get out of the house alone, or at least accompanied only by a great white silent uncrying laundry bag). She ironed sheets and Norm's shirts and paid bills and read the recipe columns of the newspapers searching for an interesting or different way to serve inexpensive foods. The thing she most notably did not do was think.

I don't know what it is like to be pregnant voluntarily. I assume it's a very different experience from that of the women I know. Maybe it's joyful—something shared between the woman and her man. But for the women I know, pregnancy was terrible. Not because it's so painful—it isn't, only uncomfortable. But because it wipes you out, it erases you. You aren't you anymore, you have to forget you. If you see a green lawn in a park and you're hot and you'd love to sit on the grass and roll over in its cool dampness, you can't; you have to toddle over to the nearest bench and let yourself down gently on it. Everything is an effort —getting a can down from a high shelf is a major project. You can't let yourself fall, unbalanced as you are, because you're responsible for another life besides your own. You have been turned, by some tiny pinprick in a condom, into a walking, talking vehicle, and when this has happened against your will, it is appalling.

Pregnancy is a long waiting in which you learn what it means completely to lose control over your life. There are no coffee breaks, no days off in which you regain your normal shape and self, and can return refreshed to your labors. You can't wish away even for an hour the thing that is swelling you up, stretching your stomach until the skin feels as if it will burst, kicking you from the inside until you are black and blue. You can't even hit back without hurting yourself. The condition and you are identical: you are no longer a person, but a pregnancy. You're like a soldier in a trench who is hot and constricted and hates the food, but has to sit there for nine months. He gets to the point where he yearns for the battle, even though he may be killed or maimed in it. You look forward even to the pain of labor because it will end the waiting.

It is this sense of not being a self that makes the eyes of pregnant women so often look vacant. They can't let themselves think about it because it is intolerable and there is nothing they can do about it. Even if they let themselves think about afterward, it is depressing. After all, pregnancy is only the beginning. Once it is over, you have really had it: the baby will be there and it will be yours and it will demand of you for the rest of your life. The rest of your life: your whole life stretches out in front of you in that great belly of yours propped on cushions. From there it looks like an eternal sequence of bottles and diapers and cries and feedings. You have no self but a waiting, no future but pain, and no hope but the tedium of humble tasks.

Saki

THE MATCH-MAKER

". . . My mother is thinking of getting married."

"Again!"

"It's the first time."

"Of course, you ought to know. I was under the impression that she'd been married once or twice at least."

"Three times, to be mathematically exact. I meant that it was the first time she'd thought about getting married; the other times she did it without thinking. As a matter of fact, it's really I who am doing the thinking for her in this case. You see, it's quite two years since her last husband died."

"You evidently think that brevity is the soul of widowhood."

"Well, it struck me that she was getting moped, and beginning to settle down, which wouldn't suit her a bit. The first symptom that I noticed was when she began to complain that we were living beyond our income. All decent people live beyond their incomes nowadays, and those who aren't respectable live beyond other people's. A few gifted individuals manage to do both."

"It's hardly so much a gift as an industry."

"The crisis came," returned Clovis, "when she suddenly started the theory that late hours were bad for one, and wanted me to be in by one o'clock every night. Imagine that sort of thing for me, who was eighteen on my last birthday."

"On your last two birthdays, to be mathematically exact."

"Oh, well, that's not my fault. I'm not going to arrive at nineteen as long as my mother remains at thirty-seven. One must have some regard for appearances."

"Perhaps your mother would age a little in the process of settling down."

"That's the last thing she'd think of. Feminine reformations always start in on the failings of other people. That's why I was so keen on the husband idea."

"Did you go as far as to select the gentleman, or did you merely throw out a general idea, and trust to the force of suggestion?"

"If one wants a thing done in a hurry one must see to it oneself. I found a military Johnny hanging round on a loose end at the club, and took him home to lunch once or twice. He'd spent most of his life on the Indian frontier, building roads, and relieving famines and minimizing earthquakes, and all that sort of thing that one does do on frontiers. He could talk sense to a peevish cobra in fifteen native languages, and probably knew what to do if you found a rogue elephant on your croquet-lawn; but he was shy and diffident with women. I told my mother privately that he was an absolute woman-hater; so, of course, she laid herself out to flirt all she knew, which isn't a little."

"And was the gentleman responsive?"

"I hear he told some one at the club that he was looking out for a Colonial job, with plenty of hard work, for a young friend of his, so I gather that he has some idea of marrying into the family."

"You seem destined to be the victim of the reformation, after all."

Clovis wiped the trace of Turkish coffee and the beginnings of a
smile from his lips, and slowly lowered his dexter eyelid. Which, being
interpreted, probably meant, "I don't think!"

Isoko and Ichiro Hatano

MOTHER AND SON,
A JAPANESE CORRESPONDENCE

(MAY 1945–APRIL 1948)

From Ichiro to his Mother

Dear Mother,
    Thank you for the skates. As it was such a long time since I asked
for them and you had stopped talking about them, I decided they were
out of the question. Yesterday I was so happy that it took me hours to
get to sleep, as it used to on the night before excursions when I was in
the junior school. I could not help chuckling to myself whenever I
thought about them.
    Whenever I shut my eyes I saw myself gliding at great speed over
the ice and that stopped me sleeping. My feet kept moving of their own
accord and I stayed awake until one o'clock in the morning.
    Today the lessons seemed endless. There are only two or three of
us, out of forty boys, who have skating-boots: the rest all use *getas*
[wooden clogs]. The other boys admired my skates (although a few
idiots were jealous and put them down) and I felt like the old Ichiro
again.
    But soon I was not enjoying myself a bit. When I went down to the
ice for the first time, I discovered that it was terribly slippery. And you
could see the bottom through the sheet of frozen water: it was terrifying
and I could not move a step. Despite my splendid boots I was glued to
the spot, while the others watched me and laughed. I was awfully embarrassed.

All the same, by the time we left the lake I had reached the point where I could move fairly well and I think, if I continue at the same rate, I shall be able to skate decently before very long.

I hope you will come and watch me, once I have really learned. Wait till you see how fast I go!

Good night for now.

Tomorrow there is an English test, but I was so happy that . . . It is the first time I have really had fun since I came to Suwa.

From Ichiro to his Mother

Dearest Mother,

This has been on my mind for some time, but I did not say anything because I was afraid to ask.

What has happened to your coat? I can't believe that you have sold it, but for several days you have been going out without a coat, though you looked frozen, and this worries me.

You can't have sold it to buy the skates, Mother? This idea suddenly came into my head yesterday when I saw you shivering as you came in.

Please tell me the whole truth, Mother.

To Ichiro from his Mother

Dear Ichiro,

You don't miss anything. I took so many precautions against anyone finding out and yet you noticed.

It may upset you to hear this, but you have guessed right. It was some time since you had asked me for skates and I wanted to buy them as soon as possible but I could not manage to find the money. And when it came to the day before all the schoolboys were going to the lake and you still said nothing I could bear it no longer. As there was a lady who had been wanting my coat for some time, I decided to let her have it.

But you need not worry about it. I still have my three-quarter length coat and the blue one—do you remember, the one that you used to like to hide in when you went to the kindergarten?

And when I see how much you are enjoying yourself, it makes me feel much warmer than if I had a coat. It is a long time since I have seen you so happy. I don't care a bit about the coat. The thing that I care about most is your heart. So if you love me, keep it always honest and upright. That is the one thing I pray for. You understand what I mean, don't you?

Go on enjoying your skating. I shall certainly come and watch you gliding over the ice.

From Ichiro to his Mother

Dearest Mother,

Have I reached adolescence at last? You will wonder what has been happening to make me ask you such a question point-blank.

Well, this is why. When we were just about to leave the junior school, our teacher, Mr. Hanaoka, told us:

"In two or three years' time you will begin to rebel against your parents or look down on them." At that time I told myself that that would never happen to *me* and I was still sure of it until quite recently; I could not imagine myself rebelling against you or looking down on you. But of late it has been different.

Obviously, since this has cropped up in matters which concern me I could not show what I felt; but there are several things about you which dissatisfy me. Even now, of course, I would never dream of looking down on you, but I feel as though you are no longer perfect in my eyes, as you were before.

If I tell you such things you will be hurt and as soon as I remember that I no longer want to say anything. Nevertheless it is a feeling I can't suppress. Does it happen to all boys who reach adolescence? If so I think it's a very sad thing—and unpleasant too. And I thought it would never happen to me! . . . When I think of this little draught getting into my heart, as though through a crevice, I lose all faith in myself.

Perhaps it would have been better not to write this. But I can't bear to feel that little draught squeezing itself in between you and me. And as I cannot manage to fight it off alone I would like you to stop up the crack from your side, Mother. I am afraid that if I were to leave things as they were, they would gradually get worse and worse.

I know you are very busy, but do please write soon to set my mind at rest.

From Ichiro, who is afraid of catching cold from this draught.

To Ichiro from his Mother

I read your letter very carefully. It is typical of you to worry because your mother is no longer perfect in your eyes, and it touches me very much indeed.

But this is something quite natural, Ichiro dear.

Just as the ripe fruit breaks off from the tree, so a time will come when you will have to break off from your mother. It's sad—sad for me too. But it's something to be glad about for your sake, since it means that you are growing up.

Only yesterday I was talking about you to your father—saying how of late you have been wearing a sulky expression which you never used to have and have taken to answering back. He said to me:

"Ichiro is reaching the difficult age."

All this is only a natural development, my dear. Do not worry about it. Of course, it makes your mother sad to receive a letter like yours, but you need not be afraid, she will not lose heart. You must not be miserable either but strive with all your might to grow into a good and brave adolescent.

Charles Chaplin

If it had not been for my mother I doubt if I could have made a success of pantomime. She was one of the greatest pantomime artists I have ever seen. She would sit for hours at a window, looking down at the people on the street and illustrating with her hands, eyes and facial expression just what was going on below. All the time, she would deliver a running fire of comment. And it was through watching and listening to her that I learned not only how to express my emotions with my hands and face, but also how to observe and study people.

It seems to me that my mother was the most splendid woman I ever knew. . . . I have met a lot of people knocking around the world since, but I have never met a more thoroughly refined woman than my mother. If I have amounted to anything, it will be due to her.

John Bird

PERCY GRAINGER

From the moment of his birth, Rose took a completely protective attitude towards Percy; protective against his father and against the world. In later years Percy often remarked that one of the strongest qualities in the relationship between him and his mother was the mutually held thought of "Us two *against* the World" or "Two Australians *against* the World." Indeed Rose was to wield such power over the heart and mind of her son that it can be said that from the beginning he was created psychologically in her own image.

The idea of incest was obsessive with Grainger for most of his life—both before and after the death of his mother. He did not, however, harbour the desire to make this physical reality with his mother. Perhaps this may have been largely due to his knowledge of Rose's syphilitic condition, but certainly other indeterminable and unrecorded factors came into play. Rose retained her youthful looks for many years and she and Percy were often taken as being sister and brother or wife and husband. Whatever the physical attractions may have been between Rose and Percy they were certainly never given an explicitly incestuous outlet, but a mere glance at any one of many thousands of letters which they exchanged can leave no doubt as to the emotional qualities of the relationship. The contents of each and every letter are drowned in the most excruciating and mawkish sentimentality and if the reader were not aware of the fact that they were between mother and son, they could easily be mistaken for the most intimate of love letters—which, of course, in many cases they were. On this subject, perhaps it is sufficient to say that even in old age Grainger described the relationship as "the only truly passionate love affair of my life."

Grainger journeyed to Bath alone and one of the most significant facts about the engagement was that it marked the first time in his life when he had been separated from his mother for more than a few days. He enjoyed every moment of this trip to Bath; the concert was a great success and whilst staying with the Heymanns he delighted in their conversation and the long walks they often took together. He was to receive a cruel and rude awakening, however, on his return to London, for when he told his mother how much he had enjoyed his music-making and the company of the Heymanns she burst into an hysterical fit of anger. This form of neurotic behaviour continued on and off for the rest of her life and was repeated in a progressively more histrionic fashion whenever her son enjoyed himself in her absence. When he returned from a recital tour of Denmark with Herman Sandby a few years later—a tour which he had thoroughly enjoyed—Rose's anger went unabated for several days. The cause of these outbursts would seem puzzling had not Grainger himself written extensively about his mother's attitude concerning them:

> Mother felt it was a disloyalty on my part to be so very happy the very first time I'd escaped from her apron strings. . . . On the other hand, she was never jealous of my happiness with such composer friends as Balfour Gardiner, Roger Quilter & Cyril Scott. What mother felt was disgust at my disloyalty, not merely my joy in being with other people than herself, but my joy in commonplace things & people. She had brought me up to enjoy superior things & people & here was I hilariously happy in getting close to common things & people. Hatred for disloyalty is not the same thing as jealousy. Alfhild [Alfhild de Luce—later to become Herman Sandby's wife] has written that Herman was hurt in his soul when he came to London to find that I had no manly freedom. What does a composer want with manly freedom? A composer needs protection so that he can forget outside things & concentrate on the much nicer things he has in his own mind.

Except for the regular visitors such as Roger Quilter, who would take tea with the Graingers each Thursday afternoon, and at the special at-homes when all his friends were invited, it became increasingly difficult for even his closest friends to gain access to Grainger during these years. Cyril Scott has written that acquaintances who wished to see him had to give advance notice and were invited to call, "punctually, please," at, say, 4:20 P.M. on a given day and not to stay after 4:40 P.M. In subsequent years, Grainger began taking piano pupils (charging one guinea an hour), and it has been recorded that if the pupil stayed one minute over his or her allotted time Rose would enter the room and start nervously pacing the floor.

Nevertheless, if Percy needed a girlfriend or on the occasions when it was felt that he needed a sex-partner it was still mostly Rose who did the choosing. And just as capriciously she would terminate any relationship which she felt was in any way a threat to the love which existed between herself and her son. In one of the many remarkably frank letters which Grainger wrote to Alfhild Sandby is to be found a paragraph which sheds much light on his passive attitude towards his mother. Alfhild had recently sent him a play in first draft form which dealt with the conflicting loyalties a young man can experience when forced to choose between the attractions of his loved one and the iron will of his mother. (Alfhild almost certainly modelled the main character of the play on Percy, at least up to the point where the play's hero chooses to elope with his beloved.) Grainger was uncompromising in his criticism of the play and compared his own life and attitudes with those of the play's hero. He wrote:

> To me as an Australian (with possibly some influence early imbibed from Japanese and Chinese thought) it seems unbelievable that 2 young people should behave as your Leon and Varenka do: live for love (or passion) in *defiance of a mother's expressed wish*. That any young man or woman should be disobedient to a parent seems to me incredibly low. (When *Mutiny on the Bounty* was shown in Japan they had to change the name to *Heroes of the Pacific* & cut out all parts of the film showing actual mutiny. It is not *decent* for a Japanese to witness any form of mutiny, not even in a film.) I feel the same way. And I blush at the mere thought that two young people could dare to wish to *live together* against the will of a parent! I (in my life) have taken love action only when *advised to do so* by my Mother. Any other thought is sickeningly repugnant to me.

Rose was completely ruthless in her demands for the most devoted filial affection and loyalty. Her bizarre and histrionic effects to "test" his love would take the most drastic forms. Often if he had been out of the house or the room, just before his return she would stretch herself out corpse-like on the floor shamming death. On discovering her in this state he would become tearful and panic-stricken and beg her to speak to him. The moment she was convinced she was not the object of indifference she would sit up and say, "That's all right. I only wanted to see if you still loved me," and go about her business as if nothing had happened. This "test" she continued till around 1920, when Percy was nearly forty. Threats to make herself ill or commit suicide were frequent.

My dear Son,

I am out of my mind and cannot think properly. I asked L. over the phone whether you told her if I had any improper love for you? I did not want to say this, and knew it was untrue, but couldn't help saying it, and then next day told her I thought she had spread the rumour. I did not mean it, but couldn't help saying it. You must tell the truth, that in spite of everything I said—I have never for one moment loved you wrongly—or you me—not for one moment nor the thought of doing so. The whole thing has driven me insane—and I have accused myself of something I have never thought of. You and I never loved one another anything but purely and right. No one will believe me—but it is the real truth, as you know. It is quite unbelievable what I have said to L—, but I am insane—not on all points, but I cannot do anything any more—and only feel like lying in bed and thinking not sleeping—but just unable to do anything. I am insane. I am oh so sorry and want to do something to help you, but cannot. I doubt whether I will be able to dress myself in a day or so. Every day gets worse—I am an idiot, and no one seems to realize it. I am so sorry—I have loved you and so many others so dearly.

Your poor insane mother.

P.S. You have tried so hard to be all that is noble—but your mad side has ruined us—dear God knows the truth—man will not believe the truth I am writing.

A LETTER IN ENGLISH FROM HENRI DE TOULOUSE-LAUTREC TO HIS MOTHER

Toulouse-Lautrec learned English at an early age and was proud of his ability to write and speak it.

Neuilly 22 Septembre 75

My dear Mamma,

I was very glad of receiving such a pretty letter and I will tell you very good news. My Greek master was very satisfied with me and he put on a piece of paper "I am very satisfied of the lessons as well of the tasks." He gave me a Latin version to do. I have read my Latin Grammar this morning and I am going to do Miss' tasks. Yesterday I went to the bath and I have looked for the plate. M. Verrier vas very satisfied with my legs. When you will return I hope you will find me well. Give my love to every one and return soon. If I had wings I should go to see you but I have no. I finish my letter by telling you that everybody sends you his compliments and particularly your boy who kisses you 1000000000000000 million times.

Your affectionate boy,

Coco de Lautrec
My kiss

P.S. Don't drawn you or send me a telegram

Oscar Wilde

A WOMAN OF NO IMPORTANCE

ACT 4

GERALD: I implore you to do what I ask you.

MRS. ARBUTHNOT: What son has ever asked of his mother to make so hideous a sacrifice? None.

GERALD: What mother has ever refused to marry the father of her own child? None.

MRS. ARBUTHNOT: Let me be the first, then. I will not do it.

GERALD: Mother, you believe in religion, and you brought me up to believe in it also. Well, surely your religion, the religion that you taught me when I was a boy, mother, must tell you that I am right. You know it, you feel it.

MRS. ARBUTHNOT: I do not know it. I do not feel it, nor will I ever stand before God's altar and ask God's blessing on so hideous a mockery as a marriage between me and George Harford. I will not say the words the Church bids us to say. I will not say them. I dare not. How could I swear to love the man I loathe, to honour him who wrought your dishonour, to obey him who, in his mastery, made me to sin? No; marriage is a sacrament for those who love each other. It is not for such as him, or such as me. Gerald, to save you from the world's sneers and taunts I have lied to the world. For twenty years I have lied to the world. I could not tell the world the truth. Who can ever? But not for my own sake will I lie to God, and in God's presence. No, Gerald, no ceremony, Church-hallowed or State-made, shall ever bind me to George Harford. It may be that I am too bound to him already, who, robbing me, yet left me richer, so that in the mire of my life I found the pearl of price, or what I thought would be so.

GERALD: I don't understand you now.

MRS. ARBUTHNOT: Men don't understand what mothers are. I am no different from other women except in the wrong done me and the wrong I did, and my very heavy punishments and great disgrace. And yet, to bear you I had to look on death. To nurture you I had to wrestle with it. Death fought with me for you. All women have to fight with death to keep their children. Death, being childless, wants our children from us. Gerald, when you were naked I clothed you, when you were hungry I gave you food. Night and day all that long winter I tended you. No office is too mean, no care too lowly for the thing we women love— and oh! how I loved you. Not Hannah, Samuel more. And you needed love, for you were weakly, and only love could have kept you alive. Only love can keep any one alive. And boys are careless often, and without thinking give pain, and we always fancy that when they come to man's estate and know us better they will repay us. But it is not so. The world draws them from our side, and they make friends with whom they are happier than they are with us, and have amusements from which we are barred, and interests that are not ours; and they are unjust to us often, for when they find life bitter they blame us for it, and when they find it sweet we do not taste its sweetness with them. . . . You made many friends and went into their houses and were glad with them, and

I, knowing my secret, did not dare to follow, but stayed at home and closed the door, shut out the sun and sat in darkness. My past was ever with me. . . . And you thought I didn't care for the pleasant things of life. I tell you I longed for them, but did not dare to touch them, feeling I had no right. You thought I was happier working amongst the poor. That was my mission, you imagined. It was not, but what else was I to do? The sick do not ask if the hand that smooths their pillow is pure, nor the dying care if the lips that touch their brow have known the kiss of sin. It was you I thought of all the time; I gave to them the love you did not need; lavished on them a love that was not theirs. . . . And you thought I spent too much of my time in going to Church, and in Church duties. But where else could I turn? God's house is the only house where sinners are made welcome, and you were always in my heart, Gerald, too much in my heart. For, though day after day, at morn or evensong, I have knelt in God's house, I have never repented of my sin. How could I repent of my sin when you, my love, were its fruit. Even now that you are bitter to me I cannot repent. I do not. You are more to me than innocence. I would rather be your mother—oh! much rather!—than have been always pure. . . . Oh, don't you see? don't you understand! It is my dishonour that has made you so dear to me. It is my disgrace that has bound you so closely to me. It is the price I paid for you—the price of soul and body—that makes me love you as I do. Oh, don't ask me to do this horrible thing. Child of my shame, be still the child of my shame!

GERALD: Mother, I didn't know you loved me so much as that. And I will be a better son to you than I have been.

Mario Puzo

THE GODFATHER

She finished her drink and got up to leave. Hagen escorted her to the hall but as he opened the door, a woman came in from outside. A short, stout woman dressed in black. Kay recognized her as Michael's mother. She held out her hand and said, "How are you, Mrs. Corleone?"

The woman's small black eyes darted at her for a moment, then the wrinkled, leathery, olive-skinned face broke into a small curt smile of greeting that was yet in some curious way truly friendly. "Ah, you Mikey's little girl," Mrs. Corleone said. She had a heavy Italian accent, Kay could barely understand her. "You eat something?" Kay said no, meaning she didn't want anything to eat, but Mrs. Corleone turned furiously on Tom Hagen and berated him in Italian ending with, "You don't even give this poor girl coffee, you *disgrazia*." She took Kay by the hand, the old woman's hand surprisingly warm and alive, and led her into the kitchen. "You have coffee and eat something, then somebody drive you home. A nice girl like you, I don't want you to take the train." She made Kay sit down and bustled around the kitchen, tearing off her coat and hat and draping them over a chair. In a few seconds there was bread and cheese and salami on the table and coffee perking on the stove.

Kay said timidly, "I came to ask about Mike, I haven't heard from him. Mr. Hagen said nobody knows where he is, that he'll turn up in a little while."

Hagen spoke quickly, "That's all we can tell her now, Ma."

Mrs. Corleone gave him a look of withering contempt. "Now you gonna tell me what to do? My husband don't tell me what to do, God have mercy on him." She crossed herself.

"Is Mr. Corleone all right?" Kay asked.

"Fine," Mrs. Corleone said. "Fine. He's getting old, he's getting foolish to let something like that happen." She tapped her head disrespectfully. She poured the coffee and forced Kay to eat some bread and cheese.

After they drank their coffee Mrs. Corleone took one of Kay's hands in her two brown ones. She said quietly, "Mikey no gonna write you, you no gonna hear from Mikey. He hide two-three years. Maybe more, maybe much more. You go home to your family and find a nice young fellow and get married."

Kay took the letter out of her purse. "Will you send this to him?"

The old lady took the letter and patted Kay on the cheek. "Sure, sure," she said. Hagen started to protest and she screamed at him in Italian. Then she led Kay to the door. There she kissed her on the cheek very quickly and said, "You forget about Mikey, he no the man for you any more."

There was a car waiting for her with two men up front. They drove her all the way to her hotel in New York never saying a word. Neither did Kay. She was trying to get used to the fact that the young man she had loved was a cold-blooded murderer. And that she had been told by the most unimpeachable source: his mother.

Marilyn French

THE WOMEN'S ROOM

One night, after they had been with her for a little over a week, Mira was sitting in the dark living room with her brandy and cigarette. The boys were in the bedroom watching TV, or so she thought. Because Clark idled in and sat down across from her. He did not speak, he only sat there, and Mira's feelings reached across to him, thankful to him for sharing her isolation, her silence, the dark.

"Thanks, Mom," he said suddenly.

"Thanks? For what?"

"For taking us around to all those places. You have a lot of other things to do. And you've been to them before. You must've been bored."

He had picked up her mood, and interpreted it as boredom. "I wasn't bored," she said.

"Well, anyway, thanks," he said.

It was no good. He had picked up her mood and if she didn't explain, would assume she had been bored, and now was merely being polite. She did not know what to do. "It was the least I could do," she heard a prissy voice saying. "I haven't much to offer you boys. Your father . . ."

"He never spends any time with us," Clark cut her off in a new, sharp voice. "We were there all summer. He took us out on the boat three times, with his wife and a whole bunch of friends. He doesn't ever talk to us. He sends us out of the room when the conversation starts to get . . . well, you know."

"No, I don't know."

"Well . . ."

"You mean when they start to talk about sex?"

"Oh, no! No, Mom" he exclaimed, and his voice was full of disgust. "Those people never talk about sex. I mean—well, when somebody talks about someone who got divorced, or a guy who cheated on his income tax . . . you know. Whenever they talk about anything *real*," he concluded, "anything beside politenesses."

"Oh!"

They were silent together.

Clark tried again. "Anyway, it was nice of you, especially when we don't act very—well, interested, you know."

"You were better this time than last. At least," she added sarcastically, "you gave signs of life this time."

She thought: he handed me a weapon and I used it. She wondered why. She wondered what she was really saying. It came to her that she was profoundly reproaching him, her son, reproaching him for existing, for being her son, for being, over the years, so much trouble and so little reward, for having needed to have his diapers changed, for waking her in the middle of the night, for chaining her to a kitchen and bathroom and house, for being her life as well as his own and not being worth it. What would be worth it? If he were a Picasso, a Roosevelt, would that repay her? But he was sixteen, and untalented.

MOTHERS
AND DAUGHTERS

George Bernard Shaw

MAN AND SUPERMAN

As a rule there is only one person an English girl hates more than she hates her eldest sister; and that's her mother.

George Bernard Shaw

TOO GOOD TO BE TRUE

No woman can shake off her mother. There should be no mother, only women.

Dr. Beverley Raphael

Being a mother is an excitement and enticement and a growth. It is the possibility that haunts and delights the young girl as she grows to womanhood. It is a part of the fantasy, both her longing for it and her fear of it. The months of pregnancy highlight all the richness of the remembered and internalised experience about mothering. The birth itself brings forth the baby, until now a fantasy, into reality. This real baby is a constant changing, crying, knowing being, and for me the delight of this experience has been one of the most important parts of my life as a woman.

Letizia Ramolino Buonaparte, Napoleon's mother

. . . my opinion is that the future good or bad conduct of a child depends on its mother.

Rudyard Kipling

OUR LADY OF THE SNOWS

Daughter am I in my mother's house,
But mistress in my own.

Shakespeare

SONNETS

Thou art thy mother's glass, and she in thee
Calls back the lovely April of her prime.

Pia Lindstrom
(Daughter of Ingrid Bergman)

I don't know why other daughters don't try to understand their mothers. It seems self-defeating to me to carry on a lengthy adolescence, so that by the time you're 20, you still can't see your parents as people. Part of growing up for me was making some of my own mistakes. It's easy to judge, when you haven't lived; perhaps that's why children are sometimes harsh on their parents. Later, when you start to make your own mistakes, when you do the wrong thing and say to yourself, "I really blew that"; when you behave in ways that you regret—that's when you begin to understand. I was married and divorced myself, before I was 22. I started to see that being a perfect person wasn't as easy as I thought.

Dorothy Pitman Hughes

(Dorothy Pitman Hughes is the founder of the West 80th Street Day Care Center and administrative director of the Westside Community Alliance, Inc., in New York City. She is presently serving on the Governor's Task Force for Human Services.)

People are always saying how different I am from my mother. Lessie Ridley spent her whole life in the tiny town of Lumpkin, Georgia, had 10 kids, and worked most of the time as a domestic, cleaning the homes of servicemen from Fort Benning. I live in New York City, where I work with people in my community, raise money from foundations, and organize programs for change; first a community-controlled child-care center and now a program of alternatives to welfare.

But it was Mother who gave me my political education. My mother, my five sisters, and I would talk for hours while we worked, especially when we quilted. It was our own personal women's group.

The church and the schools didn't teach us to be independent, so she was really alone in preparing us for life. And she warned us that we would be alone, too, unless we did something to change the society we lived in. We learned from her words, and from her example: whenever there was a family crisis or problem, she always fought it through. She was never defeated. It was my mother who taught us to stand up to our problems, not only in the world around us but in ourselves.

When I first came to New York and started to make a little money, I got Mother to stop working since her physical condition wasn't too good. Now that my father has lost his job because of the economy, she has gone back to work. But this time, she's started her own business—making and selling quilts.

Whenever I have a problem, she calls me—I used to ask her how she knew, but she would just answer, "Tell me what's wrong." As we talked, I could almost see my problem get smaller. She keeps me going.

She is very dark and very beautiful, my mother. She is slim and tall, a friend and a teacher. And she is strong.

She once wrote me a letter that started with the story of two strangers in town. The first one met an old woman and asked her, "What kind of people do you have in this town?" The old woman said, "What kind of people were in the town you just left?" The stranger said, "Oh, horrible people. Cutthroats and murderers." And the old woman replied, "Well, you will find those same people in this town." The second stranger asked the old woman the same question—and she asked the same question in return: "What kind of people were in the town you just left?" He replied, "Oh, they were wonderful people. Kind and gentle." And the old woman said, "Then you will find those same people here."

I always remembered that story. Other people become what you expect them to be, and you carry yourself with you, wherever you are —Lumpkin, Georgia, or the streets of New York. You are a success or a failure, depending on how you see yourself, on what you make happen in your life and the world around you.

My mother is a success.

Joanna Mermey

(Joanna Mermey is a regular contributor to the Village Voice *and a free-lance radio and television producer.)*

My mother, my sister, and I started our master's programs together. By the time my sister and I got our degrees, Mother was halfway into her doctorate, had written a novel, and had become head of the high school English department where she taught.

Zenna, as we have called her since she traded in housewifery for her career, is a superachiever. I always envisioned her as one of those people everyone in high school hated. Since she was editor of both the yearbook and school paper, president of the honor society, and head majorette, there wasn't much room for anyone else. I used to get terrible pangs of inferiority looking at the list of accomplishments under her smiling yearbook picture.

She and I spent much of my childhood shrieking at each other. Although marriage was part of my original game plan, and thousands of dollars were poured into pimple cream and braces, my mother was constantly drumming it into my head that I had to have a successful career.

Since I didn't know any mothers who worked and my mother was busy running to Hadassah meetings being "The Mayor-of-Hillside-New-Jersey's Wife," I couldn't understand her constant hocking about a job and a career. It wasn't until I reached my twenties that I began to understand why my mother yelled a lot. . . .

Zenna was working her way through law school, subsisting on milk shakes, when she met my father, Sidney, the dashing young lawyer. Sidney proposed and informed her "one lawyer in the family is plenty." Zenna promptly gave up a promising legal career and had me. She told me, "The idea of being supported after working seven days a week during the war was glamorous, but it soon palled."

She worked hard at raising my sister and me. She took us to lessons in dancing, singing, guitar, piano, flute, string bass, acting, personality, golf, and Hebrew. She dragged us to skin doctors, diet doctors, and the orthodontist. She gave us permanents, designed our clothes, and ripped up our English compositions until they were perfect. She tried very hard to make us beautiful, talented, creative women. She also organized my father's political campaigns, joined all groups a politician's wife is expected to join, and ran the house like a drill sergeant.

One evening during my junior year in high school, my mother announced that she was "sick and tired of breaking my neck for free." The next morning she dropped us off at school and enrolled in a nearby college to get the education credits she needed to teach.

When I left for college, my mother started a new life at 44. She got a job teaching at a ghetto school, and never went to a Hadassah meeting again. When she discovered her students had reading problems, she went to graduate school to specialize in reading disabilities. When she found there weren't any books for kids with low reading levels, she began writing them. She is currently developing curricula for exceptionally deprived youngsters, and hopes to teach college and open her own reading clinic.

I asked her why she waited so long. "I had a guilt complex. I was sure that you kids wouldn't be able to get along by yourselves," she explained. "Being a mother wasn't enough for me. But in those days, you were either a career woman or a mother. I'm sorry I didn't start working ten years earlier—look how much further ahead I'd be. And if you ever make me a grandmother—don't expect to take off and leave the kids with me. I spoiled you enough."

Jane Gardham

GOD ON THE ROCKS

"I hate my mother," she suddenly announced to the priest.

There was a sort of shuffle and glint from behind the grille and a clearing of the throat.

"He thinks I've gone wonky," she thought. "Thinks I'm a bit funny."

"Hate, loathe and detest her," she said again, loudly. (Oh, if thou hadst seen the everlasting crowns of the saints in heaven and with how great glory they now rejoice . . .)

"I despise my mother, and my brother, and I hate my life with him. There is nobody I do not hate or despise. Nobody on earth (. . . who once were esteemed in the world as contemptible. Neither wouldst thou long for this life's pleasant days . . .)."

"My child . . ." (behind the grille). "You are repenting of this?"

"No."

"I see. Then . . ."

"I am not repenting. I am telling you that I am filled with hate and that I am not repenting."

(Her age.) "My child, let me . . ."

He came out of the box and helped her up and walked her to the front pew. The church was quite empty.

"This is a shock," he said. "It's a shock, Binkie . . ."

"I've had a blow," she said and began to scream a little. " 'I've had a blow, Jane.' "

(Right off it. Round the twist.) "Binkie, I had no idea . . ."

"It was at Girton," she wept.

"Yes—yes, I know."

"It was the best time of my life. When Charles came up—the year after me, he took me about. May Balls . . ."

"I'm sure . . ." Father Carter looked about him. The twelve apostles looked unflinchingly back. "I'm sure it must be dull. Dull for you now. Here. It is a very great waste . . ."

Through her tears the words of Thomas à Kempis went straying on. "Oh if these things had a sweet savour and pierced to the bottom of thy heart how couldst thou dare so much as once to complain?" Then she thought that he had said something about her waist.

He had said she was fat.

"I was thin. I was thin as could be," she wept, looking into his face. "At Cambridge. If you'd known me then . . ."

(Oh Lord!)

"I got a good Upper Second. I had several chances to marry. But I couldn't get away, you see. Do you see? Do you know what it's like with a woman like my mother in the background? She ruins everything. Ruins. Ruins. Destroys. She sneers and watches. Even now she sneers and watches. Laughed at Charles wanting to marry Ellie. Laughed at me from the beginning because I couldn't play the piano—didn't like her beastly pictures or want to read her ghastly books. She hated us so much one summer she used to run off out of the house and walk about on the beach. Just go get away from us. She used to burst into tears at breakfast. She killed my father—he just sat wondering why he was hated. Then at Cambridge she laughed at Charles and me for being Socialists. She gave the house to charity just to watch what we'd do about it. Disinherited us, she said, 'Now see how you like equality.' She is a vile woman. She has ruined my life."

"I believe," said the priest, "that she is very sick . . ."

"And Charles's."

"Binkie—Miss Frayling—she is dying."

Red as a bull Binkie blew her nose and roared, "So are we all."

ON SIR RICHARD BURTON

Richard Burton was working on a book with the help of his wife Isabel.

It is clear from the marginal notes that Burton carefully checked her cuts, and at times where he felt her sensibility excessive he wrote an emphatic "stet" in the margin. In places this became a fascinating dialogue between husband and wife. Isabel wanted to erase the footnote where Richard had written of "the abominable egotism and cruelty of the English mother, who disappoints her daughter's womanly cravings in order to keep her at home for her own comfort"—counting it correctly a slap at her own mother. Burton with a "stet" retained it.

Sylvia Plath

THE BELL JAR

Esther is recovering in hospital from a suicide attempt.

I thought if they left me alone I might have some peace.

My mother was the worst. She never scolded me, but kept begging me, with a sorrowful face, to tell her what she had done wrong. She said she was sure the doctors thought she had done something wrong because they asked her a lot of questions about my toilet training, and I had been perfectly trained at a very early age and given her no trouble whatsoever.

That afternoon my mother had brought me the roses.

"Save them for my funeral," I'd said.

My mother's face puckered, and she looked ready to cry.

"But, Esther, don't you remember what day it is today?"

"No."

I thought it might be Saint Valentine's day.

"It's your *birth*day."

And that was when I had dumped the roses in the wastebasket.

"That was a silly thing for her to do," I said to Doctor Nolan.

Doctor Nolan nodded. She seemed to know what I meant.

"I hate her," I said, and waited for the blow to fall.

But Doctor Nolan only smiled at me as if something had pleased her very, very much, and said, "I suppose you do."

Anaïs Nin

JOURNAL OF A WIFE

March 26

. . . Regretfully I close the door upon my heaven, and I steal softly into another room. Mother lies there, weeping. I fall upon my knees—with a sorrow so piercing that it effaces all other feelings.

Mother clings to me. She murmurs vaguely that she has lost her little girl. Of life, which has been all hardness and pain for her, she expected a sole compensation, and she does not have even that. She tells me through her tears that her life is useless, that she has lost the desire to live. Her faith is broken, her courage, her health, her very heart. The unspeakable cruelty of it overwhelms me. There are times when, in horror of the grief I am causing the mother I love beyond words, I think myself mad.

My Love opens his arms; his eyes shine with love of me and the need of me. Behind him Mother's sorrow looms, immense and terrifying. I see her tear-stained face, her weak, worn figure. I am torn by the choice, torn by conflicting reasoning, by irrepressible sentiments, by pity, by rebellion, by bitterness and self-reproach.

I am impotent to preserve those I love from sorrow. Shall I be permitted to alleviate it? Why has God allowed me to be the instrument of Mother's unhappiness when I prayed night after night to be allowed to suffer for her?

April 7

. . . I should have sacrificed love for her sake.

April 13

Above all else I have desired death these past days. Not even my love of Hugo could alter my despair; it even deepened it, because I could not surrender to the charm of it wholly—always the thought of Mother, Mother holding sway over my feelings.

Hugo begs me to control these feelings, and I could if it were one feeling, but Mother's despair calls out all of them, the deepest, the most enduring and the most heartrending. There is my love for her; there is the pity I always feel strongly even towards strangers and more so when it is my mother who suffers; there is the helplessness to sustain and live for one who needs me, as Mother does; there is the intolerable pain of causing suffering. And Mother sees in our separation only the ruin of all her dreams, her hopes, her needs, her very life.

Sometimes I find strength to communicate my faith to her; at others I am carried away, and together we follow the road of our calvary. And to think that I wrote, some time ago, in the ignorance of my idealism, in the blindness of my dreams: "I see the way to a truer happiness for mother." I did not know she wanted only me, free of obligations, free to devote myself to her completely.

Anita Brookner

HOTEL DU LAC

And to Edith, at this strange juncture in her life, there was something soothing in the very existence of Mrs. Pusey, a woman so gentle, so greedy, so tranquil, so utterly fulfilled in her desires that she encouraged daring thoughts of possession, of accumulation, in others. She was, Edith thought, an embodiment of the kind of propaganda no contemporary woman could stoop to countenance, for Mrs. Pusey was not only an enchantress in her own right, she was also appreciative of such propensities in others. (She was also, by the same token, dismissive.) She had unexpected areas of imagination, of generosity. For example, she saw her daughter not as a rival, as a lesser woman might have done, but as a successor, to be groomed for the stardom which would eventually be hers by right. There was indeed a physical closeness between mother and daughter that surpassed anything Edith had ever known, and there was also love on both sides, although Edith registered that love as being mildly unrealistic. For in spite of Jennifer's physical stolidity, a stolidity which verged on opulence, it was clear that her mother still thought of her as a small girl. And Jennifer, probably now as a matter of habit as well as of fondness, continued to behave like one. . . .

Mrs. Pusey had conveniently opened the debate by referring to her husband, now unfortunately dead, but still an inspiration to her and ever in her thoughts.

"A wonderful, wonderful man," she had said, after releasing this information, the thumb and forefinger of her right hand pressed briefly above the bridge of her nose.

"Don't, Mummy," begged Jennifer, her hand stroking her mother's forearm.

Mrs. Pusey gave a shaky little laugh. "She does hate me to get upset," she said to Edith. "It's all right, darling, I'm not going to be silly." And she pulled out a fine white lawn handkerchief and dabbed at the corners of her mouth.

"Oh, but you can't think how I miss him," she confided to Edith. "He gave me everything I could possibly want. My early married life was like a dream. He used to say, 'Iris, if it'll make you happy, buy it. I'll give you a blank cheque. And don't spend it all on the house. Spend it on yourself.' But of course my lovely home came first. How I adored that house." Here the thumb and forefinger were once again applied to the bridge of the nose.

"Where do you live?" asked Edith, aware that this was an unimpressively bald question.

"Oh, but my dear, I'm talking about our first home, in Haslemere. Oh, I wish I had the photos here. Architect designed, it was. It was my dream home. And I musn't talk about it too much, because Jennifer will get upset, won't you darling? Oh, yes, it broke her heart to leave Green Tiles."

I can just see it, thought Edith. Parquet floors. Fitted cupboards. Picture windows. Every conceivable appliance in the kitchen. Gardener twice a week. Gardener's wife, devoted, in a white overall, every day. Downstairs cloakroom for the gentlemen to use after playing a round of golf. Patio, she added.

"But when my husband went to Head Office and I saw how much travelling he was going to have to do, I put my foot down. Why should he wear himself out, I said to myself, just to please his silly little wife who loves a quiet life in the country? And anyway, I knew he would want me to entertain for him. I knew that before he did. So we moved to St. John's Wood. Montrose Court. And of course it's a beautiful flat, and I have an excellent housekeeper. And it's big enough for Jennifer to have her own suite. She can invite all her friends; I leave her entirely alone. And the shops are very good."

She dabbed the corners of her mouth again. "Of course, I have everything delivered," she added.

Having assured Edith of her comfortable circumstances at home, she went on to describe to her the tenor of their life abroad. It was clear that as travelling companions, Mrs. Pusey and Jennifer were entirely compatible. Abroad was seen mainly as a repository for luxury goods. They were extensively familiar with the kind of resort which had recently but definitely gone out of fashion; hence their presence here, although that was also explained by the bank account and the fact that Mr. and Mrs. Pusey had known M. Huber when they motored over from Montreux "in the old days." But it became clear that Mr. Pusey had frequently been left at home to do whatever he did while Jennifer and her mother took off for restorative trips to Cadenabbia or Lucerne or Amalfi or Deauville or Menton or Bordighera or Estorial. Once, only once, to Palma, but that was apparently a mistake. "I never could stand the heat. After that, my husband said he wouldn't risk the Mediterranean again, not in the high season. Of course, that was before all these package tours. Pretty place. But the heat was terrible. I spent all my time in the cathedral, trying to cool down. Never again."

No, Mrs. Pusey went on, she preferred the cooler weather. And they hated crowds. And M. Huber made them so welcome. Of course, they always had the same suite. The one on the third floor, overlooking the lake.

"Then I think we must be on the same corridor," ventured Edith. "My room is 307."

"Why, yes," said Mrs. Pusey. "That little room at the end. Of course, there are very few single rooms in a place like this." She looked speculatively at Edith. "If we go up together, you can look in and see where we are," she said. Then, urging herself effortfully to the edge of her chair, she attempted to rise, and after two false starts heaved herself upright, shaking off Jennifer's arm and steadying herself on her fine ankles. This woman is getting on for seventy, thought Edith.

But it did not seem so, as she followed the shapely midnight blue back and the wake of rosy scent into the lift and out again and along the corridor. While Jennifer was allowed forward to open the door, Mrs. Pusey made herself ready to do the honours. They did indeed have a suite: their two bedrooms could be entered separately from the corridor, but, Mrs. Pusey implied, they were invariably to be found in the small

salon that connected them and which was agreeably filled with the amen-
ities which confident people accord themselves in strange places: a colour
television, a basket of fruit, flowers, several splits of champagne. And
leading the way into her bedroom, Mrs. Pusey gestured with a smile to
a negligé in oyster-coloured satin, thickly encrusted with lace, which
was laid out over the back of a chair. "My weakness," she confided. "I
do love nice things. And there's such a good shop in Montreux. That's
why we come back here every year."

She eyed Edith again and smiled. "You should buy yourself something pretty while you're here, dear. A woman owes it to herself to have
pretty things. And if she feels good she looks good. That's what I tell
Jennifer. I always see to it that she's fitted out like a queen. Don't I,
darling?"

And she held out her arms to Jennifer who walked into them and
snuggled her face against her mother's. "Ah," laughed Mrs. Pusey. "She
loves her silly mother, don't you, darling?" And they embraced lovingly
and walked to the door, still entwined, to see Edith out. "Don't be alone,
dear," said Mrs. Pusey. "You know where to find us." And the door
had closed.

Edith found herself thinking about this conversation at various moments in the night when the Spartan firmness of her mattress made her
normally light sleep more intermittent than usual. She thought too of
the Aladdin's cave she had perceived in the Puseys' suite, with its careless
deployment of pleasurable attributes. But most of all she thought of the
charming tableau of mother and daughter entwined, their arms locked
about each other, their rosy faces turned to Edith. Seeing her, they had
taken the full measure of her solitariness, and the implication of this
condition showed in their expressions which had become quite innocent
with surprise and pity. She had felt almost apologetic as, with a stiff
little bow (and that was an association and a reminiscence in itself), she
had bid them goodnight and made her way thoughtfully to her room.
And had resolved to learn and to do better, so that this particular complex of feelings might not be activated again.

Nancy Mitford

LOVE IN A COLD CLIMATE

"Let Mr. Fleetwood be, for the present. I want to know what, exactly, you are planning to do with your life. Do you intend to live at home and go mooning on like this for ever?"

"What else can I do? You haven't exactly trained me for a career, have you?"

"Oh, yes, indeed I have. I've trained you for marriage which, in my opinion (I may be old-fashioned), is by far the best career open to any woman."

"That's all very well, but how can I marry if nobody asks me?"

Of course, that was really the sore point with Lady Montdore, nobody asking her. A Polly gay and flirtatious, surrounded by eligible suitors, playing one off against the others, withdrawing, teasing, desired by married men, breaking up her friends' romances, Lady Montdore would have been perfectly happy to watch her playing that game for several years if need be, so long as it was quite obvious that she would finally choose some suitably important husband and settle down with him. What her mother minded so dreadfully was that this acknowledged beauty should appear to have no attraction whatever for the male sex. The eldest sons had a look, said, "Isn't she lovely?" and went off with some chinless little creature from Cadogan Square. There had been three or four engagements of this sort lately which had upset Lady Montdore very much indeed.

"And why don't they ask you? It's only because you give them no encouragement. Can't you try to be a little jollier, nicer with them, no man cares to make love to a dummy, you know, it's too discouraging."

"Thank you, but I don't want to be made love to."

"Oh, dear oh, dear! Then what is it you want?"

"Leave me alone, Mother, please."

"To stay on here, with us, until you are old?"

"Daddy wouldn't mind, a bit."

"Oh, yes he would, make no mistake about that. Not for a year or two perhaps, but in the end he would. Nobody wants their girl to be hanging about for ever, a sour old maid, and you'll be the sour kind, that's too obvious already, my dear, wizened-up and sour."

I could hardly believe my ears; could this be Lady Montdore speaking, in such frank and dreadful terms, to Polly, her beautiful paragon, whom she used to love so much that she was even reconciled to her being a daughter and not an heir? It seemed to me terrible, I went cold in my very backbone.

Gloria Vanderbilt

WOMAN TO WOMAN

"Society is still rocking with the sensation of the week—the revelation that 10-year-old Gloria Vanderbilt, pawn in a desperate custody battle, stated in court she preferred living with her aunt, Mrs. Harry Payne Whitney. It was a tremendous blow to the mother, Mrs. Gloria Morgan Vanderbilt, whose income is largely derived from the child's millions.

"The words fell naively and without rancor from the 10-year-old girl's lips as she rocked in a big swivel chair in the chambers of Surpreme Court Justice John F. Carew, who had previously announced that his decision would be largely determined by Gloria.

"During a three-hour examination which was disguised as a chat, Gloria dangled her long, spindly legs from the chair and talked of many things with the jurist, who has five children of his own.

"Little Gloria wanted it understood that she did not dislike her mother. It was simply, she explained, that she hadn't seen much of her. And when she was in her mother's care, they travelled so much, all over Europe. She couldn't remember much about it, but she was sure they jumped around a great deal, so much so that she never had any steady playmates."

The sensations of color and touch are accurate but the mind plays tricks with the scale. My mother's pearls looked as huge to me as quail's eggs strung together with crystal cord. That was true to a little girl's eyes and hands. Now, they are a necklace of white beads.

I really have so few memories of her from those days. I saw very little of her, actually, because she led the life often typical of women in her world. A very social life in London or Paris, out most of the night and sleeping late in the day until the round of parties began again. She was beautiful and exquisite and my memories mostly are of her dressed to go out for the evening. She was mysterious, remote, and unattainable to me. The ropes of pearls against the soft velvet of her yellow dress. How could I ever reach her or be part of her?

All my ideals of beauty in women began with my mother. She was only eighteen when I was born; my father died shortly after. Mother moved to Europe to live. Her beauty was flawless and therefore in a sense one-dimensional. I have always, because of early memories of her, been fascinated by a stylized, model type of beauty. It was only much later, when my mother's beauty was altered by her life experience, that I came to understand and appreciate her inner truth, and found her in later life touching and vulnerable and not at all the ephemeral being who floated on the periphery of my childhood.

My mother was beautiful in a haunting and intangible way that made almost bearable the sense of loss I experienced at never seeing enough of her, and therefore never really knowing her or feeling that she belonged to me. Her presence fills my memories and dreams, and what was in-complete and unfinished between us I have overcome in my work. What was painful and destructive I have made into something of my own, changed the sorrow into something vital and accessible.

ON NANCY CUNARD

Lady Diane Cooper . . . remembers Nancy saying defiantly, during some conversation about maternal prohibitions and anxieties, "My mother's having an affair with Thomas Beecham; I can do as I like." For all Lady Cunard's care not to flout conventions, her relationship with Beecham was no secret and gave Nancy an easy weapon against her.

What seemed like discretion to her mother looked more like hypocrisy to Nancy.

It seems that Nancy's hostile feelings toward her mother were beginning to be public knowledge. One ominous incident was related in a 1914 letter from one of Lady Cunard's friends, Lady Desborough, to her son Julian Grenfell. Lady Desborough was describing an evening of parlor games at Windsor Castle, where she had recently been staying as lady-in-waiting. "They were playing the game one night of who they would like to see best come into the room and Nancy Cunard said in that high voice 'Lady Cunard *dead.*' "

For all her capacity to appear lightheartedly scornful about the breach with her mother, she was still simmering. She felt compelled to put what had happened on record; she also wanted to punish her mother for her ignorance and unkindness.

The idea of a pamphlet . . . had stayed in her mind. It was as if she could not commit herself fully to her real work against race prejudice, the anthology, until she had struck a public blow against her mother and all she stood for. Also, Nancy needed to link herself directly with the cause she now felt was the most important thing in her life. She had a strong, even exaggerated, sense of her own significance; but there was nothing affected about her wish to demonstrate her feeling of solidarity with the victims of prejudice.

In the aftermath of her visit to America and her meetings with the *Crisis* editors, Nancy dashed off a short article for them called "Does Anyone *Know* Any Negroes?" The title was a remark her mother had made to her in 1930, before she fully realized that Crowder was Nancy's lover. The piece is Nancy's summary of her experiences of race prejudice since she had met Crowder in Venice in 1928, but the heart of it is her account of her mother's attitude. As an introduction, Nancy printed, in quotes, a series of remarks made by her mother. "Does anyone *know* any Negroes? I never heard of that. You mean in Paris then? No, but who receives them . . . What sort of Negroes. What do they *do?* You mean to say they go into people's houses?" The tone is mocking rather than hostile. The article was published in *Crisis* in the issue of September 1931; if, as seems likely, Lady Cunard heard about it, she must have been still more hurt and angry. But Nancy had not finished; indeed, she had hardly begun.

Shortly before Christmas [1931] she wrote and had privately printed a pamphlet, eleven pages long, entitled *Black Man and White Ladyship: An Anniversary*. There can seldom if ever have been a more savage public attack by a daughter against her mother.

The pamphlet was divided into two sections: The first, headed "Her Ladyship," opened with Nancy describing the ingredients of the situation.

> I have a Negro friend, a very close friend (and a great many other Negro friends in France, England and America). Nothing extraordinary in that. I have also a mother—whom we will at once call—Her Ladyship. We are extremely different but I had remained on fairly good (fairly distant) terms with her for a number of years. The English Channel and a good deal of determination on my part made this possible. I sedulously avoid her social circle both in France and in England. . . .

Nancy launched into a more specific tirade against her mother.

> But, your Ladyship, you cannot kill or deport a person from England for being a Negro and mixing with white people. You may take a ticket to the cracker southern states of U.S.A. and assist at some of the choicer lynchings which are often announced in advance. You may add your purified-of-that-horrible-American-twang voice to the Yankee outburst . . . No, with you it is the other old trouble, class.
>
> Negroes, besides being black (that is, from jet to as white as yourself but not so pink), have not yet "penetrated into London Society's consciousness." You exclaim: they are not "received" (You would be surprised to know just how much they are "received"). They are not found in the Royal Red Book. Some big hostess gives a lead and the trick is done.
>
> For as yet only the hefty shadow of the Negro falls across the white assembly of High Society and spreads itself, it would seem, quite particularly and agonizingly over you.

For three pages, Nancy attacked her mother at every vulnerable point. She began: "It is now necessary to see Her Ladyship in her own fort, to perceive her a little more visually." She described her as "petite and desirable as per all attributes of the nattier court lady" and in a fierce temper over a description of herself in Cecil Beaton's recently published *Book of Beauty*. She mocked her conservatism. "What is the matter with people these days? Bolshevism is going on too, England is breaking up." She presented her as bewildered by and hostile to all forms of change and vulnerable to mocking criticism." Her Ladyship may be as hard and buoyant as a dreadnought but one touch of ridicule goes straight to her heart. And she is so alone—between little lunches of sixteen, a few callers at tea and two or three invitations per night."

Her Ladyship, according to Nancy, was frequently swindled by art dealers and jewelers because she was unable to detect fakes, and she was not above cultivating rich people who would buy and sell paintings and furniture from and to each other. Her extravagance over clothes was exposed by a useful quote from the *Daily Express*. "I have not the faintest idea how much I spend on clothes every year. It may run into thousands. I have never bothered to think about it."

Nancy attacked her mother's snobbery. "If a thing is *done,* she will, with a few negligible exceptions, do it. And the last person she has talked to is generally right, providing he is *someone.* The British Museum seems to guarantee that African art is art? Some dealers too are taking it up, so the thick old Congo ivories that she thinks are slave bangles are perhaps not so hideous after all. Though still very strange; one little diamond would be better." Her mother, Nancy continued, "likes to give—and to control. It is unbearable for her not to be able to give someone something. But suppose they don't want it—what does this *mean?*"

She went on to portray her mother as inhibited and hypocritical. "Some days she will even shy at the word 'lover.' " Although she had homosexual friends, wrote Nancy, she affected ignorance of and distaste for homosexuality. Communism was another taboo topic. "Her Ladyship is the most conscientious of ostriches and when she comes up again she hopes the *un*-pleasant thing has disappeared." Her quickness of mind was mere picking of brains; she pretended to despise gossip while fomenting it; she would drop people she suddenly heard were thought undesirable. Lady Cunard's famous generosity, hospitality and wit were derided by her daughter as empty and meaningless. "Is it an amusing atmosphere? It is a stultifying hypocrisy. Yet, away from it it has no importance; it is, yet it is unreal. There is no contact, the memories of it are so many lantern slides. They move and shift together in a crazy blur of dix-huitieme, gold plate and boiserie, topped with the great capital C, conversation, rounded off with snobbery and gossip."

Patrick White

THE EYE OF THE STORM

Sister Badgery was delighted to hear of this material success. She brought a brush and began stroking her patient's hair.

"I don't believe you know my daughter's name."

"Well, 'Dorothy,' isn't it? I'm no good at those foreign names."

"I shall teach you," said Mrs. Hunter, her lips inflating as though she were tasting a delicious food, her nostrils filling with what could have been a subtle perfume. " '*Princesse de Lascabanes*' "; she laid on the French pretty thick for Sister Badgery's benefit. "Let me hear you say it."

The nurse obliged after a fashion. "But what shall I call her?" the voice whined despairingly.

"Nothing more elaborate than 'Madame.' "

" 'Mad-damn, mad-damn,' " Sister Badgery breathed in imitation, and a more sonorous variant, " 'Ma-darm!' "

Mrs. Hunter sensed she had got her nurse under control, which was where she wanted her; she also suspected Sister Badgery would refer to "Princess Dorothy" to please herself and impress her friends.

"Mad-damm, ma-darm!" Happier for its new accomplishment the voice went clucking in and out the golden morning.

Mrs. Hunter was so soothed by clocks and brandy it seemed unlikely that anybody would arrive; if they did, it might even be undesirable: her life was too closely charted.

"Open mouth! Mrs. Hunter?" It was that Badgery again. "Whatever happens, we must take our temp, mustn't we?"

What did they call it? Dettol? Cool, anyway. Sterilizing. Was it better this way: to be sterilized out of existence? I don't mind dying, Dr. Gidley, but I do expect my nurses to protect me against worse than death: such as the visitants you do not conjure up for yourself, worst of all the tender ones.

"Shall I be strong enough, I wonder?"

Holding her patient's wrist, Sister Badgery found it unnecessary to answer: the pulse was remarkably strong.

When they were both shocked, if not positively alarmed, by an interruption to their celebration.

The door opened.

"Sister, can she be seen?" It was Mr. Wyburd in something too loud for a whisper and less than his usual grammar. "The princess has arrived. Her daughter."

As if this were not enough, a second figure was pushing rustling past the one at the door: for Mrs. Hunter it was sound perfume joy despair; whereas Sister Badgery saw a tall thin hatless woman, somewhere around fifty (to be on the kind side), her dress unsurprising except for its simplicity and the pearls bounding about around her neck, and on her bosom, as she half ran half staggered.

A princess shouldn't run, the nurse recovered herself enough to disapprove; and she shouldn't have a horse face.

But Dorothy floundered, imperviously, on. "O *mon Dieu, aidez-moi!*" she gasped, before assuming another of her selves, or voices, to utter, "Mother!" and lower, "Mum!"

Then, by act of special grace, a blind was drawn over the expression the intruder was wearing for this old *mummy* propped up in bed, a thermometer sticking out of its mouth; if life were present, it was the life generated by jewels with which the rigid claws were loaded.

The princess fell against the bed, groping through the scents of Dettol and baby powder, to embrace, deeper than her mother, her own childhood.

Rejecting the thermometer with her mouth—lucky it didn't break off—Mrs. Hunter was smiling, whether in bliss or fright it was difficult to tell.

Till she giggled through her flux of tears, "Too much excitement! I think I've wet myself."

"I want to talk to my daughter—Mrs. Wyburd—privately," Mrs. Hunter said.

She knew from the sound of the knife-edged skirt that she had offended her nurse. That made two presents she would have to give: Mrs. Wyburd and Mrs. Badgery.

When the nurse had closed the door the princess felt imprisoned, not only in the room, but in her own body. In her state of foreboding she reached out for the glass of barley water Sister Badgery had removed, and tried to find comfort in sips of that mawkish stuff. She could see herself in one of the looking-glasses with which her blind mother still kept herself surrounded. If the princess had not been so terrified of what the next moment could hold, she might have noticed that her own eyes were deep and lustrous: beautiful in fact; but in the circumstances her mind could only flutter through imagined eventualities.

Actually, Mrs. Hunter was enjoying the luxury of being alone and perfectly silent with somebody she loved. (They did love each other, didn't they? You could never be sure about other people; sometimes you found they had hated you all their lives.) This state of perfect stillness was not unlike what she enjoyed in her relationship with Sister de Santis, though in essence it was different; with the night nurse she was frequently united in a worship of something too vast and selfless to describe even if your mind had been completely compos whatever it is. This other state of unity in perfect stillness, which she hoped she was beginning to enjoy with Dorothy, she had experienced finally with Alfred when she returned to "Kudjeri" to nurse him in his last illness. There were moments when their minds were folded into each other without any trace of the cross-hatching of wilfulness or desire to possess. Yet at the same time all the comfort of touch was present in their absorption. At least that was the way you had felt, and believed, or hoped for the same in someone else.

Mrs. Hunter coughed out of delicacy for the feelers extended in the direction of her silent daughter.

Dorothy said, after swallowing, "I do think, darling, they ought to get you another carpet. This one is threadbare in places, particularly at the door."

Mrs. Hunter gasped and frowned. "I haven't noticed." Then she recovered herself. "They haven't told me." She began easing one or two of her encrusting rings. "I expect they've worked it out that I'm going to die—that it wouldn't be worth while."

Dorothy was making those pained sounds.

"But I shan't die—or anyway, not till I feel like it. I don't believe anybody dies who doesn't want to—unless by thunderbolts."

"Nobody wants to suggest you're going to die, Mother."

"Then why does everybody come flying from the ends of the earth?"

The Princesse de Lascabanes knew that her eyes were threatening to overflow: because the great, the constant grudge had been against her over-controlled feelings; when the showdown came, hadn't he even accused her of being "frigid"?

"I can only—well, I'd like to explain your flying out here as lack of emotional control," Mother was still bashing. "I expect they told you I had a stroke. In that case, you were misinformed. I only had a very slight—what was hardly a stroke at all."

Dorothy Hunter plunged her hands as deep as she could into the bowels of the dusty old uncomfortable chair; she would stick it out.

"In any case you flew—to make sure you'd see me die—or to ask me for money if I didn't. Basil too."

"Oh God, Mother, don't you allow for the possibility of human affection?" The outraged daughter snatched back her hands from out of the depths of the chair: what her mother had said was the more cruel for being partly true.

"Dorothy, didn't I ever tell you of my experience in a cyclone?"

Mother was daring you not to have known. She was standing at the head of the stairs, one arm outstretched, pointing, in a dress of blinding white such as had suited her best: cold and perfect in its way. And now a mere daughter, in spite of trial by marriage, the exorcism of a number of doubts, and arrival at perhaps a few mature conclusions, was frightened to the edge of panic by whatever revelation this vision of earthly authority might be threatening her with.

"No," she protested. "You didn't tell—that is, I think I remember hearing—yes, about a storm."

Somehow she must be spared: Mother must grant her this one concession.

"If I didn't write to you at the time, I must have been too annoyed with you—flying off like that—in a rage." Mrs. Hunter sounded reasonable, calm, just. "It was when the Warmings asked us to stay on their island. They had to leave in a hurry. One of the children was sick, I think. Then you rushed away. You missed a lot of excitement—and made a fool of yourself."

Mrs. Hunter laughed gently; it sounded almost as though she still had those small but exquisite teeth. "What was the name of the professor man?"

Dorothy Hunter was frozen beyond answering. She shouldn't have been; it had happened fifteen years ago.

"Anyway, it was while I was on the island that this cyclone struck. Oh, I shall tell you—when I can find the strength. I can see the birds, just as your Russian said."

If physical strength was letting her down, her capacity for cruelty would never fail her: to drag in Edvard Pehl. At her most loving, Mother had never been able to resist the cruel thrust. To have loved her in the prime of her beauty, as many had, was like loving, or "admiring" rather, a jewelled scabbard in which a sword was hidden: which would clatter out under the influence of some peculiar frenzy, to slash off your ears, the fingers, the tongues, or worse, impale the hearts, of those who worshipped. And yet we continued to offer ourselves, if reluctantly. As they still do, it appears: to this ancient scabbard, from which the jewels have loosened and scattered, the blind sockets filled instead with verdigris, itself a vengeful semi-jewellery, the sword still sharp in spite of age and use.

She must try to define her love for her mother: it had remained something beyond her understanding.

And the cyclone: why was it given to Elizabeth Hunter to experience the eye of the storm? That too! Or are regenerative states of mind granted to the very old to ease the passage from their earthly, sensual natures into final peace and forgiveness? Of course Mother could have imagined her state of grace amongst the resting birds, just as she had imagined Mrs. Hewlett's escaped lovebird and the mad or distraught gardener. Though remembering some frightfulness the prince had forced on her mind more painfully than on her body, Dorothy de Lascabanes suspected the lovebird's murder was not an invention.

Vera Brittain

LADY INTO WOMAN

Vera Brittain's letter of dedication to her daughter Shirley Williams

My dear Daughter,

I owe you much gratitude for the title which you were resourceful enough to suggest.

You were right to propose a form of words which implies that the democratic movement described in this book has not been concerned exclusively with sex equality.

Not only has the sheltered "lady" of the Victorian epoch become the self-sufficient "woman" of today; the political and social changes of

the past half-century have brought her close in experience and under-standing to the millions of women in all past ages who were never sheltered and always had to work.

You will find that I have not attempted to be soberly impartial about the emancipation of women, past, present, or future; with Canon Raven I believe it to be more significant, and more beneficial, than any great constructive change of the past fifty years. But I do not expect every reader of this book to agree, for the backwoodsmen are still with us.

Up to date they have hardly troubled you, but unlike many of your contemporaries you do not regard the women's movment as a bygone issue. Even from your brief experience you know that it is continuing, and still has far to go.

When you were growing up you sometimes suggested, as you had every right to do, that certain aspects of your upbringing might have been better. But you have had three advantages which you do, I believe, acknowledge as likely to be of special service to you in your life and work.

First, you owe to the Infant Welfare movement in general, and the Chelsea Babies' Club in particular, the vital energy and powers of en-durance which have enabled you to show that the physical inferiority of women was a myth based upon faulty training and a traditional expec-tation of feminine weakness.

Secondly, you have been free from the implanted sense of inferiority that handicaps so many women by undermining the self-confidence which is the basis of all achievement, both masculine and feminine. You were deeply desired as a *daughter,* and it was always taken for granted by both your parents that your education and opportunities would be equal to your brother's. The women of your family had sought these benefits before you. Your paternal grandmother was a pioneer suffragist; your mother grew up with that eager generation of young feminists who were the first to inherit the freedom won for women by women. You have repaid us both by making a full and early use of your heritage.

Thirdly, you belong to a household in which a woman's work has been constantly in progress, and professional standards obeyed with the same sense of obligation by a wife and mother as by a husband and father. You have never been made to feel that the profession adopted by a woman is somehow less important than the one chosen by a man, or that her failure to do as well as she is able should be condoned and excused because of her sex.

My work, it is true, has been more interrupted than yours, I hope, will be, for I belong to a generation in which most families still took, and take, for granted that a woman's vocation should be laid aside for parental illness, the troubles of relatives, and domestic trivialities of every description.

I could have written much better if I had been interrupted much less, and should have proved altogether a more effective person had I not been obliged—and not only in my youth—to spend time and energy in learning to believe in myself and my purposes despite the enervating influence of an Edwardian childhood.

That you, who have been spared that particular battle, will live to see women ascend to heights of achievement hitherto undreamed of and make your own contribution to this future stage of a great revolution, is the constant and joyful hope of

Your Mother.

Billie Holiday

LADY SINGS THE BLUES

Our little flat was more than a home. It was a combination YMCA, boardinghouse for broke musicians, soup kitchen for anyone with a hard-luck story, community center, and after-after-hours joint where a couple of bucks would get you a shot of whisky and the most fabulous fried-chicken breakfast, lunch, or dinner anywhere in town.

Mom just loved people. Part of this might have come from never wanting to be alone, where she could only brood over Pop. Part of it must have come from her fears for me. She knew she wouldn't be around for very long to take care of me. There was damn little she could do to protect me after she was gone. All she had was me. All I had was her. She always figured if she was good to people and did things for them without any reward on this earth she was laying up good will in some heavenly bank. Then after she was gone I'd have something to draw on. And some of these people, she hoped, would be good to me in return. It hasn't worked that way. Not yet anyway. But that's the way she felt, bless her.

Mom not only loved people, she believed in them. She believed God made them, so there had to be some good in everybody. She found good in the strangest places and in the strangest people. She could find good in pimps and whores, even in thieves and murderers.

A bitch might be turning fifteen tricks a day and come to Mom in trouble, and Mom would go to bat for her, saying, "She's a good little thing deep down underneath, and that's what matters."

She'd have a fit if someone dropped their hat on the bed or dropped salt on the floor. These were things she really took seriously. But she wouldn't bat an eye at other things people did. She kept her eye on the good spots she found in them somewhere.

You could be the biggest thief and scoundrel on the face of the earth, but all you had to do was tell Mom you were a musician and give her a little story and she'd give you everything in the house that wasn't nailed down.

People took advantage of her, sure. But there wasn't a cat around in those days who didn't respect her. If Mom caught herself saying "Goddamn" she'd have to go confess it. She was that proper and respectable. The house might be full and she'd be fixing fried chicken for a party of characters, and a fracas would start—some cat would be cussing out some broad a blue streak. But he'd always stop somewhere in the middle, out of respect to Mom, and say, "Excuse me, Mom, I'm sorry, but I got to straighten this whore out."

I never got beyond the fifth grade in school—and they were Baltimore's broken-down segregated schools at that. But I guess you could call that progress. Mom was only thirteen years older than me and had never got to school at all.

In my time the Board of Education didn't care enough about it to send some social worker chasing after me. In Mom's time they didn't care at all.

One of the things we did together in those early Harlem days was hold classes. I was the teacher, Mom the pupil. And I taught her to read and write. Nothing I ever did gave me such a kick as getting a handwritten note from her later when I was on the road, or watching her fall out when she read a letter from Louis Armstrong signed "Red Beans and Ricely Yours."

One night Mom was campaigning for her damn restaurant when Brenda was at the house. Right off she offered to be an angel for the project.

It was her way of keeping tight with me, but it was what Mom wanted. So she started planning and eventually ended up with a place of her own, Mom Holiday's, on 99th Street near Columbus.

I didn't fight it because it kept Mom busy and happy and stopped her from worrying and watching over me.

It wasn't long before I was sorry. Going legit couldn't change the Duchess. Nobody could just be a customer. They were all people and she loved them. Half of Local 802 was soon hanging around. All you had to do was say you were a musician or a friend of mine and you could get anything in the joint.

Cats could come in, order themselves a big feed, then give her a story instead of money. Then sometimes Mom would give them some change on the way out. She was always giving change for money she never saw.

The best paying customer she had was me. Every time I went in the place I paid for something.

One time she'd have a long face on, waiting for me.

"The Board of Health was here," she'd say. "They said we got to have two toilets."

The damn Board of Health could pass by thousands of Harlem tenements with no damn toilets at all, then land on the Duchess and tell her she had to have two.

So it would take a few hundred bucks for that. Then the next time I'd turn around she'd say, "The Board of Health was here again. They say I can't fry hamburgers in a pan any more. I got to have a griddle."

So I handed over another few bucks for a griddle. Fifty for this. And forty for that. I don't know how much it cost me to keep the Board of Health happy, but it was plenty. And I never got back a quarter.

I only tried once. And neither me nor Mom ever forgot it. I needed some money one night and I knew Mom was sure to have some. So I walked in the restaurant like a stockholder and asked.

Mom turned me down flat. She wouldn't give me a cent. She was mad with me and I was mad with her. We exchanged a few words. Then I said, "God bless the child that's got his own," and walked out.

I stayed sore for three weeks. I thought about it and thought about it. One day a whole damn song fell into place in my head. Then I rushed down to the Village that night and met Arthur Herzog. He sat down at a piano and picked it out, phrase by phrase, as I sang it to him.

I couldn't wait to get it down and get it recorded. I told him about the fight with Mom and how I wanted to get even. We changed the lyrics in a couple of spots, but not much.

This one will gas the duchess, I thought. And it did.

GOD BLESS THE CHILD

Them that's got shall get
Them that's not shall lose
So the Bible says
And it still is news
Mama may have
Papa may have
But God bless the child that's got his own
That's got his own.

Yes, the strong gets more
While the weak ones fade
Empty pockets don't
Ever make the grade
Mama may have
Papa may have
But God bless the child that's got his own
That's got his own.

Money, you've got lots of friends
Crowding round your door
But when it's done
And spending ends
They don't come no more

Rich relations give
Crust of bread and such
You can help yourself but don't take much
Mama may have
Papa may have
But God bless the child that's got his own
That's got his own.

Saki

THE BAKER'S DOZEN

EM: We were just talking of you when you joined us.

MRS. P-P: Really! Nothing dreadful I hope.

EM: Oh, dear, no! It's too early on the voyage for that sort of thing. We were feeling rather sorry for you.

MRS. P-P: Sorry for me? Whatever for?

MAJ.: Your childless hearth and all that, you know. No little pattering feet.

MRS. P-P: Major! How dare you? I've got my little girl, I suppose you know. Her feet can patter as well as other children's.

MAJ.: Only one pair of feet.

MRS. P-P: Certainly. My child isn't a centipede. Considering the way they move us about in those horrid jungle stations, without a decent bungalow to set one's foot in, I consider I've got a heartless child, rather than a childless hearth. Thank you for your sympathy all the same. I daresay it was well meant. Impertinence often is.

EM: Dear Mrs. Paly-Paget, we were only feeling sorry for your sweet little girl when she grows older, you know. No little brothers and sisters to play with.

MRS. P-P: Mrs. Carewe, this conversation strikes me as being indelicate, to say the least of it. I've only been married two and a half years, and my family is naturally a small one.

MAJ.: Isn't it rather an exaggeration to talk of one little female child as a family? A family suggests numbers.

MRS. P-P: Really, Major, your language is extraordinary. I dare-say I've only got a little female child, as you call it, at present—

MAJ.: Oh, it won't change into a boy later on, if that's what you're counting on. Take our word for it; we've had so much more experience in these affairs than you have. Once a female, always a female. Nature is not infallible, but she always abides by her mistakes.

Edith G. Neisser

MOTHERS AND DAUGHTERS

If any conclusion is to be drawn from a search for mothers and daughters in literature it would be that in fiction and drama a dozen or more favorite themes occur repeatedly in varied, but almost always in domestic, settings. These are, of course, by no means the only themes to be found. Our own era is more interested in the relationship than earlier ones appear to have been, probably because more women read and more women write, and because women and their lives within their families have come to be recognized as interesting and important, and not only to other women. Since the tremendous influence of the relationship on the lives of the two women and on the life of everyone with whom they come in contact is recognized, perhaps before long someone will write a novel of the first rank which gives the whole sweep of the relationship throughout the lives of the two generations.

ON DIANE ARBUS

With Allan away at war, the Nemerovs were insisting that Diane move into their new apartment at 888 Park. A nice, freshly decorated room awaited her; everything would be taken care of—meals, maids, her bills.

And she could talk on the phone as much as she wanted. "Diane had telephonitis," a friend said. So she returned, a bit sullen, and within a few days she and her mother were arguing. She told Naomi Rosenbloom, "Mommy keeps telling me to wear my galoshes in the rain and I don't want to anymore."

Diane's own daughter, Doon, was born on April 3, 1945. Afterward Diane told Naomi Rosenbloom that she had forbidden her mother and sister to accompany her to the hospital. She hadn't wanted anyone close to her to witness her personal drama of "dread, guilt, and expectation." Diane was terrified of being alone, but she believed she had to be alone to really experience something. Only then would it count.

As soon as she got back to the Nemerov apartment, she bustled about, trying to act very grown-up, very much the little woman. "She became a wonderful mother," Renee says. "Tender, gentle, loving—she absolutely adored Doon and felt magically connected to her." When the baby was only a month old, Diane entwined her bassinet with fresh flowers and pasted postcards on the walls—prints of Roman ruins, Greek statues, English landscapes—"things for the baby to see and absorb when she wakes up."

She loved showing her tiny daughter off. Ben Lichtenstein dropped by the Nemerov apartment and Diane woke Doon up and put her on the floor, ordering, "Now crawl for your Uncle Ben, Doonie." And Doon wriggled across the carpet and Diane beamed. She was very proud.

Gertrude Nemerov had decided to take over the care and feeding of her granddaughter, Doon, and without consulting Diane she had hired a German nurse and insisted that Doon be bottle-fed, even though Diane had been breast-feeding her baby. Arguments ensued. Diane held her ground. Finally a compromise was reached: before every feeding the nurse would put Doon on the scales to be weighed and then Diane would attempt to breast-feed her, after which Doon would be weighed again to see if she had gained any nourishment.

Peggy says, "I felt so sorry for Diane. She was under such scrutiny that often the milk wouldn't flow. She was trembling with nerves—with the German nurse and Gertrude hovering over her." Peggy remembers that once after the feeding-and-weighing procedure Diane suddenly burst into the hall and ran up and down crying triumphantly, "Doon gained five and half ounces!"

ON MARIE ANTOINETTE

Maria Theresa to Marie Antoinette, 4 May 1770

Madame my dear daughter,
So there you are—where Providence has settled you must live. If one is
to consider only the greatness of your position, you are the happiest of
your sisters and all princesses. You will find a loving father who will
also be your friend if you deserve it. You may trust him completely;
you will risk nothing. Love him, obey him, try to guess his thoughts;
you cannot do too much of this at the time when I lose you. . . . As to
the Dauphin, I say nothing; you know how touchy I am on that point;
the wife must be completely submissive to her husband and must have
no business other than to please him and obey him. The only true
happiness in this world is a happy marriage: I can say so freely. All
depends on the wife, on her being willing, sweet, and amusing.

Maria Theresa to Marie Antoinette

Schönbrunn, 3 October 1773

My other complaint is not cleared up either . . . you are riding a great
deal, especially at the hunt . . .
　　I kept silent as long as there was no real marriage, but now that you
tell me that everything is all right, I must speak, and you must do what
you promised. A married woman can never be sure she is not pregnant,
and there is never more danger than during the first four weeks. You
can't even know whether you are or not. I stress this, not to frighten
you, but to jolt you into thinking seriously that this sport, if you go on
living together as husband and wife, is highly unsuitable.

Marie Antoinette to Maria Theresa, 31 August 1775

Madame my very dear Mother,
Your dear letter revived me. The idea that my dear Mama disapproved
of me was most upsetting to me; I hope that I will never deserve such
feelings for these suspicions. As for protections and recommendations, I
think that in *ce pays-ci* it is impossible to avoid them; it is even a matter

of etiquette that the members of my Household be given no special favors unless I have asked for them; the essential point is that my protection must always be well-placed, and I will always do my best. It would be unreasonable if I were to be annoyed at my condition [the nonconsummation of her marriage]; but I think a great deal about it and speak to the King about it quite often, although always with sweetness and measure. I am trying to make him feel he should have the little operation [circumcision], which has already been mentioned and which I believe to be necessary.

Marie Antoinette to Maria Theresa, 12 November 1775

The King seems more friendly and trusting to me than ever, and I have nothing more I can possibly want from that side. As for the important question which worries my dear mama, I am very sorry to have nothing new to report; the laziness is surely not on my side. I understand better than ever how important this point is for my future; but my dear Mama must realize that my situation is a difficult one and that patience and sweetness are my only weapons. I am still hoping, and the King often sleeps with me. . . .

Maria Theresa to Marie Antoinette, 3 October 1777

Madame my dear daughter,
Two of your letters, those of the first of last month, and of the twenty-second, have abated somewhat the great joy you gave me in that of August 30. I am not sorry about the irregularity of your period, as long as you are not used to its being late. It is a sign that nature is changing, and we must hope that God, who after so many years has granted us one important point, will also grant us the rest. I am sorry that the King doesn't like to sleep with you; I consider this a very essential point, not to have children but so as to be more closely united and trusting in each other by thus spending, every day, a few hours alone together. But you are right not to insist on it; just keep paying attention to it so as to bring it little by little to where we want it; but, my dear daughter, to do that you will have to make an effort, you must go to bed at the time which suits the King and arise also at his time. . . .

Marie Antoinette to Maria Theresa

Versailles, 18 March 1778
Lent has brought us back to our normal way of living. The King sleeps

with me three or four nights a week and behaves in such a way as to give me great hopes.

Oscar Wilde

THE IMPORTANCE OF BEING EARNEST

ACT 1

LADY BRACKNELL: Pardon me, you are not engaged to any one. When you do become engaged to some one, I, or your father, should his health permit him, will inform you of the fact. An engagement should come on a young girl as a surprise, pleasant or unpleasant, as the case may be. It is hardly a matter that she could be allowed to arrange for herself. . . . And now I have a few questions to put to you, Mr. Worthing. While I am making these inquiries, you, Gwendolen, will wait for me below in the carriage.

GWENDOLEN *(reproachfully):* Mamma!

LADY BRACKNELL: In the carriage, Gwendolen!
> *Gwendolen goes to the door. She and Jack blow kisses to each other behind Lady Bracknell's back. Lady Bracknell looks vaguely about as if she could not understand what the noise was. Finally turns round.*
Gwendolen, the carriage!

GWENDOLEN: Yes, mamma. *(Goes out, looking back at Jack.)*

LADY BRACKNELL *(sitting down):* You can take a seat, Mr. Worthing.
> *Looks in her pocket for note-book and pencil.*

JACK: Thank you, Lady Bracknell, I prefer standing.

LADY BRACKNELL *(pencil and note-book in hand):* I feel bound to tell you that you are not down on my list of eligible young men, although I have the same list as the dear Duchess of Bolton has. We work together, in fact. However, I am quite ready to enter your name, should your answers be what a really affectionate mother requires. Do you smoke?

JACK: Well, yes, I must admit I smoke.

LADY BRACKNELL: I am glad to hear it. A man should always have an occupation of some kind. There are far too many idle men in London as it is. How old are you?

JACK: Twenty-nine.

LADY BRACKNELL: A very good age to be married at. I have always been of opinion that man who desires to get married should know either everything or nothing. Which do you know?

JACK *(after some hesitation):* I know nothing, Lady Bracknell.

LADY BRACKNELL: I am pleased to hear it. I do not approve of anything that tampers with natural ignorance. Ignorance is like a delicate exotic fruit; touch it and the bloom is gone. The whole theory of modern education is radically unsound. Fortunately in England, at any rate, education produces no effect whatsoever. If it did, it would prove a serious danger to the upper classes, and probably lead to acts of violence in Grosvenor Square. What is your income?

JACK: Between seven and eight thousand a year.

LADY BRACKNELL *(makes a note in her book):* In land, or in investments?

JACK: In investments, chiefly.

LADY BRACKNELL: That is satisfactory. What between the duties expected of one during one's lifetime, and the duties enacted from one after one's death, land has ceased to be either a profit or a pleasure. It gives one position, and prevents one from keeping it up. That's all that can be said about land.

JACK: I have a country house with some land, of course, attached to it, about fifteen hundred acres, I believe; but I don't depend on that for my real income. In fact, as far as I can make out, the poachers are the only people who make anything out of it.

LADY BRACKNELL: A country house! How many bedrooms? Well, that point can be cleared up afterwards. You have a town house, I hope? A girl with a simple, unspoiled nature, like Gwendolen, could hardly be expected to reside in the country.

JACK: Well, I own a house in Belgrave Square, but it is let by the year to Lady Bloxham. Of course, I can get it back whenever I like, at six months' notice.

LADY BRACKNELL: Lady Bloxham? I don't know her.

JACK: Oh, she goes about very little. She is a lady considerably advanced in years.

LADY BRACKNELL: Ah, nowadays that is no guarantee of respectability of character. What number in Belgrave Square?

JACK: 149.

LADY BRACKNELL *(shaking her head):* The unfashionable side. I thought there was something. However, that could easily be altered.

JACK: Do you mean the fashion, or the side?

LADY BRACKNELL *(sternly):* Both, if necessary, I presume. What are your politics?

JACK: Well, I am afraid I really have none. I am a Liberal Unionist.

LADY BRACKNELL: Oh, they count as Tories. They dine with us. Or come in the evening, at any rate. Now to minor matters. Are your parents living?

JACK: I have lost both my parents.

LADY BRACKNELL: Both? . . . That seems like carelessness. Who was your father? He was evidently a man of some wealth. Was he born in what the Radical papers call the purple of commerce, or did he rise from the ranks of the aristocracy?

JACK: I am afraid I really don't know. The fact is, Lady Bracknell, I said

I had lost my parents. It would be nearer the truth to say that my parents seem to have lost me. . . . I don't actually know who I am by birth. I was . . . well, I was found.

LADY BRACKNELL: Found!

JACK: The late Mr. Thomas Cardew, an old gentleman of a very charitable and kindly disposition, found me, and gave me the name of Worthing, because he happened to have a first-class ticket for Worthing in his pocket at the time. Worthing is a place in Sussex. It is a seaside resort.

LADY BRACKNELL: Where did the charitable gentleman who had a first-class ticket for this seaside resort find you?

JACK *(gravely)*: In a hand-bag.

LADY BRACKNELL: A hand-bag?

JACK *(very seriously)*: Yes, Lady Bracknell. I was in a hand-bag—a somewhat large, black leather hand-bag, with handles to it—an ordinary hand-bag in fact.

LADY BRACKNELL: In what locality did this Mr. James, or Thomas, Cardew come across this ordinary hand-bag?

JACK: In the cloak-room at Victoria Station. It was given to him in mistake for his own.

LADY BRACKNELL: The cloak-room at Victoria Station?

JACK: Yes. The Brighton line.

LADY BRACKNELL: The line is immaterial. Mr. Worthing, I confess I feel somewhat bewildered by what you have just told me. To be born, or at any rate bred, in a hand-bag, whether it had handles or not, seems to me to display a contempt for the ordinary decencies of family life that reminds one of the worst excesses of the French Revolution. And I presume you know what that unfortunate movement led to? As for the particular locality in which the hand-bag was found, a cloak-room at a railway station might serve to conceal a social indiscretion—has probably, indeed, been used for that purpose before now—but it could hardly be regarded as an assured basis for a recognized position in good society.

JACK: May I ask you then what you would advise me to do? I need hardly say I would do anything in the world to ensure Gwendolen's happiness.

LADY BRACKNELL: I would strongly advise you, Mr. Worthing, to try and acquire some relations as soon as possible, and to make a definite effort to produce at any rate one parent, of either sex, before the season is quite over.

JACK: Well, I don't see how I could possibly manage to do that. I can produce the hand-bag at any moment. It is in my dressing-room at home. I really think that should satisfy you, Lady Bracknell.

LADY BRACKNELL: Me, sir! What has it to do with me? You can hardly imagine that I and Lord Bracknell would dream of allowing our only daughter—a girl brought up with the utmost care—to marry into a cloak-room, and form an alliance with a parcel. Good-morning, Mr. Worthing!

Lady Bracknell sweeps out in majestic indignation.

A MOTHER'S LOT—
MOTHER'S FAULT

Mrs. Margaret Whitlam

Now that I've reached the age,
or maybe the stage,
where I need my children more
than they need me,
I really understand how grand it is
to be a grandmother.

Proverb

God could not be everywhere, so he made mothers.

Dr. Anne Silcock

Motherhood is both the process of conceiving and giving birth to a separate unique individual and the challenge of providing the growing child with an environment which is optimally tuned to his particular needs and possibilities for development.

Margaret Drabble

CHILDREN—A BRIEF HISTORY OF MY ADDICTION

I used to be a reasonably careless and adventurous person before I had children: now I am morbidly obsessed by seat-belts and constantly afraid that low-flying aircraft will drop on my children's school.

Dr. Margaret Raphael

Being a mother is rewarding to one's female instincts, trying to one's nerves, physically exhausting, emotionally both frustrating and satisfying, and above all, *not* to be undertaken lightly.

Major Doris Pengilly

Motherhood is being available to your children whenever they need you, no matter what their age or their need.

William Blake

SONGS OF EXPERIENCE: "INFANT SORROW"

My mother groaned, my father wept,
Into the dangerous world I leapt;
Helpless, naked, piping loud,
Like a fiend hid in a cloud.

Milan Kundera

THE BOOK OF LAUGHTER AND FORGETTING

There had been a time when Marketa disliked her mother-in-law. When she and Karel were living with his family (her father-in-law was still alive then), she had daily run-ins with her. The woman was so hostile and ready to take offense. They couldn't stand it very long and moved out. "As far from Mother as possible" was their slogan at the time. They found a place in a town at the other end of the country and didn't have to see Karel's parents any more than once a year, if that often.

Then one day her father-in-law died, and Mother was left all alone. They saw her at the funeral. She was meek and miserable and seemed smaller to them than before. Both had the same thought: you can't stay here alone now—come live with us.

Both had the same thought, but neither could quite come out and say it. Especially since the solemn walk she took with them the day after the funeral when, miserable and shrunken as she was, she gave them a lecture of every sin they had ever committed against her—and with a vehemence they found totally inappropriate. "Nothing will ever change her," said Karel to Marketa when they were alone in the train. "Sad as it may be, 'far from Mother' still holds."

But the years rolled on, and though Mother did not in fact change, Marketa must have changed, because she suddenly felt that all the things her mother-in-law had done to hurt her were actually harmless and silly and that she was the one at fault for attaching such importance to a few hard words. Until then she had looked at Mother the way a child looks at an adult, but now the roles were reversed: Marketa was the adult, and Mother, seen from a distance at least, was as small and defenseless as a child. She felt a surge of indulgence, tolerance, and even began corresponding with her. The old woman took to it very quickly, wrote back conscientiously, and demanded more and more letters from Marketa. They were the only thing that made living alone bearable, she claimed.

The thought that had taken shape at the funeral of Karel's father began running through their minds again. And again the son checked the daughter-in-law's kind instincts. Instead of saying, "Mother, come live with us," they invited her to stay for a week.

It was Easter, and their ten-year-old son had gone off on vacation. Eva was due the next weekend, on Sunday. They were willing to spend the whole week with Mother, except for that Sunday. You can come this Saturday, they told her, and stay until the next. We've got something on for Sunday, somewhere to go. They did not say anything more definite because they were not too anxious to talk about Eva. Karel said it twice more over the phone. From this Saturday to next. We've got something on for Sunday, somewhere to go. And Mother answered, "Yes, children, that's very nice of you. You can be sure I'll leave whenever you want me to. All I ask is a bit of respite from my loneliness."

But when on Saturday evening Marketa tried to arrange a time for them to take her to the station the next morning, Mother announced clearly and simply that she would not be leaving until Monday. When Marketa looked surprised, she added, "Karel told me you had something on for Monday, somewhere to go, so I'd have to leave by Monday."

Now Marketa could certainly have said, "You've made a mistake, Mother, we're leaving tomorrow," but she didn't have the courage. She couldn't just make up a place to say they were visiting. She realized they'd been very careless about their alibi, so she didn't say anything at all and resigned herself to the fact that Mother would be staying with them all of Sunday too. Her only consolation was that the boy's room, the room they had put her in, was at the other end of the apartment and Mother would not bother them.

"Come on now, don't be mean," she said to Karel disapprovingly. "Just look at her, poor thing. She really breaks my heart."

Karel gave a resigned shrug. Marketa was right. Mother had changed. She was satisfied with everything, grateful for everything. Karel had expected a confrontation over some trifle. It never came.

Once when they were out walking, she gazed into the distance and asked, "What's the name of that pretty white village?" There was no village, just stone road markers. Karel felt an upsurge of pity when he realized how much his mother's sight had deteriorated.

But the defect in her sight seemed to explain something much more basic: what was large for them was small for her; what were stones for them were houses for her.

To tell the truth, this characteristic of hers was not entirely new, but at one time it had bothered them greatly. One night, for example, the tanks of a huge neighboring country came and occupied their country. The shock was so great, so terrible, that for a long time no one could think about anything else. It was August, and the pears in their garden were nearly ripe. The week before, Mother had invited the local pharmacist to come and pick them. He never came, never even apologized. The fact that Mother refused to forgive him drove Karel and Marketa crazy. Everybody's thinking about tanks, and all you can think about is pears, they yelled. And when shortly thereafter they moved away, they took the memory of her pettiness with them.

But are tanks really more important than pears? As time passed, Karel realized that the answer was not so obvious as he had once thought, and he began sympathizing secretly with Mother's perspective —a big pear in the foreground and somewhere off in the distance a tank, tiny as a ladybug, ready at any moment to take wing and disappear from sight. So Mother was right after all: tanks are mortal, pears eternal.

Mother used to insist on knowing everything about her son and was angry when he tried to hide any of his life from her, so this time they decided to make her happy and tell her all about what they did, what went on in their lives, what they thought about things. They soon noticed, though, that Mother was only listening to them to be polite and would respond to their stories with a remark about her poodle, which she left with a neighbor while she was away.

There was a time when he would have considered it egocentric or small-minded of her, but now he knew better. The years went by more quickly than they realized. Mother had laid down the field marshal's baton of her motherhood and moved on to a different world. On another one of their walks they had been caught in a storm. They put their arms under hers and propped her up on either side. If they had not literally carried her along, the wind would have blown her away like a feather. Karel was touched to feel how ridiculously little she weighed in his hands. He realized his mother belonged to a different order of creature: smaller, lighter, more easily blown away.

Mother had never been particularly interested in her daughter-in-law's relatives, but the words "cousin," "niece," "aunt," and "granddaughter" made her feel warm inside. They formed a comfortable sphere of intimate concepts.

And here she had another confirmation of something she had long known: her son was an incurable eccentric. How could Mother ever be in the way with a relative visiting? She could understand their wanting to talk by themselves, but it made no sense at all to send her away a day early just for that. Fortunately, she'd figured out a way to handle them. She simply made believe she'd mixed up the schedule they'd agreed on. She almost enjoyed the look on that poor girl's face as she tried to tell her to leave on Sunday.

Yes, she had to admit they were nicer than before. A few years ago Karel would have shooed her away without mercy. That little ruse of hers yesterday had actually been for their own good. One day it would spare them pangs of conscience for having needlessly packed their mother off to her loneliness a day early.

During the drive to the station Mother never stopped talking.

What did she say?

First, she thanked him. She'd had a wonderful time with her son and daughter-in-law.

Second, she lectured him. They had done her a great injustice. When he and Marketa were living with her, he had been impatient with her—coarse, even—and inconsiderate. Mother had suffered a great deal. Yes, she admitted, they'd been very nice this time, different from before. They'd changed. Yes. But why had they waited so long?

Sitting through the long litany of charges (he knew it by heart), he was not the least upset. He had been watching her from the corner of his eye and was again amazed at how tiny she was. It was as though her whole life had been a long gradual shrinking process.

But what did that shrinking process entail?

Was it the actual shrinking of a person as he abandons his adult proportions and starts down the long path through old age and death to that far-off place where all is void and without proportions?

Or was it just an optical illusion caused by the fact that Mother was moving into the distance, that she was in another place, that she looked like a lamp, a doll, a butterfly to him?

By this time they are aboard the train, and Karel is trying to find her a compartment. They all seem too crowded and uncomfortable. Finally he puts her in a first-class compartment and runs off to settle the extra fare with the conductor. And since he has his wallet ready, he takes out a hundred-crown note and puts it in Mother's hand as if Mother were a little girl going on a long, long journey, and Mother accepts the money matter-of-factly, without any show of surprise, like a schoolgirl accustomed to receiving occasional gifts of money from adults.

And then the train starts moving—Mother is at the window, Karel on the platform—and he waves for a long, long time, until the last possible moment.

Nora Ephron

CRAZY SALAD

[Review of Pat Loud: A Woman's Story, *Pat Loud with Nora Johnson*]

In 1966, she found a set of her husband's cuff links, engraved "To Bill, Eternally Yours, Kitty," and all hell broke loose. Her husband assured her he had bought the cuff links in a pawn shop, but she did not believe him. So she snuck off, had an extra set of his office keys made, and while he was off on a business trip she went to look through his files.

"It was all there," she writes, "as though it had been waiting for me for years—credit card slips telling of restaurants I'd never been to and hotels I'd never stayed at, plane tickets to places I'd never seen, even pictures of Bill and his girls as they grinned and screwed their way around the countryside."

Bill Loud returned from his business trip. Pat Loud slugged him, in front of the children. He slugged her back, in front of the children. They both went to see a psychiatrist. They both stopped seeing the psychiatrist. They spent night after night getting drunk as Bill Loud recited the intimate sexual details of his infidelities. The subject of open marriage was introduced. Pat Loud began going to local bars during lunch and picking up businessmen. "We would have a few drinks and some tortillas," she recalls. "Then we would let nature take its course." She threatened divorce. He started seeing his women again. And in the midst of this idyllic existence, Craig Gilbert, a film-maker with a contract from public television, came into their home and told them he was looking for "an attractive, articulate California family" to do a one-hour special about.

It is impossible to read this book and not suspect that Craig Gilbert knew exactly what he was doing when he picked the Louds, knew after ten minutes with them and the clinking ice in their drinks that he had found the perfect family to show exactly what he must have intended to show all along—the emptiness of American family life. Occasionally, in the course of this book, Pat Loud starts to suspect this, nibbles around it, yaps like a puppy at the ankles of truth, then tosses the idea aside in favor of loftier philosphical pronouncements. "If he knew it," she concludes, "it was not necessarily because he actively smelled it about us, but because he knew in a way what we didn't—that life is lousy and its tragic and it's supposed to be and you can pretend otherwise if you want, but if you do, you're wrong."

Gilbert had no trouble persuading the Louds to cooperate. Bill had always been outgoing and exhibitionistic. Pat, for her part, saw the show as a way to appear as she had always wanted to—the perfect mother, cheerfully beating egg whites in her copper bowls.

Jeffrey Bernard

I'm racking my brains trying to think just how low I stooped in the old days but apart from regularly stealing from my mother's handbag I can't think of anything particularly awful. Anyway, that's what mothers' handbags are for.

Queen Victoria

to her daughter

Osborne, May 26, 1858

On the afternoon of my birthday (which was a wet one) I received your dear letter of the 22nd with such dear, warm, hearty expressions of love and affection for which 1000 thanks. I have no doubt dearest child that you can now much better appreciate Mama's love and affection and understand how all that you grumbled and struggled and kicked against was for your good, and meant in love!—your love and affection you know, dearest child, I never doubted, I only was often grieved and hurt at your manner, your temper.

John Kennedy Toole

A CONFEDERACY OF DUNCES

"Just who the hell are you to try to tell me what to do, Ignatius?" Mrs. Reilly stared at her huffing son. She was disgusted and tired, disinterested in anything that Ignatius might have to say. "Claude is dumb. Okay. I'll grant you that. Claude is all the time worrying me about them communiss. Okay. Maybe he don't know nothing about politics. But I ain't worried about politics. I'm worried about dying half-way decent. Claude can be kind to a person, and that's more than you can do with all your politics and all your graduating smart. For everything nice I ever done for you, I just get kicked around. I want to be treated nice by somebody before I die. You learnt everything, Ignatius, except how to be a human being."

"It's not your fate to be well treated," Ignatius cried. "You're an overt masochist. Nice treatment will confuse and destroy you."

"Go to hell, Ignatius. You broke my heart so many times I can't count them up no more."

"That man shall never enter this house while I am here. After he had grown tired of you, he would probably turn his warped attentions on me."

"What's that, crazy? Shut up your silly mouth. I'm fed up. I'll take care of you. You say you wanna take a rest? I can fix you up with a nice rest."

"When I think of my dear departed father barely cold in his grave," Ignatius murmured, pretending to wipe some moisture from his eyes.

"Mr. Reilly died twenty years ago."

"Twenty-one," Ignatius gloated. "So. You've forgotten your beloved husband."

"Pardon me," Mr. Levy said weakly. "May I speak with you, Mr. Reilly?"

"What?" Ignatius asked, noticing for the first time the man standing up on the porch.

"What you want with Ignatius?" Mrs. Reilly asked the man. Mr. Levy introduced himself. "Well, this is him in person. I hope you didn't believe that funny story he give you over the phone the other day. I was too tired to grab the phone out his hands."

"Can we all go in the house?" Mr. Levy asked. "I'd like to speak with him privately."

"It don't matter to me," Mrs. Reilly said disinterestedly. She looked down the block and saw her neighbors watching them. "The whole neighborhood knows everything now."

But she opened the front door and the three of them stepped into the tiny entrance hall. Mrs. Reilly put down the paper bag she was carrying that contained her son's scarf and cutlass, and asked, "What you want, Mr. Levy? Ignatius! Come back here and talk to this man."

"Mother, I must attend to my bowels. They are revolting against the trauma of the last twenty-four hours."

"Get out that bathroom, boy, and come back here. Now what you want with crazy, Mr. Levy?"

"Mr. Reilly, do you know anything about this?"

Ignatius looked at the two letters that Mr. Levy produced from his jacket and said, "Of course not. That is your signature. Leave this house immediately. Mother, this is the fiend who fired me so brutally."

"You didn't write this?"

"Mr. Gonzalez was extremely dictatorial. He would never permit me near a typewriter. Actually, he cuffed me once rather viciously when my eyes chanced to stray across some correspondence which he was composing in rather dreadful prose. If I was permitted to shine his cheap shoes, I was grateful. You know how possessive he is about that cesspool company of yours."

"I know. But he says he didn't write this."

"An obvious untruth. His every word is false. He speaks with a forked tongue!"

"This man wants to sue us for a lot of money."

"Ignatius done it," Mrs. Reilly interrupted a little rudely. "Whatever went wrong, Ignatius done it. He makes trouble everyplace he goes. Go on, Ignatius. Tell the man the truth. Go on, boy, before I knock you in the head."

"Mother, make this man leave," Ignatius cried, trying to push his mother against Mr. Levy.

"Mr. Reilly, this man wants to sue for $500 thousand. That could ruin me."

"Ain't that awful!" Mrs. Reilly exclaimed. "Ignatius, what you done this poor man?"

As Ignatius was about to discuss the circumspection of his behavior at Levy Pants, the telephone rang.

"Hello?" Mrs. Reilly said. "I'm his mother. Of course I'm sober." She glared at Ignatius. "He is? He did? What? Aw, no." She stared at her son, who was beginning to rasp one paw against the other. "Okay, mister, you'll get your stuff, all except the earring. The bird got that. Okay. Of course I can remember what you telling me. I ain't drunk!" Mrs. Reilly slammed down the telephone and turned on her son with, "That was the weenie man. You're fired."

"Thank God," Ignatius sighed. "I couldn't stand that cart again, I'm afraid."

"What you told him about me, boy? You told him I was a drunk?"

"Of course not. How ludicrous. I don't discuss you with people. No doubt he's spoken with you previously when you were under the influence. You've probably had a date with him for all I know, a drunken spree in several hot dog boites."

"You can't even peddle hot dogs in the streets. Was that man angry. He says you gave him more trouble than any vendor he ever had."

"He resented my worldview rather actively."

"Oh, shut up before I slap you again," Mrs. Reilly screamed. "Now tell Mr. Levy here the truth."

What a squalid homelife, Mr. Levy thought. This woman certainly treated her son dictatorially.

"Why, I am telling the truth," Ignatius said.

"Lemme see that letter, Mr. Levy."

"Don't show it to her. She reads rather dreadfully. She'll be confused for days."

Mrs. Reilly knocked Ignatius in the side of the head with her purse.

"Not again!" Ignatius cried.

"Don't hit him," Mr. Levy said. The kook's head was already bandaged. Outside of the prizefighting ring, violence made Mr. Levy ill. This Reilly kook was really pitiful. The mother ran around with some old man, drank, wanted the son out of the way. She was already on the police blotter. That dog was probably the only thing that the kook had ever really had in his life. Sometimes you have to see a person in his real environment to understand him. In his own way Reilly had been very interested in Levy Pants. Now Mr. Levy was sorry that he had fired Reilly. The kook had been proud of his job at the company. "Just let him alone, Mrs. Reilly. We'll get to the bottom of this."

"Help me, sir," Ignatius slobbered, grabbing histrionically at the lapels of Mr. Levy's sports jacket. "Fortuna only knows what she will do to me. I know too much of her sordid activities. I must be eliminated. Have you thought of speaking to that Trixie woman? She knows far more than you suspect."

"That's what my wife says, but I never believed her. After all, Miss Trixie is so old. I wouldn't think she could write a grocery list."

"Old?" Mrs. Reilly asked. "Ignatius! You told me Trixie was the name of some cute girl worked at Levy Pants. You told me you two liked each other. Now I find out she's a grammaw can't hardly write. Ignatius!"

It was sadder than Mr. Levy had thought at first. The poor kook had tried to make his mother think he had a girlfriend.

"Please," Ignatius whispered to Mr. Levy. "Come into my room. I must show you something."

"Don't believe a word Ignatius says," Mrs. Reilly called after them as her son dragged Mr. Levy through the door into the musty chamber.

"Just let him alone." Mr. Levy said to Mrs. Reilly somewhat firmly. This Reilly woman wouldn't even give her own child a chance. She was as bad as his wife. No wonder Reilly was such a wreck.

ON JAMES EARL RAY

Jimmy may all day have seemed to be idolizing his father, to be following the movement of those billiard balls around the table as Speedy skillfully pocketed them. But in the night, his feelings sprang loose from their conscious censorship, and other kinds of feelings came out.

It is not surprising that Jimmy's dreams had to do with the other side of his admiration, with his fear and his Oedipal feelings toward Speedy. In fact, his nightmares were pointed directly at the Oedipal dilemma.

That prison psychiatrist, the one Jimmy had told about his nightmares, learned that Jimmy "at the age of ten awoke one night and thought he had lost his eyesight." This is what happened to King Oedipus in the myth on which the psychological insight is based: King Oedipus blinded himself in self-punishment for murdering his father to wed his mother.

The emotion that set Jimmy apart from this brothers and sisters, from others for the rest of his life, was the quality of his anger.

The source of some of but not all of this anger in Jimmy was in his feelings about Speedy, that were lodged in the deepest recesses of his being, ready to produce anger, deep, sullen, hateful, even murderous anger.

Most of us defiantly refuse to acknowledge such explanations of our behaviour. We find them offensive, sinister in their implications and, though we seldom admit it even to ourselves, quite unsettling. But just when we have safely put these "theories" behind us, they pop up in front of us, they find their substance in some vagrant, unexpected piece of evidence like James Earl Ray's dream.

He remembered the nightmare for thirty years.

"If the cops had me pinned down," Ray said, "I'd pretend to give up. I'd throw my gun down. Then when they stepped up to take me, I'd take them with me. I'd do it with maybe two ounces, maybe four ounces of nitroglycerin."

What do these reveries mean, what do they reveal about Ray and his inner life, his unconscious, and do they tell about the motives that led to his conscious acts? His concern for children and his hatred of adults, the way that either seemed to set off explosions of feeling in him, show that his passions came from his own childhood, more exactly from his infant experiences. It's perfectly plausible when you think about it why the first relationship one has in life is so important. The nourishment you get from your mother is your first exchange with another human being. As the months pass, if all goes well, you are less and less dependent on a direct physical contact with your mother, and eventually, if your emotions develop as they should, you are able to sustain the pleasure and reassurance you felt when you were with your mother, when she is no longer around. The feelings you have learned from her are now a part of you; you have "internalized" them.

But if your mother hasn't met the needs of her infant, if she is erratic or barren of tenderness, the result is devastating for you. You haven't seen any consistent cause-and-effect pattern in your emotional world. You learn that you cannot trust your mother, and you conclude that you cannot trust anyone, or life itself.

As an infant, James Earl Ray suffered from this loss. One clue that he did is the fact that from the earliest time anybody seems to remember him, he had an uncontrollable temper, quick flashes of anger, rage beyond any explicable provocation. Another clue is his reaction to the TV movie on India. To Ray there are no "good" adults; "adult" stands for people who don't take care of children. The intensity of his rage directed at these adults who stand to him for parents has its explanation in the fact that Ray was deprived of parental love and affection at the moment when he was utterly dependent on his parents, on adults, for warmth.

To Ray all children are people who have not received their due, who have been treated unjustly; infancy and childhood stand to him as periods of unhappiness. His daydream of starting an orphan asylum proves that he felt unloved and unwanted in some way that was important to him.

It all goes back to Ceal [his mother] (for whom we cannot have enough compassion): a woman who, as the lives of her children prove, had little to give them; married to Speedy, a man who gave her and the children nothing. It was not the economic poverty of Ray's infancy and childhood that seared his psyche; it was the poverty of warmth, of affection, that created within him his murderous feeling of deprivation.

But why did Martin Luther King magnetize and become the focal object of these emotions?

Martin Luther King stirred Ray's feelings by being a figure who offered love and warmth to thousands of people. King reminded Ray in a pointedly bitter way of how he had not been taken care of. In this sense, King became, in the symbolic functions of the mind, the mother Ray had not had; King performed the functions that Ceal did not.

Dale Spender

WOMEN OF IDEAS

Freud was a great enemy of women. . . . Thanks to Freud, the whole of the United States is covered with millions and millions of grown men grizzling about the way they were treated by their mothers, who are usually dead.

Anonymous

A WOMAN IS A WORTHY THING

I am as lighte as any roe
To preise womene where that I go.
To onpreise womene it were a shame,
For a woman was thy dame.
Our blessed lady bereth the name
Of all womene where that they go.

A woman is a worthy thing;
They do the washe and do the wringe;
"Lullay, lullay!" she dothe thee singe;
And yet she hath but care and wo.

A woman is a worthy wight;
She serveth a man both daye and night;
Thereto she putteth alle her might;
    And yet she hath but care and wo.

ON GEORGE ORWELL

On 24 June he was called urgently, but not unexpectedly, to Southwold. On 28 June his father, Richard Walmesley Blair, died of cancer. The death certificate futher notes: "E. A. Blair, son, present at the death."

Three days later he returned to Wallington, thus almost immediately after the funeral. Although he felt deeply for his mother, visiting home more often than many of his contemporaries, he, like the rest of the Blairs, seemed to practise an ethic of practicality, having little liking for or apparent need of emotional gestures. One imagines that he asked his mother after the funeral if there was anything he could do for her, and she replied no, in the customary manner with them: so he left to get back to his book of essays.

John Nicholson

MEN AND WOMEN

WORKING MOTHERS

Women may be able to survive without having children, but the great majority of them want to experience motherhood and I very much doubt whether this will change. What has changed is that most women now want to combine being a mother with having a career. This brings us to a very important question: is it damaging for children to be brought up in a home where a mother is at work? A report put out by the World Health Organization (WHO) thirty years ago produced the axiom that mother-love in infancy is as essential for normal psychological development as vitamins are for normal physical development. The principal author of the report subsequently made it clear that he did not believe that only a child's biological mother was equipped to bring him up, or that her absence—for any length of time, and for whatever reason—must inevitably harm him. But these were the ideas that took root in the public consciousness.

The practical consequences of the report were enormous. Welfare agencies based their policies on the assumption that it must be less damaging for a child to be brought up by incompetent—or even downright malevolent—parents than by foster parents or in an institution. More importantly, mothers of that generation were led to believe that it would be irresponsible for them to return to work until all their children were at school, however pressing the economic or personal reasons for wanting to take a job earlier.

Most psychologists now agree that the WHO report which introduced the concept of maternal deprivation greatly overstated its effects. This was not, as some feminists have suggested, part of an international conspiracy to keep women out of the labour-force at a time of high unemployment, but simply because the report was based on incomplete information, and was too strongly influenced by the results of studies of children who had been brought up in institutions in which the quality of child care fell far below modern standards. Unfortunately, the report was produced before child psychologists had developed techniques for studying the detailed workings of the relationship between a baby and his or her parents, at a time when we knew much less about how successful child rearing is carried out, let alone why it sometimes fails.

Partly as a result of interest generated by this report, the relationship between human babies and their parents has been examined in minute detail over the last twenty years. Child psychologists have spent many thousands of hours observing how parents and their babies actually behave towards each other, and we are now in a much better position to assess how much a baby is likely to be affected by having a mother who works, and to look again at the all-important question, Are women uniquely well equipped to bring up their own children? I call this question all-important because the fact that women are men's equals in so many respects will count for very little—and may well be a source of frustration—if it really is true that children inevitably suffer when their mothers are not present all the time throughout the pre-school years.

We saw earlier that there is not much evidence that women have an irresistible biological instinct to produce babies and must suffer if they deny it.. But it is still possible that when a woman does have a baby, biological factors make her the best person to bring it up. We know that the maternal behaviour of a female rat is at least partly controlled by its sex hormones, and we also know that the production of oestrogen in pregnant women is stepped up during the five weeks before they give birth. It has not yet been proved that this has any effect on the way they treat their babies, but we might take it as suggestive evidence that mothers are biologically prepared for the birth of a child, and perhaps as an indication that they are likely to be the best person to look after it. It would not however prove that they are the only people who could do the job, and there are two qualifications which have to be borne in mind when trying to gauge the significance of a mother's hormones for the well-being of her child.

The first is that, even in rats, hormones only influence maternal behaviour before and for a short period after giving birth. The female rat soon comes to rely on the presence of her pups to remind her to behave in a suitably maternal fashion and there is convincing evidence that a human mother, too, often finds it difficult to form a close relationship with a baby who is taken away from her at birth and placed in an incubator because it has been born prematurely or as a result of some other complication. Interestingly, fathers are also more likely to play a major role in looking after a child if they have been present when it was born, and during the first days of its life.

The second thing to bear in mind is that by no means all mothers in industrialized countries breast-feed their babies (in Britain, figures released in November 1982 suggest that about a third do not). Since we know that the act of breast-feeding produces a physiological response even in adoptive mothers, we must assume that mothers who do not breast-feed thereby reduce any impact which hormones might otherwise have had on their behaviour.

There is some evidence that breast-feeding strengthens that emotional bond between a mother and her child. But the fact that so many mothers form a perfectly satisfactory relationship with their children without breast-feeding them, while the relationship can break down when breast-feeding is employed, argues against attaching too much importance to this aspect of a mother's rapport with her child. It is also

striking how quickly and easily adoptive parents take to their new role, even though the adoptive mother has not been pregnant with the child, and so will neither have experienced the hormonal changes of pregnancy nor breast-fed the child.

There is no way of being certain how much—if any—of a mother's behaviour towards her baby is innate, and how much the result of learning. John Watson, the founding father of behaviourist psychology, spent some time observing mothers and concluded that nursing is the only ready-made activity. As he put it, "the mother is usually about as awkward as she can be. The instinctive factors are practically nil." Other observers have disputed his view. Most mothers seem to have a standard way of touching their new-born babies, beginning with the arms and legs and then stroking the back and stomach. They also tend to hold their babies so that they can look into each other's eyes. When holding or feeding the baby, they bring its face to within about a foot of their own, which happens to be the distance at which a new-born baby's eyes focus best. More significantly, even adults without children consistently hold babies at a distance at which the baby's—though not necessarily their own—eyes are best in focus. Mothers also pitch their voices higher when talking to their babies, and we know (though mothers may not) that babies are more responsive to high-pitched sounds.

However, the fact that mothers everywhere seem to treat their babies in the same way in many respects does not prove that the behaviour is instinctive. And even if it is, there is evidence that fathers too behave in a fairly standard way when first confronted by their own children, which suggests that it is not just mothers but parents who are biologically programmed to treat babies in a certain way.

ON ELIZABETH CADY STANTON

. . . Elizabeth Cady Stanton changed . . . from being a young bride in cosmopolitan London to being a careworn mother in relatively isolated Seneca Falls. On her return to America, Stanton lived in Chelsea "with beautiful views of Boston Bay, and here where she had good *servants* and good company—and only two children—she was somewhat unsympathetic about the drudgery of housework, as she herself states. "I tried to give an artistic touch to everything, and hence enjoyed it. I never could understand how housekeepers could rest with rubbish all round their back doors. . . ."

The similarities with our own time should not go unnoted; it seems that even in the 1840s the intellectual arguments were not always sufficient protection against the seductive myth of marriage and motherhood, and if today some assert that entry to the women's movement is by way of disillusionment with domesticity, Elizabeth Cady Stanton would readily have accepted the validity of such an explanation. "In Seneca Falls [where she and her family moved in 1847] my life was comparatively solitary," she says, "and the change from Boston was somewhat depressing." The house was old, had been unoccupied for a few years, was in need of repairs and had a very overgrown garden; it was on the outskirts of town, there were no footpaths ("sidewalks") and the road was often muddy. "Mr. Stanton was frequently away from home, I had poor servants, and an increasing number of children. To keep a house and grounds in good order, purchase every article for daily use, keep the wardrobes of half a dozen human beings in proper trim, take the children to dentists, shoemakers and different schools, or find teachers at home, altogether made sufficient work to keep one brain busy, as well as all the hands I could impress into the service."

ON IDA WELLS-BARNETT

In 1896 the National Association of Colored Women was formed and this constituted a significant step in the organization of black women. A convention was held in Washington. . . . In attending this convention, Ida Wells-Barnett typified the problematic existence confronting women who wished to participate in public life, and who had children—in a society where provision was not made for such basic aspects of existence. Refusing to handle the problem so that it remained invisible (and therefore could continue *without* provision being made), Wells-Barnett took her child (at this stage, four months old) with her. In all she had four children and, while generally adopting the policy that her baby went with her to whatever meeting she attended, there were times when the pressure got too great, and she temporarily "retired" from public life.

ON FLORENCE NIGHTINGALE

That it is obligatory for a woman to be happy, to present a contented and cheerful disposition to her master in order that he can feel satisfied with the arrangement and secure in the knowledge of his own psychological (as well as financial) indispensability, is a lesson that mothers unwaveringly teach their daughters, argues [Florence] Nightingale. The only way such a lesson can be taught successfully is by the systematic denial and removal of *passion* from women. If emotion were allowed to reside in women, says Nightingale, women could not bear their lives, so women go round teaching their daughters that "women have no passions." In the conventional society, which men have made for women, and women have accepted, they *must* have none, they *must* act the farce of hypocrisy, the lie that they are without passion—and therefore what else can they say to their daughters, without giving the lie to ·themselves?

Marilyn French

THE WOMEN'S ROOM

It's easy enough to blame men for the rotten things they do to women, but it makes me a little uncomfortable. It's too close to the stuff I read in the fifties and sixties when everything that went wrong in a person's life was Mother's fault. All of it. Mothers were the new devil. Poor mothers, if only they realized how much power they had! Castraters and smotherers, they were unpaid servants of The Evil One.

"Kids, mothers," Val muttered. "You're not supposed to feel your own feelings so that you can be a perpetual bandage to everybody else's."

Jan Power

POSITIONS VACANT
WOMEN & GIRLS

WANTED: female for mother, no experience necessary, no pre-training given. Hours: 24 hour shift for life of child. Salary: meager, government subsidised, $3.79 per week. Holiday and sick leave negotiable, but not encouraged. Thorough grounding an advantage in:

    nursing
    catering
    philosophy
    psychiatry
    sex
    religion
    carpentry
    dressmaking
    marketing & finance
    media appreciation (incl. TV repairs)
    taxi driving
    arts
    science
    and sport

End result highly unpredictable, product non-exchangeable and non-returnable. Could be fun and rewarding.

MOTHERS OBSERVED

ON J. A. M. WHISTLER

James Whistler (1834–1903) was a painter most closely associated with modernism, and known widely for his famous portrait of his mother.

In 1878, in the little essay he called "The Red Rag," he would write: "Art should be independent of all claptrap—should stand alone, and appeal to the artistic sense of eye or ear without confounding this with emotions entirely foreign to it, as devotion, pity, love, patriotism, and the like. . . . Take the picture of my mother, exhibited at the Royal Academy as an *Arrangement in Grey and Black*. Now that is what it is. To me it is interesting as a picture of my mother; but what can or ought the public to care about the identity of the portrait?" Yet at a slightly later date, in a private conversation and with just a hint of his usual air of listening to his own phrases, he himself came close to taking the side of "claptrap," and an alert friend noted the betrayal with relish: ". . . we were looking at the *Mother*. I said some string of words about the beauty of the face and figure, and for some moments Jimmy looked and looked, but he said nothing. His hand was playing with that tuft upon his nether lip. It was, perhaps, two minutes before he spoke. 'Yes,' very slowly, and very softly—'yes, one does like to make one's mummy just as nice as possible.' "

Philip Roth

PORTNOY'S COMPLAINT

"He eats French fries," she says, and sinks into a kitchen chair to Weep Her Heart Out once and for all. "He goes after school with Melvin Weiner and stuffs himself with French-fried potatoes. Jack, you tell him, I'm only his mother. Tell him what the end is going to be. Alex," she says passionately, looking to where I am edging out of the room, "*tate-lah*, it begins with diarrhea, but do you know how it ends? With a sensitive stomach like yours, do you know how it finally ends? *Wearing a plastic bag to do your business in!*"

Who in the history of the world has been least able to deal with a woman's tears? My father. I am second. He says to me, "You heard your mother. Don't eat French fries with Melvin Weiner after school."

"Or ever," she pleads.

"Or ever," my father says.

"Or hamburgers out," she pleads.

"Or hamburgers out," he says.

"*Hamburgers*," she says bitterly, just as she might say *Hitler*, "where they can put anything in the world in that they want—and he eats them. Jack, make him promise, before he gives himself a terrible *tsura*, and it's too late."

"I *promise*!" I scream. "I *promise*!" and race from the kitchen—to where? Where else.

I tear off my pants, furiously I grab that battered battering ram to freedom, my adolescent cock, even as my mother begins to call from the other side of the bathroom door. "Now this time don't flush. Do you hear me. Alex? I have to see what's in that bowl!"

Doctor, do you understand what I was up against? My wang was all I really had that I could call my own. You should have watched her at work during polio season! She should have gotten medals from the March of Dimes! Open your mouth. Why is your throat red? Do you have a headache you're not telling me about? You're not going to any baseball game, Alex, until I see you move your neck. Is your neck stiff? Then why are you moving it that way? You ate like you were nauseous, are you nauseous? Well, you ate like you were nauseous. I don't want you drinking from the drinking fountain in that playground. If you're thirsty wait until you're home. Your throat is sore, isn't it? I can tell how you're swallowing. I think maybe what you are going to do, Mr. Joe Di Maggio, is put that glove away and lie down. I am not going to allow you to go outside in this heat and run around, not with that sore throat, I'm not. I want to take your temperature. I don't like the sound of this throat business one bit. To be very frank, I am actually beside myself that you have been walking around all day with a sore throat and not telling your mother. Why did you keep this a secret? Alex, polio doesn't know from baseball games. It only knows from iron lungs and crippled forever! I don't want you running around, and that's final. Or eating hamburgers out. Or mayonnaise. Or chopped liver. Or tuna. Not everybody is careful the way your mother is about spoilage. You're used to a spotless house, you don't begin to know what goes on in restaurants. Do you know why your mother when we go to the Chink's will never sit facing the kitchen? Because I don't want to see what goes on back there. Alex, you must wash everything, is that clear? Everything! God only knows who touched it before you did.

Morris Bishop

THERE'S MONEY
IN MOTHER AND FATHER

We all know Mumsy was vague and clumsy,
Dithering, drunken and dumb.

Elias Canetti

AUTO DA FÉ

If a mother could be content to be nothing but a mother; but where would you find one who would be satisfied with that part alone?

John Rae

THE CUSTARD BOYS

A mother has an innate ability for aggravating the wounds of her off-spring's pride. This is inevitable since the relationship between mother and child is a most unnatural one; other species have the good sense to banish their young at an early age.

READER'S DIGEST, 1955

There are two kinds of mothers: those who place a child's bouquet in a milk bottle on top of the refrigerator, and those who enthrone it in a vase on the piano.

Cardinal Mermillod

A mother is she who can take the place of all others but whose place no one else can take.

Commissioner Mary C. Beasley

Motherhood—an incident, an occupation, or a career
According to the mettle of the women.

Mrs. Rosemary Foot, M.P.

What price success if one fails as a mother?

Alice S. Rossi

EQUALITY BETWEEN THE SEXES: AN IMMODEST PROPOSAL

Full time motherhood is neither sufficiently absorbing to the woman nor beneficial to the child to justify a contemporary woman's devoting fifteen or more years to it as her exclusive occupation. Sooner or later—and I think it should be sooner—women have to face the question of who they are besides their children's mother.

PROVERBS 31: 26–28

She openeth her mouth with wisdom; and in her tongue is the law of kindness. She looketh well to the ways of her household. And eateth not the bread of idleness. Her children arise up, and call her blessed; her husband also, and he praiseth her.

Judith Pugh

Motherhood is a wonderful thing—what a pity to waste it on children.

Anne Deveson

. . . I think it's time we moved away from singling out mothers as if they were holy cows, and we started talking about parents. Fathers should also be seen as well as heard.

Jane Austen

PRIDE AND PREJUDICE

From this day you must be a stranger to one of your parents. Your mother will never see you again if you do *not* marry Mr. Collins, and I will never see you again if you *do*.

Charles Dickens

OUR MUTUAL FRIEND

O Mrs. Higden, Mrs. Higden, you was a woman and a mother, and a mangler in a million million.

John Gay

FABLES

Where yet was ever found a mother,
Who'd give her booby for another?

OVERHEARD ON A BUS

Of course, the trouble with my mother is that she never had any children . . .

Erik Erikson

INSIGHT AND RESPONSIBILITY

Defenseless as babies are, they have mothers at their command, families to protect the mothers, societies to support the structure of families, and traditions to give a cultural continuity to systems of tending and training.

Sylvia, Lady Brooke

QUEEN OF THE HEAD HUNTERS

Nobody who was not Somebody meant a thing to my father. It was not so much that he was a snob as that he enjoyed Royalty and titles, and was genuinely and shamelessly impressed with Earls and Dukes and Duchesses, who paraded through his spacious rooms and elegant gardens, while my mother paid homage to the great whom "her Reggie" had invited there. I thought her self-effacement was weak and foolish in those days. Now, when I look back at the memory of them and their fifty years and more of perfect human harmony, I realize that two such brilliant stars could not have shone in the same house without the ultimate destruction of them both. So she stood meekly in the shadow of his glory and let her personality pale and fade against his. She was, I think, almost as clever and colourful as he was, but she dimmed her light to strengthen his because he was the god at whose shrine she humbly worshipped. They were never really happy when away from one another and unless she went with him to London he felt lost, like an actor without an audience. Then, when they returned to "Orchard Lea" there was my brother Maurice who was always very close to my father. Sometimes I could see jealousy rise like a flash in my mother's large dark eyes and she would say something sarcastic to her beloved Reggie that she would afterward regret.

Sue Townsend

THE SECRET DIARY OF ADRIAN MOLE AGED 13¾

Tuesday January 20
Full Moon

My mother is looking for a job!

Now I could end up a delinquent roaming the streets and all that. And what will I do during the holidays? I expect I will have to sit in a launderette all day to keep warm. I will be a latchkey kid, whatever that is. And who will look after the dog? And what will I have to eat all day? I will be forced to eat crisps and sweets until my skin is ruined and my teeth fall out. I think my mother is being very selfish. She won't be any good in a job anyway. She isn't very bright and she drinks too much at Christmas.

I rang my grandma up and told her, and she says I could stay at her house in the holidays, and go to the Evergreens' meetings in the afternoons and stuff like that. I wish I hadn't rung now.

Thursday February 12
Lincoln's Birthday

I found my mother dyeing her hair in the bathroom tonight. This has come as a complete shock to me. For thirteen and three-quarter years I have thought I had a mother with red hair, now I find out that it is really light brown. My mother asked me not to tell my father. What a state their marriage must be in! I wonder if my father knows that she wears a padded bra? She doesn't hang them on the line to dry, but I have seen them shoved down the side of the airing cupboard. I wonder what other secrets my mother has got?

Sunday March 8
First in Lent

My mother has gone to a woman's workshop on assertiveness training.

Men aren't allowed. I asked my father what "assertiveness training" is. He said, "God knows, but whatever it is, it's bad news for me."

We had boil-in-the-bag cod in butter sauce and oven-cooked chips for Sunday dinner, followed by tinned peaches and Dream-topping. My father opened a bottle of white wine and let me have some. I don't know much about wine but it seemed a pleasant enough vintage. We watched a film on television, then my mother came home and started bossing us around. She said, "The worm has turned," and "Things are going to be different around here," and things like that. Then she went into the kitchen and started making a chart dividing all the housework into three. I pointed out to her that I already had a paper round to do, an old age pensioner to look after and a dog to feed, as well as my school work, but she didn't listen, she put the chart on the wall and said, "We start tomorrow."

Peggy Guggenheim

OUT OF THIS CENTURY:

CONFESSIONS OF AN ART ADDICT

My mother was much more conventional than I, and she was forever inviting Laurence and me to the Ritz to her parties. On the other hand, she seemed to enjoy our Bohemian parties as well. She had made great friends with Mrs. Vail and was dragged into the American Women's Club which was Mrs. Vail's stronghold. My mother was probably at her best at this time, because she could at last have a life of her own. She was no longer tormented by father's infidelities, and all her children were married. But she never actually relinquished her daughters. She used to phone me every morning and tell me it was cold or raining and that I should wear a warm coat or rubbers, as the case might be. This drove me frantic, but what I hated most of all were the conventional parties at the Ritz and being perpetually told that I led the wrong kind of life. Anyone who was not rich she referred to as a beggar, and any

woman who had a lover she called N.G., meaning no good. She was greatly disappointed that I had not married a Jewish millionaire. Nevertheless, she liked Laurence because he flirted with her. She herself had had various proposals, which she turned down. One was from a Sicilian duke, who wrote to ask her to lend him a return ticket to America, at the same time lamenting the fact that although he would like to marry her he regretted that he was not rich enough "to keep her in her usual luxury stand." She was, I am afraid, a one-man woman and, after the bad luck she had encountered with my father, she put all her energies into making matches for other people.

She had a strange habit of repeating everything three times. Once when we were dining with her at the Ritz, Laurence tickled her leg under the table; her only comment to this was, "Shush, Peggy will see, Peggy will see, Peggy will see." Once when she went to a milliner to order a hat with a feather, she said, "I want a feather, feather, feather." She is reported to have received a hat that bore three feathers. In New York when finally at the age of fifty she learned to drive a car, she was stopped by a policeman in a one-way street for going against the traffic. Her reply, if inconsistent, was correct. She said, "I am only driving one way, one way, one way." She not only repeated everything three times, but she also always carried three coats with her which she was perpetually changing. In a heat wave she wore two silver foxes and fanned herself to keep cool. She always carried three watches, one was a wristwatch, one she wore around her neck as a necklace, and the third one formed part of a lorgnon. The latter she could not use as she could see only with the lorgnon.

J. R. Ackerley

MY FATHER AND MYSELF

I have reason to believe that I often wear a frown. Our public faces can be known to us only by hearsay and I have been given several clues to my own. A preoccupied anxious look seems to be my most settled guise, tinged by sadness. A charming smile: "sunshine through tears," some-one once described it to me. My fine blue eyes can emit a piercing stare, I am told, though what on earth they pierce I have no notion, they certainly did not manage to pierce my father. And, as I say, a frown may darken my face. My mother would sometimes make it worse by trying to smooth it away with her fingers. "It will spoil your beautiful brows," she said. I was told later, to my sorrow, that love me though she did she was rather scared of me ("Do you lov your little mother?" she would say, as though the full word were too much to ask for), and I expect I gave her cause; with her ceaseless chatter she invited defence, the raised barricading newspaper, the yawn, the frown, the offhand manner, the bored, inattentive face. A friend once remarked to me, "It's wonderful how rude one can be to your mother without her even noticing it."

To stay alive and well was problem enough for her, and the recipe for that was to keep the bowels open, to try to be cheerful and light-hearted, to take plenty of exercise (inside the house was safer than outside), not to lean out of railway-carriage windows, or spill the salt, or walk under ladders, to hide the knives and drape the mirrors at the approach of thunderstorms, and always to spit if there was a bad smell. One of my few early recollections of her is raising her veil to spit vigorously in the street, exhorting us to do likewise. I remember too a time when, before going to sleep, she would place her loose cash and rings on a chair outside her bedroom door, together with a note to burglars generally, which read: "Take my money but spare our lives." She wrote always with a quill, a large dashing hand, full of exclamation marks and under-linings.

I don't remember ever having had a serious, intimate conversation with my mother in my life; yet when I think of her, as I sometimes do, or look at her photos with that sad face she always put on for photogra-phers, I take much of her psychology to myself.

John Mortimer

CLINGING TO THE WRECKAGE

Much of my mother's life went underground when she married my father, although we were visited occasionally by a red-bearded painter who had been her fellow student. He and my mother used to sit up talking after my father, who held strong views about visitors, had gone to bed. Once, when I was about ten years old, I came downstairs and burst into the living-room, ostensibly to search for burglars, but really to stop my mother committing adultery, the thought of which, I am now convinced, had never entered her head.

I always found my mother's attitude to me curiously disconcerting. She seemed to find most of the things I did slightly comic ("killing" was the word she most often used). Long after my father had died I rang her up to tell her that I had been asked to go to some distant town to sit as a Judge, hoping that she might be impressed. "*You,* a Judge?" She started to giggle. "*You?* Whatever do they think they're doing, asking *you* to be a Judge?" and then she laughed so much that she had to put down the telephone receiver. From time to time she seemed to find it hard to remember essential things about me, such as whether I took sugar, or my name. In later years she often looked at me vaguely and called me "Daisy," which was my aunt's name. Not until she was very old did I find some short stories which she had written, which showed her concern about me and her anxiety, no doubt entirely justified, about what I got up to when out of her sight.

Simone Signoret

NOSTALGIA
ISN'T WHAT IT USED TO BE

Among the other vivid images of that time is my mother's reflection in a mirror—or rather in many different mirrors—and here is the reason. At the time, my hair was cut in a pageboy style, rather like Joan of Arc, and my mother took me to have it cut in barbershops. In the plural. We must have gone through half a dozen of them between my fifth and sixth years. We would arrive; I would be set on a pile of telephone directories between two customers being shaved and trimmed; my mother would make sure the cotton wool wedged between my neck and the big wrap was quite clean—which would upset the artist to whom she gave her instructions—and then she would sit down and smile reassuringly at me in the mirror. She would pick up the available reading matter; without fail there'd be something called *Le Rire* or *Le Sourire*—smutty and very French, a kind of equivalent of *Playboy*. She would leaf through the magazine with an air of disgust, and then replace it ostentatiously on the little table she had removed it from.

As long as our artist was busy with my fringe and locks, all would go well, except for the clippings that would fall into my eyes and on my nose, which he would flick off with a kind of shaving brush. But come the moment to do the back: two hard, expert fingers pushed my head forward. I could no longer see my mother's face, but I knew I'd hear this phrase—it never varied: "May I ask you, monsieur, to kindly pass your instrument through a flame," at precisely the moment he would start clicking his clippers preparatory to an attack on the back of my neck. A sudden pause in the snipping. My head still down, I saw nothing. And then the artist would reply along these lines: "Madame, this salon is run with the greatest care." My mother would get up and approach the two flaming little jets of gas on either side of the mirror, and she would begin to launch forth on a condensed lecture on human hygiene, from which it would emerge that I was but a child, that frequently adults are carriers of grievous germs, and that in any case the gas jets had not been installed merely for decorative purposes. All this would be delivered with exquisite politeness. Then she would sit down again. The artist thereupon singed his instrument, with a smirk at his two colleagues which never escaped my attention. He would rub up the back of my neck, and then there would be no sound except the click of the still warm clippers on my neck. When it was all over, no little massage was proposed, no lotion or free soap samples, he would just peel off the big wrapper. We paid and left, and as soon as we were outside my mother would say: 'Well, we'll never set foot in there again!'

I was an only child, and overprotected. I never had a cat because a little neighbor had her eye put out by hers. I never was allowed a pair of roller skates because one of my mother's cousins fractured his skull on the edge of a sidewalk in Arles in 1911. But I had canaries and goldfish. When they died the fact would be hidden from me, and they would be replaced the same night by live ones, which were not always the same size or color.

One summer, in Le Pouliguen, on the Atlantic coast, we became shrimp saviors. I had caught three shrimps and a little crab. That evening we put a pailful of sea water on the bedroom mantel in our *pension de famille;* and my mother settled down in bed with a book. She was not one of those ladies who put their children to bed and then go out dancing. I began to cry, and explained that I wanted to put my three shrimps and the crab back into the sea. She dressed me again in my rompers, and we took the pail and emptied the contents into the harbor. I was blissfully happy . . . and she was too.

Hal Porter

THE WATCHER
ON THE CAST-IRON BALCONY

In the country Mother changes. Or rather, so far as I am concerned, she appears as another kind of Mother.

Since the time I wholly saw her first, lifting the spotted veil back from her powdered face under the winged hat, the cloud earlier concealing her has thinned, shredded away, vanished. She is now a woman almost always in an apron of black Italian cloth, her blouse sleeves rolled back above her beautiful forearms which turn day by day from white to country brown, a woman labelled with the names of days.

She is Monday as she helps the washerwoman whose hands are as pleated and bleached and sodden as some tripe-like fungus, a hook-nosed, hook-chinned, toothless woman as witch-like in appearance as behaviour as she prods with the pot-stick through the smoke and steam at the outdoor copper of boiling garments.

She is Tuesday as she sprinkles pillow-slips, Father's shirts, my sisters' starched sun-bonnets, and the boys' cotton sou'westers, for her flat-irons. These have already been clashed down on the top of the kitchen range so hot that a mirage almost forms above its blackleaded surface. While the irons are heating, a peaceful overture to the rites begins. Mother and the washerwoman take each bedsheet separately and, one gripping the bottom edge, one the top, retreat backwards from each other, straining the sheet horizontally taut in a version of domestic tug-o'-war, inclining their heads to scan it for signs of wear, then, this done, mincing towards each other with uplifted arms to begin the folding. On the day of this grave pavane we invariably have for dinner a succulent hash made from Sunday's cold joint. This Mother calls a German Fry—a dish her Switzer father badgered her English mother into learning how to make.

She is Wednesday, her hair concealed beneath a worn, old-fashioned head-dress, once her mother's, and called a fascinator, as she shakes the little fringed furry mats that lie before each inside door, as she mops fluff from under beds, sprinkles damp tea-leaves on the Brussels carpet before brushing it, sweeps the verandas, hunts cobwebs, polishes the brass taps and door-handles, rearranges dust with a feather duster.

She is green-fingered Thursday, and happiest, dividing her violet and primrose plants; manuring her five precious azaleas with the horse-droppings I have shovelled from the road, or cow-droppings from The Common; making a scarecrow that, wearing Father's old clothes, subtly resembles him, and to which, hopping about like a Pearlie Queen, she sings in imitation cockney, "I wouldn't leave my little wooden hut for you-oo-oo . . ."; crushing a handful of lemon verbena leaves or eau-de-Cologne mint between her palms, and inhaling the scent of her hands which must smell also of earth and thyme and toil and happiness. Thursday reveals most of all that she is country-bred, and that her passion for the country imbues her too deeply for denial: she knows a thousand delicately brutal tricks to circumvent birds and caterpillars, wasps and slugs, frost and midsummer, from despoiling her rows of peas, her lettuce and Frau Karl Druschki roses, her Lazy Wife beans and maidenhair fern, her hydrangeas and carrots and Sweet William and chives and almost sacred camellia tree. Her bible is Mrs. Rolf Boldrewood's *The Flower Garden in Australia* (A Book for Ladies and Amateurs dedicated by permission to the Countess of Jersey). Her favourite seeds come from Vilmorin-Andrieux et Cie, Marchands-Grainiers, Quai de la Mégisserie 4, Paris. So absurd is nostalgia and my persisting desire to complete the circles of experience that when, years later, I visit Paris, I eschew the Tour Eiffel and other turismo lures first to find the Quai de la Mégisserie where I compel myself not to cry.

She is Friday, curling-pinned, slap-dashing vivaciously and deftly through domesticity so that she can dress herself up, flee from her family into the after-dinner twilight, and go shopping. Friday is late shopping night. What she shops for on these evenings is nothing essential, nothing mundane. The baker, the bloody butcher in a nimbus of flies, the milkman, canter into Mitchell Street daily; the grocer, the fishmonger, the rabbit-oh, the John Chinaman greengrocer and fruiterer, the iceman and the egg-woman appear once or twice weekly; the knife-grinder, the tinker, the chimney-sweep, the clothes-prop man, and old clo'man, the clothes-peg gipsy and the Afghan pedlar drift through as regularly on time as the seasons, and the dust-laying water-waggon, and the ice-cream carts, and the swallows or their children which build their demi-cups of mud under the wooden shade over my bedroom window. Powdered and scented (eau-de-Cologne or Lily of the Valley), in her best earrings and gloves and dazzling polished shoes, her enamelled watch pinned to her bust, chewing a Sen-sen or a clove, Mother goes shopping for . . . for what? The tumpti-tiddily-tumpti of the Shire Band aloft in the hexagonal bandstand at the end of Main Street? The displays of xylonite hairpin boxes of imitation tortoise-shell? The Gaby Deslys figurines with thistle-down hair? The celluloid kewpies dressed in Bairnsdale football colours? The elegantly cruel spurs and plaited whips in the saddler's? The dusty witch-balls and fuchsia-coloured paper bells suspended over the soda-fountain and marble table-tops of Russo's? The glamour of gaslight, and electric light, and the passing and repassing between the wax dummies in the shop-windows and the spurred and slouch-hatted blokes rolling cigarettes and spitting with neat good manners between their feet as they lean against every Main Street veranda-post?

She returns home at nine-thirty sharp, her eyes glittering, refreshed by artificial light or moonlight or starlight, exhilarated to girlishness, crying out gaily, "Tea! Tea! Tea!" And, taking off her shoes new filmed with the dust of roads and adventure, "My corn is giving me Larry Dooley!" "I heard a mopoke," she says, prodding the fire, removing the stove-lid, and pushing the kettle over the hole. "I saw a falling star. Someone is dead," she says, or, "I sneaked a piece of that variegated honeysuckle over Coster's fence: I think it'll strike," or, "The band was playing 'The Blue Danube' tonight," and, "One, two, three. One, two, three," she sings whirling in her beautifully darned stockinged feet. She reveals what she has bought, other than excitement, from among the moustache cups and hurricane lamps and enamel bowls and winceyette night-gowns and glass-rubied gilt studs of Main Street. Maybe there are liquorice straps or blood oranges or little china canaries we children are to fill with water and, then, blowing down their hollow tails, make bubbling music. Whatever she buys is for us children: transfers, packets of compressed bits which expand to Japanese flowers on the surface of saucers of water, marbles of which I once knew the names, a bag of sugar-coated Paris Almonds, white and pink—simple gifts, payment that haunts now, for her several hours of freedom for the weekly promenade.

Once only does she lose her head, and buy herself a hideous white china rose, beautiful, for some reason, to her. "When you dance to-night," I hear her sometimes sing—oh, mockingly—as she lifts the atrocity—oh, gently, gently—to dust about it, "wear a rose of white. 'Twill show you forgive me again . . ." What is she really saying in song, for she is saying something?

She is Saturday and, breakfast over, a sergeant-major. Before break-fast, each child has had its weekly dose of Gregory Powder, a nauseous gunpowder-coloured purgative. Now, purged and fed, each child has its Saturday task. Her voice heightened, her movements brisk, she hurries about chivvying us, less because we are really of much help than that our being made to do something has its moral and disciplinary value, and is, moreover, a custom of that class in that era. Mother's humble hoard of real silver, and the electroplated silver, is cleaned with God-dard's Plate Powder and methylated spirits: the tea service, the salt-cellars and mustard-pot, the two cruets, the spoons and forks, the four biscuit-barrel rims and lids and handles, the salt spoons, soup ladles, fish-slice, cake pedestals, the rose-bowl and the trumpet vases. The fire-irons and fender are polished, and the steel knives are burnished with a sort of gritty cocoa rubbed on with a large cork set in a wooden handle like a drawer-handle. Butcher's paper is scissored into squares for the lavatory, and into cut-out filigree resembling Richelieu embroidery for the pantry shelves. Howsoever good I am, howsoever rapidly and competently I perform my part in these duties, I burn to escape and race reinless into the elm-lined streets, the Tannies, the river-flats, the miles-wide paddocks surrounding Bairnsdale.

Saturday afternoon is for baking. This is a labour of double nature: to provide a week's supply of those more solid delicacies Australian mothers of those days regarded as being as nutritiously necessary as meat twice daily, four vegetables at dinner, porridge and eggs and toast for breakfast, and constant cups of tea. Empty biscuit-barrels and cake-tins being as unthinkable as beds not made before eleven A.M., Mother, therefore, constructs a great fruit cake, and a score or more each of rock cakes, Banburies, queen cakes, date rolls and ginger nuts. These conventional solidities done, she exercises her talent for ritual fantasy, for the more costly and ephemeral dainties that are to adorn as fleetingly as day-lilies the altar of the Sunday tea-table. Now appear three-storeyed sponge cakes mortared together with scented cream and in whose seductive icing are embedded walnuts, silver cachous, glacé cherries, strawberries, segments of orange and strips of angelica. Now appear cream puffs and éclairs, creations of the most momentary existence, deliberately designed neither for hoarding against a rainy day nor for social showing-off. Sunday tea is the frivolous and glittering crown of the week; there is the impression given of throwing away money like delicious dirt; there is the atmosphere rather than the fact of luxury; Sunday tea is, above all, my parents' statement to each other and their children that life is being lived on a plane of hard-earned and justifiable abundance. I watch abundance which means that I watch Mother, its actual as well as its symbolic impulse.

At this stage, astute within a vague placidity, so head-over-heels am I in harum-scarum content that my inner eye drifts away from observation of myself so that I become as blurred in outline to myself as my parents once were to me. In this mood, lasting years which all seem the same year, I appear, now, looking back, to have catalogued Mother more than any human being even though that catalogue must have been made in a by-the-way fashion. This may be a natural habit of eldest sons, or mere sons. It may only be the habit of sons who are driven by their natures to write. I suspect so, but am unsure. I do not even know if an eldest son, writer or shearer's cook or accountant, be the best or worst judge of his mother. I never shall know. I am discovering as I write these words that my autobiography, at this period, is my mother's biography. Outside her formal pattern of Monday as washing-day, Tuesday as ironing-day, etcetera, Mother is constantly making time almost in the same way as she makes Cornish Pasties. She makes it, between the crevices of her daily plan, in many patterns, and lays it aside, lays aside tangible and visible samples of the hours: a mound of darned socks, a dozen jars of quince jelly, a dead-straight line of weeded onions, a varnished meat pie decorated with a pastry rose and its serrated pastry leaves. Sometimes, as men and boys do, as Father and I do, she fills in time. She too fishes in the river, comes mushrooming and black-berrying, shrieks and splashes and dog-paddles at beach-picnics. This filling-in is, however, apparent only: the picnic-hamper holds the too much she has made to eat, there is always time's essence in blackberry tarts and blackberry jam, a dish of stewed mushrooms and jars of dried ones, or a platter of fried bream. In making time thus three-dimensional in many forms she creates the illusion of abundance for us.

She sings still, as constantly, as cheekily, the same songs but whereas, before, the song seems foremost and she a vaporous shape gesturing through some task behind the melody, now it is she and the task that fill the foreground, piling up riches, weaving, like a spider, from the threads of her own strength of will, and love, and ability to serve, a web of plenty. She knows that we can scarcely afford to keep up with the Joneses, let alone impress them. She sees to it that we afford to impress ourselves.

Abundance! Plenty!

To me, now, the years between six and ten are cards of the same suit. The total impression remaining is this one of copiousness. Never for one second do I realize that what I count as such is not so to many. Not only does it seem so in my dreamily watchful, belly-filled, soft-bedded, unruffled home life, it seems more so in that country outside the country town. It is a magnification of Dr. Moss's pittosporum with its bees and butterflies and blossoms and gusts of scent. From waking to sleeping, from January to December, from year to year, it is impossible for me not to be aware of fecundity: the grass thicker than wool and gorged with globules of dew or mated with frost; the late twilight air flowing in currents of moths and Christmas beetles and cockchafers as we play on The Common under a sky closely gravelled with planets and stars; the footpaths and paddocks glaring yellow with capeweed through which we paddle until boots or bare feet are mustard-coloured with pollen; the birds gibbering and squealing and squeaking a million-fold in every elm in every street at sunrise and sunset, and, late, late at night, when one is in bed, and the candle blown out, the crowing of roosters from every direction, from near, from nearly near, from over the hills and far far away, cry answering cry repeatedly in sounds so threadlike, so distant, so weary, as to be almost the cry of silence itself. I see fecundity everywhere—the seed-boxes of poppies shaking out their pepper, the winter-defrocked trees blotted with nests, the summer trees bearing billions of leaves, the vast mushroom-rings, the grapelike bunches of blackberries overhanging the paths and ditches along the river, Mother's fingers and mine stained emerald with the green blood of uncountable aphides we have squashed from the buds of the rosebushes.

Fecundity! Plenty! Abundance!

Gerald Durrell

MY FAMILY AND OTHER ANIMALS

I should like to pay a special tribute to my mother, to whom this book is dedicated. Like a gentle, enthusiastic, and understanding Noah, she has steered her vessel full of strange progeny through the stormy seas of life with great skill, always faced with the possibility of mutiny, always surrounded by the dangerous shoals of overdraft and extravagance, never being sure that her navigation would be approved by the crew, but certain that she would be blamed for anything that went wrong. That she survived the voyage is a miracle, but survive it she did, and, moreover, with her reason more or less intact. As my brother Larry rightly points out, we can be proud of the way we have brought her up; she is a credit to us. That she has reached that happy Nirvana where nothing shocks or startles is exemplified by the fact that one week-end recently, when all alone in the house, she was treated to the sudden arrival of a series of crates containing two pelicans, a scarlet ibis, a vulture, and eight monkeys. A lesser mortal might have quailed at such a contingency, but not Mother. On Monday morning I found her in the garage being pursued round and round by an irate pelican which she was trying to feed with sardines from a tin.

"I'm glad you've come, dear," she panted; "this pelican is a little difficult to handle."

When I asked her how she knew the animals belonged to me, she replied: "Well, of course I knew they were yours, dear; who else would send pelicans to me?"

It was Larry, of course, who started it. The rest of us felt too apathetic to think of anything except our own ills, but Larry was designed by Providence to go through life like a small, blond firework, exploding ideas in other people's minds, and then curling up with cat-like unctuousness and refusing to take any blame for the consequences. He had become increasingly irritable as the afternoon wore on. At length, glancing moodily round the room, he decided to attack Mother, as being the obvious cause of the trouble.

"Why do we stand this bloody climate?" he asked suddenly, making a gesture towards the rain-distorted window. "Look at it! And, if it comes to that, look at us . . . Margo swollen up like a plate of scarlet porridge . . . Leslie wandering around with fourteen fathoms of cotton-wool in each ear . . . Gerry sounds as though he's had a cleft palate from birth . . . And look at you: you're looking more decrepit and hag-ridden every day."

Mother peered over the top of a large volume entitled *Easy Recipes from Rajputana*.

"Indeed I'm not," she said indignantly.

"You are," Larry insisted; "you're beginning to look like an Irish washerwoman . . . and your family looks like a series of illustrations from a medical encyclopedia."

Mother could think of no really crushing reply to this, so she contented herself with a glare before retreating once more behind her book.

"What we need is sunshine," Larry continued; "don't you agree, Les? . . . Les . . . Les!"

Leslie unravelled a large quantity of cotton-wool from one ear.

"What d'you say? he asked.

"There you are!" said Larry, turning triumphantly to Mother. "It's become a major operation to hold a conversation with him. I ask you, what a position to be in! One brother can't hear what you say, and the other one can't be understood. Really, it's time something was done. I can't be expected to produce deathless prose in an atmosphere of gloom and eucalyptus."

"Yes, dear," said Mother vaguely.

"What we all need," said Larry, getting into his stride again, "is sunshine . . . a country where we can grow."

"Yes, dear, that would be nice," agreed Mother, not really listening.

"I had a letter from George this morning—he says Corfu's wonderful. Why don't we pack up and go to Greece?"

"Very well, dear, if you like," said Mother unguardedly.

Where Larry was concerned she was generally very careful not to commit herself.

"When?" asked Larry, rather surprised at this cooperation.

Mother, perceiving that she had made a tactical error, cautiously lowered *Easy Recipes from Rajputana*.

"Well, I think it would be a sensible idea if you were to go on ahead, dear, and arrange things. Then you can write and tell me if it's nice, and we all can follow," she said cleverly.

Larry gave her a withering look.

"You said that when I suggested going to Spain," he reminded her, "and I sat for two interminable months in Seville, waiting for you to come out, while you did nothing except write me massive letters about drains and drinking-water, as though I was the Town Clerk or something. No, if we're going to Greece, let's all go together."

"You do exaggerate, Larry," said Mother plaintively; "anyway, I can't go just like that. I have to arrange something about this house."

"Arrange? Arrange what, for heaven's sake? Sell it."

"I can't do that, dear," said Mother, shocked.

"Why not?"

"But I've only just bought it."

"Sell it while it's still untarnished, then."

"Don't be ridiculous, dear," said Mother firmly; "that's quite out of the question. It would be madness."

So we sold the house and fled from the gloom of the English summer, like a flock of migrating swallows.

For some time Mother had greatly envied us our swimming, both in the daytime and at night, but, as she pointed out when we suggested she join us, she was far too old for that sort of thing. Eventually, however, under constant pressure from us, Mother paid a visit into town and returned to the villa coyly bearing a mysterious parcel. Opening this she astonished us all by holding up an extraordinary shapeless garment of black cloth, covered from top to bottom with hundreds of frills and pleats and tucks.

"Well, what d'you think of it?" Mother asked.

We stared at the odd garment and wondered what it was for.

"What is it?" asked Larry at length.

"It's a bathing-costume, of course," said Mother. "What on earth did you think it was?'

"It looks to me like a badly-skinned whale," said Larry, peering at it closely.

"You can't possibly wear that, Mother," said Margo, horrified, "why, it looks as though it was made in nineteen-twenty."

"What are all those frills and things for?" asked Larry with interest.

"Decoration, of course," said Mother indignantly.

"What a jolly idea! Don't forget to shake the fish out of them when you come out of the water."

"Well, I like it, anyway," Mother said firmly, wrapping the monstrosity up again, "and I'm going to wear it."

"You'll have to be careful you don't get waterlogged, with all that cloth around you," said Leslie seriously.

"Mother, it's awful; you can't wear it," said Margo. "Why on earth didn't you get something more up to date?"

"When you get to my age, dear, you can't go around in a two-piece bathing suit . . . you don't have the figure for it."

"I'd love to know what sort of figure that was designed for," remarked Larry.

"You really are hopeless, Mother," said Margo despairingly.

"But I like it . . . and I'm not asking you to wear it," Mother pointed out belligerently.

"That's right, you do what you want to do," agreed Larry; "don't be put off. It'll probably suit you very well if you can grow another three or four legs to go with it."

Mother snorted indignantly and swept upstairs to try on her costume. Presently she called to us to come and see the effect, and we all trooped up to the bedroom. Roger was the first to enter, and on being greeted by this strange apparition clad in its voluminous black costume rippling with frills, he retreated hurriedly through the door, backwards, barking ferociously. It was some time before we could persuade him that it really was Mother, and even then he kept giving her vaguely uncertain looks from the corner of his eye. However, in spite of all opposition, Mother stuck to her tent-like bathing-suit, and in the end we gave up.

In order to celebrate her first entry into the sea we decided to have a moonlight picnic down at the bay, and sent an invitation to Theodore, who was the only stranger that Mother would tolerate on such a great occasion. The day for the great immersion arrived, food and wine were prepared, the boat was cleaned out and filled with cushions, and everything was ready when Theodore turned up. On hearing that we had planned a moonlight picnic and swim he reminded us that on that particular night there was no moon. Everyone blamed everyone else for not having checked on the moon's progress, and the argument went on until dusk. Eventually we decided that we would go on the picnic in spite of everything, since all the arrangements were made, so we staggered down to the boat, loaded down with food, wine, towels, and cigarettes, and set off down the coast. Theodore and I sat in the bows as look-outs, and the rest took it in turn to row while Mother steered. To begin with, her eyes not having become accustomed to the dark, Mother skillfully steered us in a tight circle, so that after ten minutes' strenuous rowing the jetty suddenly loomed up and we ran into it with a splintering crash. Unnerved by this, Mother went to the opposite extreme and steered out to sea, and we would eventually have made a landfall somewhere on the Albanian coastline if Leslie had not noticed in time. After this Margo took over the steering, and she did it quite well, except that she would, in a crisis, get flurried and forget that to turn right one had to put the tiller over to the left. The result was that we had to spend ten minutes straining and tugging at the boat which Margo had, in her excitement, steered on to, instead of away from, a rock. Taken all round it was an auspicious start to Mother's first bathe.

Eventually we reached the bay, spread out the rugs on the sand, arranged the food, placed the battalion of wine-bottles in a row in the shallows to keep cool, and the great moment had arrived. Amid much cheering Mother removed her housecoat and stood revealed in all her glory, clad in the bathing-costume which made her look, as Larry pointed out, like a sort of marine Albert Memorial. Roger behaved very well until he saw Mother wade into the shallow water in a slow and dignified manner. He then got terribly excited. He seemed to be under the impression that the bathing-costume was some sort of sea monster that had enveloped Mother and was now about to carry her out to sea. Barking wildly, he flung himself to the rescue, grabbed one of the frills dangling so plentifully round the edge of the costume, and tugged with all his strength in order to pull Mother back to safety. Mother, who had just remarked that she thought the water a little cold, suddenly found herself being pulled backwards. With a squeak of dismay she lost her footing and sat down heavily in two feet of water, while Roger tugged so hard that a large section of the frill gave way. Elated by the fact that the enemy appeared to be disintegrating, Roger, growling encouragement to Mother, set to work to remove the rest of the offending monster from her person. We writhed on the sand, helpless with laughter, while Mother sat gasping in the shallows, making desperate attempts to regain her feet, beat Roger off, and retain at least a portion of her costume. Unfortunately, owing to the extreme thickness of the material from which the costume was constructed, the air was trapped inside; the effect of water made it inflate like a balloon, and trying to keep this airship of frills and tucks under control added to Mother's difficulties. In the end it was Theodore who shooed Roger away and helped Mother to her feet. Eventually, after we had partaken of a glass of wine to celebrate and recover from what Larry referred to as Perseus's rescue of Andromeda, we went in to swim, and Mother sat discreetly in the shallows, while Roger crouched nearby, growling ominously at the costume as it bulged and fluttered round Mother's waist.

Günter Grass

THE TIN DRUM

But let us get back to the days when I escaped periodically from our court with its carpet beating and its soup chefs, thanks to my mama, who took me every two weeks to Sigismund Markus's store, where I was permitted to select a new drum. Sometimes Mama let me come even when my old drum was in relatively good condition. How I relished those afternoons in the multi-coloured old city; there was always a pealing of bells from one church or another.

Usually our excursions were pleasantly monotonous. There were always a few purchases to be made at Leisher's, Sternfeld's, or Machwitz's; then we went to Markus's. It had got to be a habit with Markus to pay Mama an assortment of the most flattering compliments. He was obviously in love with her, but as far as I know, he never went any further than to clutch my mother's hand, ardently described as worth its weight in gold, and to impress a silent kiss upon it—except for the time I shall speak of in a moment when he fell on his knees.

Mama, who had inherited Grandma Koljaiczek's sturdy, imposing figure and her lovable vanity tempered with good nature, put up with Markus's attentions. To some extent, no doubt, she was influenced by the silk stockings—he bought them up in job lots but they were of excellent quality—which he sold her so cheap that they were practically gifts. Not to mention the drums he passed over the counter every two weeks, also at bargain prices.

Regularly at half past four Mama would ask Sigismund if she might leave me, Oskar, in his care, for it was getting late and she still had a few important errands. Strangely smiling, Markus would bow and promise with an ornate turn of phrase to guard me, Oskar, like the apple of his eye, while she attended to her important affairs. The mockery in his tone was too faint to give offense, but sometimes it brought a blush to Mama's cheeks and led her to suspect that Markus knew what was what.

As for me, I knew all about the errands that Mama characterized as important and attended to so zealously. For a time she had let me accompany her to a cheap hotel in Tischlergasse, where she left me with the landlady and vanished up the stairs for exactly three-quarters of an hour. Without a word the landlady, who as a rule was sipping half-and-half, set a glass of some foul-tasting soda pop before me, and there I waited until mama, in whom no particular change was discernible, returned. With a word of good-bye to the landlady, who didn't bother to look up from her half-and-half, she would take me by the hand. It never occurred to her that the temperature of her hand might give me ideas. Hand in over-heated hand, we went next to the Café Weitzke in Wollwebergasse. Mama would order mocha, Oskar lemon ice, and they would wait, but not for long, until Jan Bronski should happen by, and a second cup of mocha should be set down on the soothingly cool marble table-top.

Christopher Milne

THE ENCHANTED PLACES

I enjoyed playing with my mother. This was something she was good at. There were plenty of things she couldn't do, had never been taught to do, didn't need to do because there was someone to do them for her, and she certainly couldn't have coped alone with a tiny child. But provided Nanny was at hand in case of difficulty, she was very happy to spend an occasional half hour with me, playing on the floor, sitting me on her lap to show me how the gentleman rides, reciting (for the hundredth time) Edward Lear's "Calico Pie."

My mother in the garden. Trowel in hand planting Darwin tulips by the hundred. Secateurs in hand snipping at roses. Crouched down, weeding, weeding, weeding. Pouring jugs of hot water over the ants. Exhorting Tasker to ever greater efforts. Teaching me the names of the flowers— lovely names like salpiglossis and spiraea Anthony Waterer, difficult names like eschscholtzia which were fun to spell. But mostly I remember her just quietly, happily, brooding over it all, alone in the half dark.

You can love the country in two quite different ways, as a cat loves it and as a dog loves it. My mother was like a cat. She responded to the beauty, the peace and the solitude that it offered. She found this in her garden and she found it too in the countryside beyond. Solitude. She was happiest alone. Once, when she was going for a walk, I asked if I could come with her. "No," she said, "but come and meet me on my way back. I like best being met." And so we spent a lot of time meeting her. She would walk to the village and half an hour later my father and I would set off up the hill and hope that somewhere before we reached the top we would see her coming round the corner. Or it might be the other way round, and she would meet us as we drove home (choosing the pretty way, of course) after spending the morning playing golf. At night, before going to bed, she would walk up to the forest, two miles along the road, until she was level with Gills Lap. On these occasions I sometimes accompanied her. It was different in the dark. You could be with someone and they would be there if you felt you wanted them, and if you didn't you could forget them. Now and again, on our way, a car would come by: blinding lights, a roar and a whoosh of wind that seemed to suck you out into the road in their wake. We clung to each other, standing against the hedge, until they were gone. Then on again. We both loved the country at night, the black shapes of the trees, the tiny spots of light from wayside cottages, the sound of the wind bustling about its invisible business. We scarcely talked, absorbed in our private thoughts.

Dorothy [his mother] was not brainy. No one expected her to shine at algebra. But this still left plenty of things that she could have learnt and which she would have enjoyed doing and done well if only this had been proper. In the 1914–18 war when it was all right for nicely brought up young ladies to do manual work for the sake of our gallant boys, my mother had learnt to tie up parcels. I'm not sure what went inside them, probably comforts for the troops, Balaclava helmets and socks lovingly knitted by other young ladies. This was, almost certainly, the only practical thing she was ever properly taught how to do in her whole life, and the result was that she did it both then and ever afterwards exceedingly well. If today I am an expert parcel tier myself—and I may say that I am an expert parcel tier—it is because I learnt the craft at my mother's knee. I used to watch her, fascinated: the brisk competent folding of the paper that pressed the misshapen contents into a neat, firm rectangular form; the string tied so quickly, so tightly and with such an economy of knots; the result so solid and symmetrical that it seemed wrong that anyone should ever want to open it. Today from time to time I try to pass on this skill to others, but I know that, however hard I try, all they will be able to manage in the end is a squashy brown bundle loosely slung in a hammock of string. Pick it up at the wrong end, give it a shake, and all has to be done again.

But if my mother was taught to tie up parcels, she was (naturally) never taught to untie them. She was at the supplying end, not the receiving end. And anyway undoing parcels was not really a thing that needed lessons. So she taught herself. She did it by the light of nature. She merely reversed the process of tying up. It took about half an hour if the knots were tight. It left my father and myself jumping up and down with impatience if the parcel was an exciting one. "Oh, go on. *Cut* it!" But no. String was precious. You can't buy string. At least my mother wouldn't have known how to set about trying to buy it. And you can't buy paper. So it all had to be saved. "Anyway, I like undoing parcels," she said as she wound up the string on her hand. "Don't rush me," she said as she carefully flattened the crumples out of the paper.

Jean Renoir

MY LIFE AND MY FILMS

My memory goes far enough back for me to be able to recall that the world in those days was divided for me into two parts. My mother was the tiresome part, the person who ordered me to eat up my dinner, to go to the lavatory, to have a bath in the sort of zinc tub which served for our morning ablutions. And Bibon [his nanny] was for fun, walks in the park, games in the sand-heap, above all piggy-back rides, something my mother absolutely refused to do.

George Barker

TO MY MOTHER

Most near, most dear, most loved and most far,
Under the window where I often found her
Sitting as huge as Asia, seismic with laughter,
Gin and chicken helpless in her Irish hand,
Irresistible as Rabelais, but most tender for
The lame dogs and hurt birds that surround her,
She is a procession no one can follow after
But be like a little dog following a brass band.

She will not glance up at the bomber, or condescend
To drop her gin and scuttle to a cellar,
But lean on the mahogany table like a mountain
Whom only faith can move, and so I send
O all my faith and all my love to tell her
That she will move from mourning into morning.

Osbert Sitwell

LAUGHTER IN THE NEXT ROOM

William, I remember, took the design Severini had made for *Façade* to
Florence: but he could never afterwards remember the address of the
scene-painter to whom it had been entrusted for reproduction on the
curtain or anything about him except that his name was Barone, that he
was about thirty-five and the son of a man who had formerly worked

for my father at Montegufoni. As the day grew nearer and the curtain, promised for a certain date, failed to arrive, anxiety grew. A day or two before the performance, my mother said to Edith, "You leave it to me. I'll find the curtain. But I'd like you to come with me in the motor." She then drove to Florence, to the hotel where she and my father often stayed in the winter, and sent the driver in to inform the concierge that she required the names and addresses of all the Barones in Florence: this message the porter misunderstood, taking it to mean that she wanted a catalogue of all those of the rank of Baron, and accordingly he returned with the list; a large list, albeit fortunately the fact that Baron was a comparatively new title in Italy curtailed it. My mother did not look at it, but said, "Guido, drive to every address in turn." On arrival at each, she told the chauffeur to ring the bell, and ask if the owner was in, and inform him in the Italian style that two Noble Ladies awaited him outside. Barones, of one sort or another, would appear, startled, wondering what could be amiss. My mother, who spoke no Italian, fixed each poor nobleman with her dark gaze, and after examining him closely, if he were old, imperturbably announced, "It's not you we want," or, if it seemed likely that he might have a son of the right age and sort, would pronounce the esoteric message:

"Your son has my daughter's curtain!"

"But, madam, I 'ave not got 'im!" some of them would reply.

ON J. A. M. WHISTLER

The complete change of mood, from the artificial flamboyance of the *Six Projects* to the quiet sincerity of *The Artist's Mother,* must partly have been determined by the sitter's character. Quiet, reserved, pious and shy, Anna Mathilda's friends spoke of her as "one of the saints upon earth," and in company she would seek out the corners of rooms and sit quietly sewing. Whistler originally conceived of a portrait of his mother in 1867 and this may explain why, unlike some of his portraits, it was completed in a matter of months when eventually painted in 1871. He originally intended to paint her standing, but a recent illness had left her too weak to hold the pose. Her inner quietness made her an ideal subject and she sat patiently while her nervous son rubbed out one attempt after another in his search for perfection. She, meanwhile, prayed for a miracle. Finally, the portrait was completed to Whistler's satisfaction and he kissed his mother. He had achieved his results with the most limited means, the paint in places merely staining the canvas, the transparency of the head-dress suggested by thinly-scumbled paint, the delicate, uneven grey-green on the wall behind achieved by use of glazes and the whole brought to life by the dancing pattern of lines and dots, a kind of visual figure, on the curtain to the left of the figure. In keeping with the sitter's deep religious convictions, the portrait exudes a mood of quiet devotion.

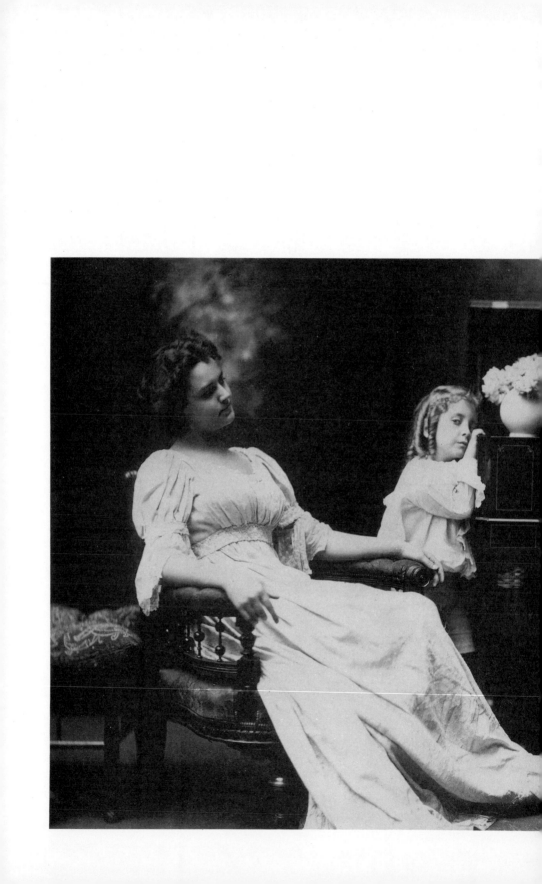

THINGS MY MOTHER TAUGHT ME

Majorie Nelson (Jackson)

Oh God, make me a better parent. Teach me to understand my children, to listen patiently to what they have to say, and to answer all their questions kindly. Keep me from interrupting them, talking back to them, and contradicting them. Make me as courteous to them as I would have them be to me. May I grant them all their wishes that are reasonable, and have the courage always to withhold a privilege which I know will do them harm.

Kate Samperi

Before becoming a mother I had a hundred theories on how to bring up children. Now I have seven children and only one theory: love them, especially when they least deserve to be loved.

Mary G. L. Davis

. . . love them, feed them, discipline them and let them go free. You may have a life-long good relationship.

ON SALVADOR DALÍ

Although Dalí was clearly a sturdy, healthy little boy, his mother's anxiety did not seem to abate. Whenever he played in the park she would remain standing, the better to watch him. He would be allowed to leave her side but the distance he could travel would be carefully defined and he would be warned not to get hurt. Dalí was four years old by the time his sister was born, yet she has clear memories of her brother's tears and storms if he awoke in the middle of the night to find himself alone. "My mother had to pick him up again because he would only quiet down in her arms. She often passed long nights, seated on the bed, her child on her knees. Scarcely would she fall asleep than he would wake up and start crying again."

This smothering attention ensured that Dalí would be kept in a state of infantile dependence, denied the forays into autonomy and self-reliance normal for his age. When he was old enough for school he would watch in helpless admiration as his playmates demonstrated their mastery of shoelaces. For example, "[I] was capable of remaining locked up in a room a whole afternoon, not knowing how to turn the door-handle to get out; I would get lost as soon as I got into any house, even those I was familiar with; I couldn't even manage . . . to take off my sailor blouse which slipped over the head, a few experiments in this exercise having convinced me of the danger of dying of suffocation." Such dangerous solo ventures had to be avoided at all costs for fear of their terrible consequences. Elsewhere in his autobiography he noted casually that, to his family, he was always "the child."

Jane Gardham

GOD ON THE ROCKS

Mrs. Marsh, Margaret's mother, was a great breast-feeder at a time when it was fashionable to be otherwise. Nor had she shingled her hair nor seen to her waist-line. She was a largish, loose-jointed, still-young woman much given to God and sympathy and immensely loving to babies. She sat hour after hour in her bedroom, knees apart in a nicely-made but antique sort of a skirt, deeply-waved brown hair falling round her face untidily.

Sometimes she had flour on her face for she seldom looked in the glass and was fond of cooking. As she fed the baby she looked into its face all the time with a very gentle deep expression. When Margaret came into the room she would raise her head with a long and understanding look.

"Going out, dear?"

"No."

"I thought it was Wednesday."

"It is. That's this afternoon."

"What, dear?"

"Going out."

Mrs. Marsh, dazed about times of day, detached herself from the baby, drawing herself back and mopping about with a cloth. She lifted the baby up on her shoulder where a huge towelling nappy lay, hanging a little way down her back for the baby to be sick on. She massaged its back which was like the back of a duck, oven-ready. The baby's unsteady head and swivelling eyes rolled on her shoulder, its round mouth slightly open, wet and red. It seemed, filmily, to be trying to take in Margaret who was fiddling with things on the mantelpiece behind her mother. She looked down at it with a realistic glare. The baby under the massage let air come out of its mouth in a long explosion and pale milk ran out and over its chin.

"Filthy," said Margaret.

"There's my little lovekin," said Mrs. Marsh. She lifted the baby into the air before her, both hands under the armpits, and let it hang like dough about to drop. "What did you say, dear? It's your treat-day with Lydia, isn't it?"

"This afternoon," said Margaret, dropping the baby's bottle of gripe water and smashing it to bits on the mottled cream tiles of the fireplace. Glass flew everywhere in splinters and the baby after jerking as if it had received an electric shock began to cry like a new lamb. "Lair, lair, lair," it went, scarlet in the face and flushing quickly to purple all over its bald head, its eyes in two directions.

Mrs. Marsh was not upset, though she had jumped as violently as her son. Margaret saw her take the decision to be understanding rather than annoyed. "There now," she said. Placing the lamenting child over her other, nappiless, shoulder she drew Margaret to her to lean upon the other one. "Never mind, dear. Just an accident."

Margaret—her mother smelled of milk and baby powder—pulled away and made a face. "It's like a pig," she said.

Mrs. Marsh looked yet more understanding.

"Darling, you do know how much we love you, don't you? He's your baby too, you know, just as much as ours. Look—you hold him. You're such a big girl. He's going to love you so much."

"What's so marvellous?"

"Marvellous?"

"About that? Why do I have to be pleased that he's going to love me? I don't need him."

"He will need you."

"No, he won't. If I wasn't here he wouldn't know anything about me."

"But you are here."

"I'm not here for him. I managed with me. Nobody was here for me when I was born and I was all right."

Mrs. Marsh, trying slowly to digest this empirical point, wrapped the child very tight in a cloth with its arms crossed over its chest tight beneath it, then put it on its face in the flounced organdy of the crib.

It did not look up to its surroundings. More like a trussed duck than ever.

"It can't be good for it, bound up like that," said Margaret, and Mrs. Marsh brightened at a sign of possible concern.

"Oh yes it is, dear. It says so in Truby King. They like to feel safe."

"I don't see why you feel safe if you're tied up."

"Not tied up, dear. Just well wrapped round. Babies come from a very warm place," she said, coy but emancipated. "Safe in a little nest in their mummies' tummies."

"I wouldn't say a little nest," said Margaret. "It was huge. And all rippling about. You could see it even, at the end. When some of the Saints came in just before that Sunday I was nearly sick. You ought to have been ashamed. All huge."

"Now why ashamed?" asked Mrs. Marsh, very bright. She had secretly found some Freud to read in the Public Library during pregnancy, as well as Truby King. "Now why ashamed? It's quite natural. After all, it's how we all came, darling."

"Pity we did."

"Now, Margaret, how silly."

"It would be better without people."

"There would be no love, darling, without people. God made us so that there might be love. Er—one John four-er-twelve, isn't it? No—John one fourteen—but . . ."

"Why bother? The world was all right before, it seems to me. If we didn't exist we weren't missing things. Ice and fire and snow and glaciers and then plants. It would have been enough you'd think. Well perhaps dinosaurs. If I'd been God I'd have left it at dinosaurs. I'd have been satisfied looking down at all that."

Mrs. Marsh said very carefully, "Margaret, I don't think you ought to talk about dinosaurs. You know what Father thinks. I suppose this is school."

"No. It's just real. They've found the bones. Father doesn't underst . . ."

"Of course Father knows there were dinosaurs. But you know that we believe in Genesis here, don't you? You've known this for a long time. You especially, Margaret, with your wonderful memory. Most people nowadays don't, they believe in a very old-fashioned idea that was disproved years ago by people your father knows all about. Most people believe in myths—you know what myths are?—invented by Sir Charles Darwin about how we grew out of fishes and monkeys and things. Doesn't that seem silly? But in this house we believe that God put us down all complete, Adam and Eve in the garden, so that we could share all the lovely things God had made."

"Very kind," said Margaret, "but . . ."

"Exactly!" Mrs. Marsh looked really delighted now whereas, considering dinosaurs, she had seemed uncertain. "Exactly. Kind."

"Unnecessary," said Margaret. "God and the world would have done. Like me before the baby came."

"Now, Margaret dear, I know you don't realise it but that is blasphemy."

"What's blasphemy?"

"But you hear about blasphemy every week at the Primal Hall!"

"Is it what Father talks? I thought what Father talked . . ."

"Margaret! Blasphemy is taking the name of God in vain."

"In vain. A lot of things are in vain."

"No. It means lightly. You are taking the name of God lightly."

"Better than heavily."

"God," said Mrs. Marsh going rather red in the cheeks and buttoning her dress after adjusting a massive camisole beneath and easing herself to an even balance, "made us in his own image." She looked at the trussed baby, face down, its red head like a tilted orange rearing up and down on the undersheet as if desperately attempting escape. Giving up, it let its head drop into suffocation position and there was another explosion followed by a long, liquid sputtering from further down the cot: and a smell. "Oh dear," said Mrs. Marsh contented, "now I'll have to start all over again with a new nappy. Could you hand me the bucket, darling?"

"His own image," said Margaret watching the horrible unwrapping. "If God looks like us . . . What's the point?"

"You must speak," said Mrs. Marsh sternly, "to your father."

P. G. Wodehouse

INDISCRETIONS OF ARCHIE

"Say! Do you want to hear the best thing I've ever done?"

"Indubitably," said Archie, politely. "Carry on, old bird!"

"I wrote the lyric as well as the melody," said Wilson Hymack, who had already seated himself at the piano. "It's got the greatest title you ever heard. It's a lallapaloosa! It's called 'It's a Long Way Back to Mother's Knee.' How's that? Poor, eh?"

Archie expelled a smoke-ring doubtfully.

"Isn't it a little stale?"

"Stale? What do you mean, stale? There's always room for another song boosting mother."

"Oh, is it boosting mother?" Archie's face cleared. "I thought it was a hit at the short skirts. Why, of course, that makes all the difference. In that case, I see no reason why it should not be ripe, fruity, and pretty well all to the mustard. Let's have it."

Wilson Hymack pushed as much of his hair out of his eyes as he could reach with one hand, cleared his throat, looked dreamily over the top of the piano at a photograph of Archie's father-in-law, Mr. Daniel Brewster, played a prelude, and began to sing in a weak, high, composer's voice. All composers sing exactly alike, and they have to be heard to be believed.

"One night a young man wandered through the glitter of
     Broadway:
His money he had squandered. For a meal he couldn't pay."

"Tough luck!" murmured Archie, sympathetically.

"He thought about the village where his boyhod he had spent,
And yearned for all the simple joys with which he'd been con-
     tent."

"The right spirit!" said Archie, with approval. "I'm beginning to like this chappie!"

"Don't interrupt!"

"Oh, right-o! Carried away and all that!"

"He looked upon the city, so frivolous and gay:
And, as he heaved a weary sigh, these words he then did say:
     It's a long way back to mother's knee,
                              mother's knee,
                              mother's knee:
     It's a long way back to mother's knee,
          Where I used to stand and prattle
          With my teddy-bear and rattle
     Oh, those childhood days in Tennessee,
     They sure look good to me!
     It's a long, long way, but I'm gonna start today!
          I'm going back,
               Believe me, oh!
          I'm going back
               (I want to go!)
          I'm going back—back—on the seven-three
          To the dear old shack where I used to be!
          I'm going back to mother's knee!"

Wilson Hymack's voice cracked on the final high note, which was of an altitude beyond his powers. He turned with a modest cough.

"That'll give you an idea of it!"

"It has, old thing, it has!"

"Is it or is it not a ball of fire?"

"It has many of the earmarks of a sound egg," admitted Archie. "Of course—"

"Of course, it wants singing."

"Just what I was going to suggest,"

"It wants a woman to sing it. A woman who could reach out for that last high note and teach it to take a joke. The whole refrain is working up to that. You need Tetrazzini or someone who would just pick that note off the roof and hold it till the janitor came round to lock up the building for the night."

"I must buy a copy for my wife. Where can I get it?"

"You can't get it! It isn't published. Writing music's the darndest job!" Wilson Hymack snorted fiercely. It was plain that the man was pouring out the pent-up emotion of many days. "You write the biggest thing in years and you go round trying to get someone to sing it, and they say you're a genius and then shove the song away in a drawer and forget about it."

Archie lit another cigarette.

"I'm a jolly old child in these matters, old lad," he said, "but why don't you take it direct to a publisher? As a matter of fact, if it would be any use to you, I was foregathering with a music-publisher only the other day. A bird of the name of Blumenthal. He was lunching in here with a pal of mine, and we got tolerably matey. Why not let me tool you round to the office tomorrow and play it to him?"

"No thanks. Much obliged, but I'm not going to play that melody in any publisher's office with his hired gang of Tin Pan Alley composers listening at the keyhole and taking notes. I'll have to wait till I can find somebody to sing it. Well, I must be going along. Glad to have seen you again. Sooner or later I'll take you to hear that high note sung by someone in a way that'll make your spine tie itself in knots round the back of your neck."

"I'll count the days," said Archie, courteously. "Pip-pip!"

Mr. Brewster, looming over the table like a thundercloud, regarded Archie with more than his customary hostility. Life was no pleasant thing for the proprietor of the Cosmopolis just now. Once a man starts building hotels, the thing becomes like dram-drinking. Any hitch, any sudden cutting-off of the daily dose, has the worst effects; and the strike which was holding up the construction of his latest effort had plunged Mr. Brewster into a restless gloom. In addition to having this strike on his hands, he had had to abandon his annual fishing-trip just when he had begun to enjoy it; and, as if all this were not enough, here was his son-in-law sitting at his table. Mr. Brewster had a feeling that this was more than man was meant to bear.

"What do you want?" he demanded.

"Hallo, old thing!" said Archie. "Come and join the party!"

"Don't call me old thing!"

"Right-o, old companion, just as you say. I say, I was just going to suggest to Mr. Connolly that we should all go up to my suite and talk this business over quietly."

"He says he's the manager of your new hotel," said Mr. Connolly. "Is that right?"

"I suppose so," said Mr. Brewster, gloomily.

"Then I'm doing you a kindness," said Mr. Connolly, "in not letting it be built."

Archie dabbed at his forehead with his handkerchief. The moments were flying, and it began to seem impossible to shift these two men. Mr. Connolly was as firmly settled in his chair as some primeval rock. As for Mr. Brewster, he, too, had seated himself, and was gazing at Archie with a weary repulsion. Mr. Brewster's glance always made Archie feel as though there were soup on his shirt-front.

And suddenly from the orchestra at the other end of the room there came a familiar sound, the prelude of "Mother's Knee."

"So you've started a cabaret, Dan?" said Mr. Connolly, in a satisfied voice. "I always told you you were away behind the times here!"

Mr. Brewster jumped.

"Cabaret!"

He stared unbelievingly at the white-robed figure which had just mounted the orchestra dais, and then concentrated his gaze on Archie.

Archie would not have looked at his father-in-law at this juncture if he had had a free and untrammelled choice; but Mr. Brewster's eye drew his with something of the fascination which a snake's has for a rabbit. Mr. Brewster's eye was fiery and intimidating. A basilisk might have gone to him with advantage for a course of lessons. His gaze went right through Archie till the latter seemed to feel his back-hair curling crisply in the flames.

"Is this one of your fool-tricks?"

Even in this tense moment Archie found time almost unconsciously to admire his father-in-law's penetration and intuition. He seemed to have a sort of sixth sense. No doubt this was how great fortunes were made.

"Well, as a matter of fact—to be absolutely accurate—it was like this—"

"Say, cut it out!" said Mr. Connolly. "Can the chatter! I want to listen."

Archie was only too ready to oblige him. Conversation at the moment was the last thing he himself desired. He managed with a strong effort to disengage himself from Mr. Brewster's eye, and turned to the orchestra dais, where Miss Spectatia Huskisson was now beginning the first verse of Wilson Hymack's masterpiece.

Miss Huskisson, like so many of the female denizens of the Middle West, was tall and blonde and constructed on substantial lines. She was a girl whose appearance suggested the old homestead and fried pancakes and pop coming home to dinner after the morning's ploughing. Even her bobbed hair did not altogether destroy this impression. She looked big and strong and healthy, and her lungs were obviously good. She attacked the verse of the song with something of the vigour and breadth of treatment with which in other days she had reasoned with refractory mules. Her diction was the diction of one trained to call the cattle home in the teeth of Western hurricanes. Whether you wanted to or not, you heard every word.

The subdued clatter of knives and forks had ceased. The diners, unused to this sort of thing at the Cosmopolis, were trying to adjust their faculties to cope with the outburst. Waiters stood transfixed, frozen in attitudes of service. In the momentary lull between verse and refrain Archie could hear the deep breathing of Mr. Brewster. Involuntarily he turned to gaze at him once more, as refugees from Pompeii may have turned to gaze upon Vesuvius; and, as he did so, he caught sight of Mr. Connolly, and paused in astonishment.

Mr. Connolly was an altered man. His whole personality had undergone a subtle change. His face still looked as though hewn from a living rock, but into his eyes had crept an expression which in another man might almost have been called sentimental. Incredible as it seemed to Archie, Mr. Connolly's eyes were dreamy. There was even in them a suggestion of unshed tears. And when with a vast culmination of sound Miss Huskisson reached the high note at the end of the refrain and, after holding it as some storming-party, spent but victorious, holds the summit of a hard-won redoubt, broke off suddenly, in the stillness which followed there proceeded from Mr. Connolly a deep sigh.

Miss Huskisson began the second verse. And Mr. Brewster, seeming to recover from some kind of a trance, leaped to his feet.

"Great Godfrey!"

"Sit down!" said Mr. Connolly, in a broken voice. "Sit down, Dan!"

"He went back to his mother on the train that very day:
He knew there was no other who could make him bright and gay:
He kissed her on the forehead and he whispered, 'I've come home!'
He told her he was never going any more to roam.
And onward through the happy years, till he grew old and grey,
He never once regretted those brave words he once did say:
It's a long way back to mother's knee—!"

The last high note screeched across the room like a shell, and the applause that followed was like a shell's bursting. One could hardly have recognized the refined interior of the Cosmopolis dining-room. Fair women were waving napkins; brave men were hammering on the tables with the butt-end of knives, for all the world as if they imagined themselves to be in one of those distressing midnight-revue places. Miss Huskisson bowed, retired, returned, bowed, and retired again, the tears streaming down her ample face. Over in a corner Archie could see his brother-in-law clapping strenuously. A waiter, with a display of manly emotion that did him credit, dropped an order of new peas.

"Thirty years ago last October," said Mr. Connolly, in a shaking voice, "I—"

Mr. Brewster interrupted him violently.

"I'll fire that orchestra-leader! He goes tomorrow! I'll fire—" he turned on Archie. "What the devil do you mean by it, you—you—"

"Thirty years ago," said Mr. Connolly, wiping away a tear with his napkin, "I left me dear old home in the old country."

"My hotel a bear-garden!"

"Frightfully sorry and all that, old companion—"

"Thirty years ago last October! 'Twas a fine autumn evening, the finest ye'd ever wish to see. Me old mother, she came to the station to see me off."

Mr. Brewster, who was not deeply interested in Mr. Connolly's old mother, continued to splutter inarticulately, like a firework trying to go off.

" 'Ye'll always be a good boy, Aloysius?' she said to me," said Mr. Connolly, proceeding with his autobiography. "And I said: 'Yes,

mother, I will!' " Mr. Connolly sighed and applied the napkin again.
" 'Twas a liar I was!" he observed, remorsefully. "Many's the dirty I've
played since then. 'It's a long way back to mother's knee.' 'Tis a true
word!" He turned impulsively to Mr. Brewster. "Dan, there's a deal of
trouble in this world without me going out of me way to make more.
The strike is over! I'll send the men back tomorrow! There's me hand
on it!"

Mr. Brewster, who had just managed to coordinate his views on
the situation and was about to express them with the generous strength
which was ever his custom when dealing with his son-in-law, checked
himself abruptly. He stared at his old friend and business enemy, wondering if he could have heard aright. Hope began to creep back into Mr.
Brewster's heart, like a shamefaced dog that has been away from home
hunting for a day or two.

"You'll what!"

"I'll send the men back tomorrow! That song was sent to guide
me, Dan! It was meant! Thirty years ago last October me dear old
mother—"

Mr. Brewster bent foward attentively. His views on Mr. Connolly's dear old mother had changed. He wanted to hear all about her.

" 'Twas that last note that girl sang brought it all back to me as if
'twas yesterday. As we waited on the platform, me old mother and I,
out comes the train from the tunnel, and the engine lets off a screech the
way ye'd hear it ten miles away. 'Twas thirty years ago—"

Archie stole softly from the table. He felt that his presence, if it had
ever been required, was required no longer. Looking back, he could see
his father-in-law patting Mr. Connolly affectionately on the shoulder.

Archie and Lucille lingered over their coffee. Mr. Blumenthal was
out in the telephone-box settling the business end with Wilson Hymack.
The music-publisher had been unstinted in his praise of "Mother's
Knee." It was sure-fire, he said. The words, stated Mr. Blumenthal,
were gooey enough to hurt, and the tune reminded him of every other
song-hit he had ever heard. There was, in Mr. Blumenthal's opinion,
nothing to stop the thing selling a million copies.

Jean-Paul Sartre

WORDS

I was still unable to read but I was snobbish enough to insist on having my books. My grandfather went along to his scoundrel of a publisher and was given *Les Contes* by Maurice Bouchor, the poet, tales drawn from folklore and adapted to children's tastes by a man who, so they said, still had the eyes of a child. I wanted to begin my appropriation ceremonies on the spot. I took the two small volumes, sniffed at them, felt them, opened them casually "at the right page" and made them creak. It was no good: I did not feel that I owned them. I tried without greater success to treat them as dolls, cradle them, kiss them and beat them. On the verge of tears, I finally laid them on my mother's lap. She looked up from her work: "What do you want me to read, darling? About the Fairies?" I asked incredulously: "Are there Fairies in there?" I knew the tale well: my mother often told it to me while she was washing my face, breaking off to massage me with eau-de-Cologne or to pick up, from under the bath, the soap which had slipped from her hands, and I would listen with half an ear to an all-too-familiar story; all I wanted to see was Anne-Marie, the young girl of my mornings; all I wanted to hear was her voice, disturbed by servitude; I loved her half-completed sentences, her always slow-to-come words and her brusque confidence, quickly defeated and put to rout, which disappeared with a pleasant fraying sound, and then re-established itself after a silence. The story was secondary: it was the link between her soliloquies. All the while she was talking, we were alone and private, far from man, gods and priests, two does in the wood, with those other does, the Fairies; I never could believe that a whole book could have been written to feature this episode in our profane life, which smelt of soap and eau-de-Cologne.

Anne-Marie made me sit down in front of her, on my little chair; she leant over, lowered her eyelids and went to sleep. From this mask-like face issued a plaster voice. I grew bewildered: who was talking? about what? and to whom? My mother had disappeared: not a smile or trace of complicity. I was an exile. And then I did not recognize the language. Where did she get her confidence? After a moment, I realized: it was the book that was talking. Sentences emerged that frightened me: they were like real centipedes; they swarmed with syllables and letters, span out their diphthongs and made their double consonants hum; fluting, nasal, broken up with sighs and pauses, rich in unknown words, they were in love with themselves and their meanderings and had no time for me: sometimes they disappeared before I could understand them; at others, I had understood in advance and they went rolling on nobly toward their end without sparing me a comma. These words were obviously not meant for me. The tale itself was in its Sunday best: the woodcutter, the woodcutter's wife and their daughters, the fairy, all those little people, our fellow-creatures, had acquired majesty; their rags were magnificently described, words left their mark on objects, transforming actions into rituals and events into ceremonies. Someone began to ask questions: my grandfather's publisher, who specialized in putting out school editions, lost no opportunity of exercising the intelligence of his young readers. It was as if a child were being quizzed. What would he have done in the woodcutter's place? Which of the two sisters did he prefer? Why? Did he agree with Babette's punishment? But this child was not entirely me and I was afraid to reply. I did reply, though; my feeble voice grew faint and I felt I was turning into someone else. Anne-Marie, too, with her blind soothsayer's look, was someone else: it was as if I were every mother's child and she were every child's mother. When she stopped reading, I quickly took back the books and carried them off under my arm without a word of thanks.

Edmund Gosse

FATHER AND SON

Left to my Mother's sole care, I became the centre of her solicitude. But there mingled with those happy animal instincts which sustain the strength and patience of every human mother and were fully present with her—there mingled with these certain spiritual determinations which can be but rare. They are, in their outline, I suppose, vaguely common to many religious mothers, but there are few indeed who fill up the sketch with so firm a detail as she did. Once again I am indebted to her secret notes, in a little locked volume, seen until now, nearly sixty years later, by no eye save her own. Thus she wrote when I was two months old:

> We have given him to the Lord; and we trust that He will really manifest him to be His own, if he grow up; and if the Lord take him early, we will not doubt that he is taken to Himself. Only, if it please the Lord to take him, I do trust we may be spared seeing him suffering in lingering illness and much pain. But in this as in all things His will is better than what we can choose. Whether his life be prolonged or not, it has already been a blessing to us, and to the saints, in leading us to much prayer, and bringing us into varied need and some trial.

The last sentence is somewhat obscure to me. How, at that tender age, I contrived to be a blessing "to the saints" may surprise others and puzzles myself. But "the saints" was the habitual term by which were indicated the friends who met on Sunday mornings for Holy Communion, and at many other times in the week for prayer and discussion of the Scriptures, in the small hired hall at Hackney, which my parents attended. I suppose that the solemn dedication of me to the Lord, which was repeated in public in my Mother's arms, being by no means a usual or familiar ceremony even among the Brethren, created a certain curiosity and fervour in the immediate services, or was imagined so to do by the fond, partial heart of my Mother. She, however, who had been so much isolated, now made the care of her child an excuse for retiring still further into silence. With those religious persons who met at the Room, as the modest chapel was called, she had little spiritual and no intellectual sympathy. She noted:

> I do not think it would increase my happiness to be in the midst of the saints at Hackney. I have made up my mind to give myself up to Baby for the winter, and to accept no invitations. To go when I can to the Sunday morning meetings and to see my own Mother.

Now, and for the first time in my life, I no longer slept in her room, no longer sank to sleep under her kiss, no longer saw her mild eyes smile on me with the earliest sunshine. Twice a day, after breakfast and before I went to rest, I was brought to her bedside; but we were never alone, other people, sometimes strange people, were there. We had no cosy talk; often she was too weak to do more than pat my hand: her loud and almost constant cough terrified and harassed me. I felt, as I stood, awkwardly and shyly, by her high bed, that I had shrunken into a very small and insignificant figure, that she was floating out of my reach, that all things, but I knew not what nor how, were coming to an end. She herself was not herself; her head, that used to be held so erect, now rolled or sank upon the pillow; the sparkle was all extinguished from those bright, dear eyes. I could not understand it; I meditated long, long upon it all in my infantile darkness, in the garret, or in the little slip of a cold room where my bed was now placed; and a great, blind anger against I knew not what awakened in my soul.

The two retreats which I have mentioned were now all that were left to me. In the back-parlour some one from outside gave me occasional lessons, of a desultory character. The breakfast-room was often haunted by visitors, unknown to me by face or name,—ladies, who used to pity me and even to pet me, until I became nimble in escaping from their caresses. Everything semed to be unfixed, uncertain; it was like being on the platform of a railway-station waiting for a train. In all this time, the agitated, nervous presence of my Father, whose pale face was permanently drawn with anxiety, added to my perturbation, and I became miserable, stupid, as if I had lost my way in a cold fog.

Had I been older and more intelligent, of course, it might have been of him and not of myself that I should have been thinking. As I now look back upon that tragic time, it is for him that my heart bleeds,—for them both, so singularly fitted as they were to support and cheer one another in an existence which their own innate and cultivated characteristics had made little hospitable to other sources of comfort. This is not to be dwelt on here. But what must be recorded was the extraordinary tranquillity, the serene and sensible resignation, with which at length my parents faced the awful hour. Language cannot utter what they suffered, but there was no rebellion, no repining; in their case even an atheist might admit that the overpowering miracle of grace was mightily efficient.

When the very end approached, and her mind was growing clouded, she gathered her strength together to say to my Father, "I shall walk with Him in white. Won't you take our lamb and walk with me?" Confused with sorrow and alarm, my Father failed to understand her meaning. She became agitated, and she repeated two or three times: "Take our lamb, and walk with me!" Then my Father comprehended, and pressed me forward; her hand fell softly upon mine and she seemed content. Thus was my dedication, that had begun in my cradle, sealed with the most solemn, the most poignant and irresistible insistence, at the death-bed of the holiest and purest of women. But what a weight, intolerable as the burden of Atlas, to lay on the shoulders of a little fragile child!

Simone de Beauvoir

MEMOIRS OF A DUTIFUL DAUGHTER

"Physical" questions sickened her so much that she never attempted to discuss them with me; she did not even warn me about the surprises awaiting me on the threshold of puberty. In all other matters, she accepted my father's ideas without ever appearing to find any difficulty in reconciling them with her religion. My father was constantly astonished by the paradoxes of the human heart, by the playful tricks of heredity, and by the strangeness of dreams; I never saw my mother astonished by anything.

In complete contrast to my father's negligence, she was profoundly conscious of her responsibilities, and took to heart the duties of mother and counselor. She sought guidance from the Union of Christian Mothers, and often attended their meetings. She took me to school, attended my classes and kept a strict eye on my homework and my lessons; she learned English and began to study Latin in order to be able to follow my progress. She supervised my reading, and accompanied me to Mass and compline; my mother, my sister, and I performed our devotions together, morning and evening. At every instant of the day she was present, even in the most secret recesses of my soul, and I made no distinction between her all-seeing wisdom and the eye of God Himself.

I did not look upon her as a saint, because I knew her too well and because she lost her temper far too easily; but her example seemed to me all the more unassailable because of that: I, too, was able to, and therefore ought to, emulate her in piety and virtue. The warmth of her affection made up for her unpredictable temper. If she had been more impeccable in her conduct, she would have been more remote, and would not have had such a profound effect upon me.

Her hold over me stemmed indeed a great deal from the very intimacy of our relationship. My father treated me like a fully developed person; my mother watched over me as a mother watches over a child; and a child I still was. She was more indulgent toward me than he: she found it quite natural that I should be a silly little girl, whereas my stupidity only exasperated my father; she was amused by my childish sayings and scribblings; he found them quite unfunny. I wanted to be taken notice of; but fundamentally I needed to be accepted for what I was, with all the deficiencies of my age; my mother's tenderness assured me that this wish was a justifiable one. I was flattered most by praise from my father; but if he complained because I had made a mess in his study, or if he cried: "How stupid these children are!" I took such censure lightly, because he obviously attached little importance to the way it was expressed. On the other hand, any reproach made by my mother, and even her slightest frown, was a threat to my security: without her approval, I no longer felt I had any right to live.

If her disapproval touched me so deeply, it was because I set so much store by her good opinion. When I was seven or eight years old, I kept no secrets from her, and spoke to her with complete freedom. I have one very vivid memory which illustrates this lack of sophistication. My attack of measles had left me with a slight lateral curvature of the spine; a doctor drew a line down my vertebral column, as if my back had been a blackboard, and he prescribed Swedish exercises. I took some lessons with a tall, blond gymnastic instructor. As I was waiting for him one afternoon I did a little practice on the horizontal bar; when I sat astride the bar, I felt a curious itching sensation between my thighs; it was agreeable and yet somehow disappointing; I tried again; the phenomenon was repeated. "It's funny," I told Mama, and then described my sensation to her. With a look of complete indifference on her face she began talking of something else, and I realized that I had asked one of those tiresome questions to which I never received any answer.

After that, my attitude seemed to change. Whenever I wondered about the "ties of blood" which were often mentioned in books, or about the "fruit of thy womb" in the Hail Mary, I did not turn to my mother for confirmation of my suspicions. It may be that in the meanwhile she had countered some of my questions with evasions I have now forgotten. But my silence on these subjects arose from a more general inhibition: I was keeping a watch on my tongue and on my behavior as a whole. My mother rarely punished me, and if ever she was free with her hands her slaps did not hurt very much. However, without loving her any less than before, I had begun to fight shy of her. There was one word which she was fond of using and which used to paralyze my sister and me: "It's ridiculous!" she would cry. We often heard her making use of this word whenever she was discussing with Papa the conduct of a third person; when it was applied to us, it used to dash us from the cozy heights of our family empyrean into the lowest depths where the scum of humanity lay grovelling. Unable to foresee what gesture or remark might unleash this terrible word upon us, we learned to look upon any kind of initiative as dangerous; prudence counseled us to hold our tongues and stay our hands. I recall the surprise we felt when, after asking Mama if we might take our dolls on holiday with us, she answered simply: "Why not?" We had repressed this wish for years. Certainly the main reason for my timidity was a desire to avoid her derision. But at the same time, whenever her eyes had that stormy look or even when she just compressed her lips, I believe that I feared the disturbance I was causing in her heart more than my own discomfiture. If she had found me out telling a lie, I should have felt the scandal it created even more keenly than any personal shame: but the idea was so unbearable, I always told the truth. I obviously did not realize that my mother's promptness to condemn anything peculiar or new was a forestalling of the confusion that any dispute aroused in her: but I sensed that careless words and sudden changes of plan easily troubled her serenity. My responsibility toward her made my dependence even greater.

And that is how we lived, the two of us, in a kind of symbiosis. Without striving to imitate her, I was conditioned by her. She inculcated in me a sense of duty as well as teaching me unselfishness and austerity. My father was not averse to the limelight, but I learned from Mama to keep in the background, to control my tongue, to moderate my desires, to say and do exactly what ought to be said and done. I made no demands on life, and I was afraid to do anything on my own initiative.

When we got back to Paris, my sister, less inhibited than myself, ventured to ask Mama if babies came out of one's navel. "Why do you ask such silly questions?" my mother said, rather tartly. "You know everything already." Aunt Helene had apparently tipped her off. Relieved at having negotiated this initial barrier we pressed Mama for more details; she gave us to understand that little babies came out of the anus, quite painlessly. She spoke in a detached tone of voice; but we were not encouraged to make further inquiries: I never again discussed these problems with her, and she never said another word to us about them.

If she had often stood in my way, I think she would have provoked me to open rebellion. But in the really important things—my studies, and the choice of my friends—she very rarely meddled; she respected my work and my leisure too, only asking me to do little odd jobs for her like grinding the coffee or carrying the refuse bin downstairs. I had the habit of obedience, and I believed that, on the whole, God expected me to be dutiful: the conflict that threatened to set me against my mother did not break out; but I was uneasily aware of its underlying presence. My mother's whole education and upbringing had convinced her that for a woman the greatest thing was to become the mother of a family; she couldn't play this part unless I played the dutiful daughter, but I refused to take part in grown-up pretense as much as I did when I was five years old. At the Cours Désir, on the eve of our First Communion, we were exhorted to go and cast ourselves down at our mothers' feet and ask them to forgive our faults; not only had I not done this, but when my sister's turn came I persuaded her not to do so either. My mother was vexed about it. She was aware of a certain reticence in me which made her bad-tempered, and she often rebuked me. I held it against her for keeping me so dependent upon her and continuing to impose her will upon me. In addition, I was jealous of the place she held in my father's affections because my own passion for him had continued to grow.

But my real rival was my mother. I dreamed of having a more intimate relationship with my father; but even on the rare occasions when we found ourselves alone together we talked as if she was there with us. When there was an argument, if I had appealed to my father, he would have said: "Do what your mother tells you!" I only once tried to get him on my side. He had taken us to the races at Auteuil; the course was black with people, it was hot, there was nothing happening, and I was bored; finally the horses were off: the people rushed toward the barriers, and their backs hid the track from my view. My father had hired folding chairs for us and I wanted to stand on mine to get a better view. "No!" said my mother, who detested crowds and had been irritated by all the pushing and shoving. I insisted that I should be allowed to stand on my folding chair. "When I say no, I mean no!" my mother declared. As she was looking after my sister, I turned to my father and cried furiously: "Mama is being ridiculous! Why can't I stand on my folding chair?" He simply lifted his shoulders in an embarrassed silence, and refused to take part in the argument.

At least this ambiguous gesture allowed me to assume that as far as he was concerned my father sometimes found my mother too domineering; I persuaded myself that there was a silent conspiracy between us. But I soon lost this illusion. One lunchtime there was talk of a wild-living cousin who considered his mother to be an idiot: on my father's own admission she actually was one. Yet he declared vehemently: "A child who sets up as a judge of his mother is an imbecile." I went scarlet and left the table, pretending I was feeling sick. I was judging my mother, and my father had struck a double blow at me by affirming their solidarity and by referring to me indirectly as an imbecile.

With my father away, Mama and my cousins were all together like birds of a feather, all professing the same highly devout principles without asking any dissident voice to disturb their perfect harmony; speaking freely of spiritual matters in my presence, they seemed to involve me in a complicity which I didn't dare to challenge: I had the feeling that they were doing violence to my soul.

One afternoon, when I was alone in the study, my mother came in and sat down opposite me; she hesitated, blushed, and then said: "There are certain things you ought to know!" I blushed too: "I know all about that," I hurriedly replied. She displayed no curiosity as to where I had obtained my knowledge, and to our mutual relief the conversation was not pursued any further. A few days later she called me into her room and asked me, with some embarrassment, how I stood "from the religious point of view." My heart began to pound: "Well," I said, "for some time now I haven't believed in God." Her face fell: "My poor darling!" she said. She went to shut the door, so that my sister might not overhear the rest of our conversation; in a pleading voice she embarked on a demonstration of the truth of God's existence; then, with a helpless gesture, her eyes full of tears, she stopped suddenly. I was sorry to have hurt her, but I felt greatly relieved: at last I would be able to live without a mask.

ON QUEEN VICTORIA

George IV was kind but distant towards her [Princess Victoria], his brother William was genuinely fond of her. He wished her to assume a position at Court, make herself known to her future subjects, and generally prepare herself for the important fate that lay before her.

A powerful obstacle stood in the path of the King's good intentions. This was none other than Victoria's mother, whose dislike and distrust of William IV was cordially returned by the Monarch himself. From the first she jealously guarded the young Princess from any contact with the Court, even with society at large. The King disliked Victoria's Uncle Leopold on private and political grounds, and during the last years of his reign did everything he could to thwart Leopold's ever-growing influence over their young niece. The Coburgs were always of a managing disposition, and Leopold had early cast his lot with the Whigs, whom King William tolerated but did not affect. The quarrel between the King and Duchess inevitably centred round the person of Victoria. As the late Sir Charles Webster wrote in his famous essay on the 1837 Accession, "the Duchess assumed complete control over her daughter and William was denied by her the usual rights of both uncle and sovereign. He always resented it. And the quarrel was developing into a public scandal when he died."

The Duchess was a weak and foolish woman, much in the hands of her Comptroller, Sir John Conroy. This sinister person, whose name is absent from the *Dictionary of National Biography,* and occurs only once in these letters, played a great part in the circumstances of the Princess's childhood.

The Duchess's attitude to Conroy was so equivocal, Webster relates, that only one conclusion could be drawn from it. "There is much evidence," he goes on, that Conroy "had the design of exploiting for his own purposes the position that Victoria must one day hold. . . . For long he seemed to have a great game to play, and Victoria was kept so far as possible from influences that would rival that of her mother, and thus his own."

ON D. H. LAWRENCE

Lydia [D. H. Lawrence's mother] was high-minded and pious. She had been a schoolteacher and had written poetry. She hated dirt and drink and poverty. It was an attraction of opposites which could not last. Arthur [his father] was irresponsible and poor. He rarely went to chapel when he ceased to be in the Brinsley church choir. She loved reading and talking more than anything, but she could not talk to him. He could hardly write and his reading never went beyond the newspapers. He understood little of what he could read. "Lass, what's meanin' o' this 'ere," he would ask his wife, who would impatiently explain. He was inarticulate, almost taciturn (at least at home) and when he did speak had a slight stammer.

He described himself to her as a mining contractor. It sounded rather grand. It was the official term for what the men called a butty. The butties had a stall and were responsible for hiring the day men to work it. The butties would be paid on Friday for all the coal got out that week, would pay off the day men at the agreed rate, then share what remained between themselves. The butty was slightly better off than the day man, but his income could fluctuate alarmingly, and he was just as much a face-worker. The first time Arthur returned home from work Lydia did not recognize him. She thought he was a Negro. He would wash only his hands before eating, insisting that it was "clean dirt." Afterwards she had to scrub his back. She thought she could make him teetotal, but he could not keep it up for long. For years she shuddered when, after closing-time, she heard the gang of miners stumbling down the hill singing "Lead, kindly light." Ada Lawrence recalled:

> Mother would wait up for him all night, her rage seething, until on his arrival it boiled over in a torrent of biting truths which turned him from his slightly fuddled and pleasantly apologetic mood into a brutal and coarse beast.

Nor could Lydia have anticipated the poverty. Arthur would abuse the managers in the pub. This got back to them, and he found himself with worse and worse stalls. And children were coming, George in 1876, William Ernest in 1878, Emily in 1882. Yet they never lacked for any-

thing. Mrs. Lawrence incurred no debts and paid her husband's. She made continued sacrifices to keep her sons out of the mine and give them a good education. The house was always spotless, and somehow superior to the neighbouring houses, for Mrs. Lawrence preferred bareness to anything cheap or tawdry. But she never forgave her husband for bringing her to this. In Ada's words:

> She did not recover from the shock of realizing that her life would be one of almost ceaseless monotony among ugliness and dirt. She escaped into herself and when the children came, lived alone with them. He was a stranger in the house.

In 1885 the Lawrences were living in Victoria Street, Eastwood. Mrs. Lawrence used her front room, with its enlarged window, as a shop, selling aprons, lace and linen. Willie Hopkin was passing one day and saw Mrs. Lawrence pushing a pram with her newest baby, "like a skinned rabbit." "I'm afraid I s'll never rear him," she said. She reared him to become the greatest writer of his time.

ON SAMUEL JOHNSON

Because of his physical disabilities, Sam needed special encouragement. Even more than most children he required devoted care and understanding from both his parents, and above all the feeling of security which grows out of being part of a happy family group. Unfortunately there was not much warmth and security in the Johnson household. There was little appreciation of the child's emotional needs, and the approach to disciplinary problems was faulty. Neither Michael nor Sarah had any conception of the best ways to offset his deficiencies or to strengthen his self-confidence. It was natural that he should be thrown most with his mother, who alternately spoiled and punished him. She would "gratify his appetite" by giving him coffee which she could ill afford, and indulge many of his childish whims. At the same time she was always trying to teach him rigid ideas of morality and behaviour, but her admonitions went beyond empty formulas. "My mother," said he, "was always telling me that I did not behave myself properly; that I should endeavour

to learn behavior, and such cant: but when I replied, that she ought to tell me what to do, and what to avoid, her admonitions were commonly, for that time at least, at an end." From his own experience Johnson looked on older people as "very unfit to manage children; for being most commonly idle themselves" they occupied themselves "by tormenting the young folks with prohibitions not meant to be obeyed and questions not intended to be answered."

Since Johnson later remarked that "no attention can be obtained from children without the infliction of pain, and pain is never remembered without resentment," it is probable that he had some unhappy memories of early physical punishments. If so, they did not alienate him from his mother. There can be no doubt of his love for her. In later life he wrote of his "dear mother" with obvious feeling. On the other hand, his was not a blind, unreasoning devotion. "Poor people's children," he commented, "never respect them: I did not respect my own mother, though I loved her: and one day, when in anger she called me a puppy, I asked her if she knew what they called a puppy's mother."

Sam's earliest instruction, religious and secular, came from his mother. Some time shortly after the eventful trip to London he was first informed about "a future state." "I remember, that being in bed with my mother one morning, I was told by her of the two places to which the inhabitants of this world were received after death; one a fine place filled with happiness, called heaven; the other a sad place, called hell. That this account much affected my imagination, I do not remember." In order that it might be better fixed in his memory, however, she sent him to repeat it to Thomas Jackson, their manservant.

If he was too young at this time to grasp the full significance of what his mother was saying, she must subsequently have made the dangers of future punishment clear enough. Sarah's approach to the Bible was literal and devout. Since her own father's taste in reading had run to evangelical sermons, it may be that she had absorbed some of his Calvinism. Hell was real, and damnation no mere symbolic device. So well did her son learn the lesson that he was never rid of the terrors of the other world. In the very year of his death, when Dr. Adams mildly asked him what he meant by being damned, Johnson passionately burst out, "Sent to hell, Sir, and punished everlastingly."

ON AUBREY BEARDSLEY

Aubrey Vincent Beardsley entered life inauspiciously. He was sickly from the start, and his mother's confinement, instead of being concluded by his birth, was extended by puerperal fever. When Mrs. Beardsley was at last able to come downstairs, it was assumed she was well enough to be told that her husband had lost all his money. It was only one more of her marital misfortunes, the earliest of which would seem to have occurred when she first met Vincent Paul Beardsley on the Pier in Brighton.

A Brighton beauty, Ellen Pitt—because of her extreme slenderness she was known locally as "the bottomless Pitt"—should have been impervious to the tinsel charms of resort romance among the piers and pavilions; yet she continued to see Beardsley, usually in the Pavilion Gardens. Their meetings often had to be clandestine. Her parents objected to the match, for although Vincent Beardsley—the son of a jeweler—called himself a gentleman, it was not so much because he had some unearned income as because he had no trade. Nevertheless, romance won out over prudence, and the marriage took place in Brighton, in the Church of St. Nicholas, on October 12, 1870. On their honeymoon Beardsley was sued for breach of promise by the widow of a clergyman. To keep the scandal from becoming more public than it already was, the bride's family intervened and forced the bridegroom to sell some houses along the Euston Road which had been left to him. Thus the damages were paid, and an uneasy marriage begun.

Witty, charming and musically gifted, Ellen Pitt Beardsley at first had little chance to use her talents. Ten months after the wedding her daughter Mabel was born, followed almost exactly a year later, on August 21, 1872, by the birth of Aubrey, whose christening was delayed for several months because of the illness of his mother. By that time Vincent Beardsley had managed to complete the squandering of his grandfather's modest fortune. As soon as she was in better health, Ellen had to find employment so that she could help maintain her children. For a while she worked as a governess and music teacher for children of her friends; and her husband, finding no satisfactory alternative to employment, worked first for the West India and Panama Telegraph Company, and then spent nearly ten years in the employ of brewers in the London area—jobs his wife obtained for him through her relatives.

Work made Vincent Beardsley even more difficult. He was jealous of his wife's friendships, brought his salary home irregularly, had a vicious temper and beat his children. When her finances were particularly desperate, Ellen would work all day on a penny bun and a glass of milk, then come home to care for her home and her two frail children. Her earliest memories of Aubrey as a toddler were associated with his fragility. He was "like a delicate piece of Dresden china" to her, and once as a child, she remembered, he used a twig to help himself up a steep flight of stairs.

Ellen Beardsley thought she recognized musical precocity in her son before he was a year old, for he would crawl to the piano when she was playing, and—so she liked to think—"beat perfect time" with a block. When he grew older she gave him piano lessons in the early evening after she returned from work. He was already playing Chopin for her while he was still too young for school.

There was also a sort of home music-appreciation course, probably not nearly so burdensome as it might seem to us today, for it was the pre-electronic age of home entertainment. In the evening, Mrs. Beardsley gave piano concerts for her husband and children from a book of miniature programs she had made up, each six pieces in length. "In this way they did not hear the same thing too often," she remembered. ". . . I would not let them hear rubbish, and it was the same with books. I would not let them read rubbish." Books seemed always to have been part of Aubrey's existence, perhaps because in his loneliness as a child he had such need of them; one of his schoolmasters was later told that "he never in a sense learnt to read, but seemed to be perfectly conversant with the English language from the first moment of handling a book." If the awesome tale meant anything at all, it at least indicated that Aubrey was able to read at an impressively early age.

At four he was taken to a symphony concert at the Crystal Palace, and once accompanied his mother to Westminster Abbey for a service; Mrs. Beardsley was a "sermon-taster" and would visit any church where the preaching was reputed to be good. Aubrey, bored as we may imagine with the homilies, could at least admire the stained-glass windows and the forest of busts. When they left the Abbey, Aubrey tugged his mother's hand and wondered, "Mummy, shall I have a bust or a stained-glass window when I am dead? For I may be a great man someday."

"Which would you like, darling?"

ON DOUGLAS MACARTHUR

There was always a tremendous amount of saluting by the MacArthur children. She insisted on it. The occasion didn't much matter—the ascent and descent of the flag, a visit by any adult, even a newspaper story about the arrival of the Statue of Liberty in New York—as long as it was done well. At bedtime her last words to Doug would be: "You must grow up to be a great man," and she would add either "like your father" or "like Robert E. Lee." The fact that his father and Lee had fought on opposite sides counted for nothing. The fact that both had fought well was everything.

At Selden, he would recall late in life, his mother began tutoring him in the three Rs, at the same time instilling in him "a sense of obligation." He remembered: "We were to do what was right no matter what the personal sacrifice might be. Our country was always to come first. Two things we must never do: never lie, never tattle." She also guided his reading. His father was a walking encyclopedia of political, military, and economic facts, but a small boy could not be expected to make head or tail of manifest destiny, Clausewitz, or J. S. Mill. He could understand heroism, however, and she saw to it that her sons never lacked books about martial heroes. In her lap they learned the virtue of physical courage and the disgrace of cowardice. Once she told Doug that men do not cry. He protested that his father's eyes were often moist at the retreat ceremony. That was different, she quickly explained; that was from love of country; that was allowed. But tears of fear were forbidden.

His mother was to remain close to him until he was in his fifties, but her influence on him was naturally greatest in these early years. If his father provided him with an example of manliness and a love of language, Pinky contributed other qualities that would distinguish him to the end of his life. Some were superficial: the courtly manner he acquired and the fastidiousness which, she would later tell him, he had inherited from his plantation forebears. Others were more subtle, because she herself was a complex woman, being both meek and tough, petulant and sentimental, charming and emotional. Under her mannered, pretty exterior she was cool, practical, and absolutely determined that her children would not only match but surpass the achievements of her father-in-law and her husband. Americans of a later generation may find it hard to fathom a woman who could realize her ambitions through the exploits of her men, particularly when they wore a uniform she had hated in her youth. Nevertheless it remains true that in her own complicated way Mary Pinkney MacArthur was resolved to defeat the Yankees on a battleground of her own choosing, with her own weapons, under a flag she alone could see.

She dressed Doug in skirts and kept his hair in long curls until he was eight, thus extending his childhood and his dependence on her.

Garrison Keillor

LAKE WOBEGON DAYS

"You stopped breathing once when you were five weeks old. Did I ever tell you that?"

No, she certainly hadn't.

"I was about to take a bath and then I thought I'd better check the crib, so I went in and you weren't moving at all. I thought you were dead. I snatched you up and tore out of the house to the Jensens and pounded on the door, and right then you let out a cry. Anyway, we took you to the doctor."

"What did the doctor say?"

"He wasn't sure. He didn't think it was a seizure. I guess it was just one of those things that happens sometimes." Then she got up to make a salad for supper.

That's how Mother told stories. Never enough detail, and she always left you hanging at the end. If she had gone ahead and run the bath water, I'd be dead right now. And it was "just one of those things that happens sometimes"? I felt a little weak myself. I had about gotten over the fear that I'd stop breathing during the night, all those years I used to remind myself to breathe, and now this. So it wasn't dumb to think that your breath could stop at any time. It could happen right now, sitting on a white kitchen chair in a cool breeze and drinking iced tea. Fall over dead on the linoleum. Thirteen years old, dead.

ON CHARLES DICKENS

The mothers of great men is a subject that has been handled often, and eloquently. How many of those who have achieved distinction can trace their inherited gifts to a mother's character, and their acquired gifts to a mother's teaching and influence. Mrs. Dickens seems not to have been a mother of this stamp. She scarcely, I fear, possessed those admirable qualities of mind and heart which one can clearly recognize as having borne fruit in the greatness and goodness of her famous son. So far as I can discover, she exercised no influence upon him at all.

Sylvia Plath

LETTERS HOME

Your last big morale-building letter was most appreciated. You are the most wonderful mummy that a girl ever had, and I only hope I can continue to lay more laurels at your feet. Warren and I both love you and admire you more than anybody in the world for all you have done for us all our lives. For it is you who has given us the heredity and the incentive to be mentally ambitious. Thank you a million times!

Your very own Sivvy

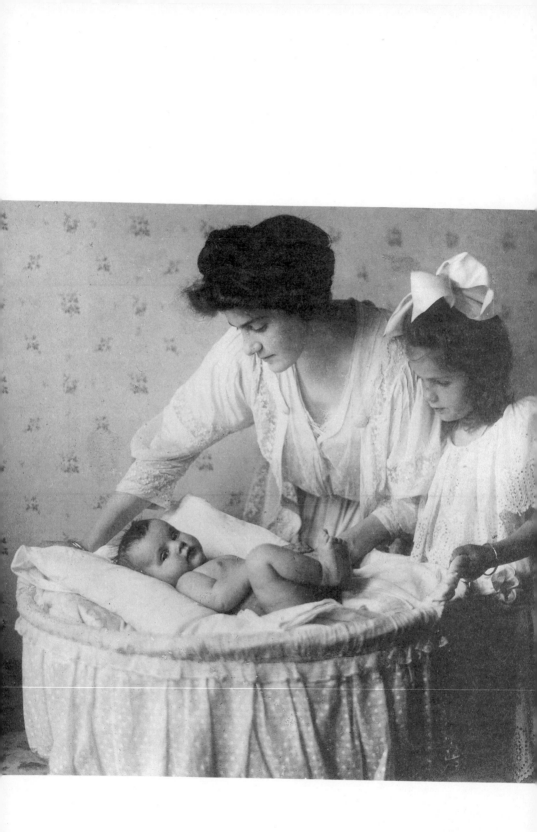

IN THE BEGINNING

D. W. Winnicott

The precursor of the mirror is the mother's face.

Pope Paul VI

The mother . . . the mysterious source of human life, where nature still receives the breath of God . . .

Harriet Beecher Stowe

UNCLE TOM'S CABIN

"Who was your mother?" "Never had none," said the child, with another grin. "Never had any mother? What do you mean? Where were you born?" "Never was born," persisted Topsy; "never had no father, nor mother, nor nothin'. I was raised by a speculator."

Billie Holiday

LADY SINGS THE BLUES

It's a wonder my mother didn't end up in the workhouse and me as a foundling. But Sadie Fagan loved me from the time I was just a swift kick in the ribs while she scrubbed floors. She went to the hospital and made a deal with the head woman there. She told them she'd scrub floors and wait on the other bitches laying up there to have their kids so she could pay her way and mine. And she did. Mom was thirteen that Wednesday, April 7, 1915, in Baltimore when I was born.

By the time she worked her way out of hock in the hospital and took me home to her folks, I was so big and smart I could sit up in a carriage.

Judith Wright

WOMAN TO CHILD

You who were darkness warmed my flesh
where out of darkness rose the seed.
Then all a world I made in me;
all the world you hear and see
hung upon my dreaming blood.

There moved the multitudinous stars,
and coloured birds and fishes moved.
There swam the sliding continents.
All time lay rolled in me, and sense,
and love that knew not its beloved.

O node and focus of the world;
I hold you deep within that well
you shall escape and not escape —
that mirrors still your sleeping shape;
that nurtures still your crescent cell.

I wither and you break from me;
yet though you dance in living light
I am the earth, I am the root,
I am the stem that fed the fruit,
the link that joins you to the night.

Sylvia Plath

THREE WOMEN:
A POEM IN THREE VOICES

(excerpt)

FIRST VOICE:

Who is he, this blue, furious boy,
Shiny and strange, as if he had hurtled from a star?
He is looking so angrily!
He flew into the room, a shriek at his heel.
The blue colour pales. He is human after all.
A red lotus opens in its bowl of blood;
They are stitching me up with silk, as if I were a material.

What did my fingers do before they held him?
What did my heart do, with its love?
I have never seen a thing so clear.
His lids are like the lilac-flower
And soft as a moth, his breath.
I shall not let go.
There is no guile or warp in him. May he keep so.

THIRD VOICE:

I see her in my sleep, my red, terrible girl.
She is crying through the glass that separates us.
She is crying, and she is furious.
Her cries are hooks that catch and grate like cats.
It is by these hooks she climbs to my notice.
She is crying at the dark, or at the stars
That at such a distance from us shine and whirl.

I think her little head is carved in wood,
A red, hard wood, eyes shut and mouth wide open.
And from the open mouth issue sharp cries
Scratching at my sleep like arrows,
Scratching at my sleep, and entering my side.
My daughter has no teeth. Her mouth is wide.
It utters such dark sounds it cannot be good.

FIRST VOICE:

What is it that flings these innocent souls at us?
Look, they are so exhausted, they are all flat out
In their canvas-sided cots, names tied to their wrists,
The little silver trophies they've come so far for.
There are some with thick black hair, there are some bald.
Their skin tints are pink or sallow, brown or red;
They are beginning to remember their differences.

I think they are made of water; they have no expression.
Their features are sleeping, like light on quiet water.
They are the real monks and nuns in their identical garments.
I see them showering like stars on to the world —
On India, Africa, America, these miraculous ones,
These pure, small images. They smell of milk.
Their footsoles are untouched. They are walkers of air.

Can nothingness be so prodigal?
Here is my son.
His wide eye is that general, flat blue.
He is turning to me like a little, blind, bright plant.
One cry. It is the hook I hang on.
And I am a river of milk.
I am a warm hill.

THIRD VOICE:

She is a small island, asleep and peaceful,
And I am a white ship hooting: Goodbye, goodbye.
The day is blazing. It is very mournful.
The flowers in this room are red and tropical.
They have lived behind class all their lives, they have been cared
        for tenderly.
Now they face a winter of white sheets, white faces.
There is very little to go into my suitcase.

There are the clothes of a fat woman I do not know.
There is my comb and brush. There is an emptiness.
I am so vulnerable suddenly.
I am a wound walking out of hospital.
I am a wound that they are letting go.
I leave my health behind. I leave someone
Who would adhere to me: I undo her fingers like bandages: I go.

SECOND VOICE:

I am myself again. There are no loose ends.
I am bled white as wax, I have no attachments.
I am flat and virginal, which means nothing has happened,
Nothing that cannot be erased, ripped up and scrapped, begun
        again.
These little black twigs do not think to bud,
Nor do these dry, dry gutters dream of rain.
This woman who meets me in windows—she is neat.

So neat she is transparent, like a spirit.
How shyly she superimposes her neat self
On the inferno of African oranges, the heel-hung pigs.
She is deferring to reality.
It is I. It is I —
Tasting the bitterness between my teeth.
The incalculable malice of the everyday.

FIRST VOICE:

How long can I be a wall, keeping the wind off?
How long can I be

Gentling the sun with the shade of my hand,
Intercepting the blue bolts of a cold moon?
The voices of lonelines, the voices of sorrow
Lap at my back ineluctably.
How shall it soften them, this little lullaby?

How long can I be a wall around my green property?
How long can my hands
Be a bandage to his hurt, and my words
Bright birds in the sky, consoling, consoling?
It is a terrible thing
To be so open: it is as if my heart
Put on a face and walked into the world.

First Voice:

Dawn flowers in the great elm outside the house.
The swifts are back. They are shrieking like paper rockets.
I hear the sound of the hours
Widen and die in the hedgerows. I hear the moo of cows.
The colors replenish themselves, and the wet
Thatch smokes in the sun.
The narcissi open white faces in the orchard.

I am reassured. I am reassured.
These are the clear bright colors of the nursery,
The talking ducks, the happy lambs.
I am simple again. I believe in miracles.
I do not believe in those terrible children
Who injure my sleep with their white eyes, their fingerless hands.
They are not mine. They do not belong to me.

I shall meditate upon normality.
I shall meditate upon my little son.
He does not walk. He does not speak a word.
He is still swaddled in white bands.
But he is pink and perfect. He smiles so frequently.
I have papered his room with big roses,
I have painted little hearts on everything.

I do not will him to be exceptional.
It is the exception that interests the devil.
It is the exception that climbs the sorrowful hill

Or sits in the desert and hurts his mother's heart.
I will him to be common,
To love me as I love him,
And to marry what he wants and where he will.

Gail Sheehy

PASSAGES

Thirty-five brings the biological boundary into sight. Probably for the first time a woman glimpses that vague, uncharted realm ahead leading to what demographers so aridly call the end of her "fecund and bearing years." The deferred nurturer is running out of time to defer. The unmarried achiever must face the motherhood issue squarely. The greatest number of single-mother adoptions are made by women between thirty-five and thirty-nine. And some of the most high-powered, late-boozing, unmarried, and unsentimental career women simply stop in their tracks and fall in love with the new experience of being pregnant.

Irma Kurtz is a free-lance journalist who made exactly that decision at the age of thirty-seven. An unmarried, witty, and egocentric American who had reached the top of her profession in England, she'd never had time to have a child before. "This was my last chance," she has written. She loved being pregnant. "It was my first act of devotion." There were also moments of panic when she could see only endings: "an end to vanity and adventure, an end to freedom, an end to my own egocentric childhood." But there is a certain seemingly universal comfort in pregnancy once the baby begins to kick. One is on an express train. One can settle back and enjoy going to the end of the line. "It was delicious to enter an entirely new area of information and interest," this journalist wrote, "at just about the age when one feels all feasible experiences have been explored."

ON *REBECCA WEST* AND *H. G. WELLS*

Rather early in the course of my mother's pregnancy—just about as soon as he had come to realise that there was no chance at all of his being able to talk her into an abortion—my father managed to persuade himself to believe that it need not change anything between them. Once it was all over they would be able to take up their game of being free spirits and the best of good companions and go on with it as before. He ignored the problems that he was going to be faced with as he retraced the route that he had travelled so disastrously with Amber Reeves, managing to throw the dust into his own eyes by concentrating on one of them to the exclusion of all others. He told himself that the business with Amber had gone so terribly wrong because far too many people had known about it: everything would be all right this time if the coming event was to be kept as far as was possible a secret, known only to their very closest friends and a few relatives. My mother consequently found herself being pushed through a series of weirdly complicated manoeuvres in the opening weeks of January 1914. They required numerous and sudden changes of address, the use of assumed names, and frequent resort to stratagems that seemed to belong to the world of Feydeau's farces—journeys made to identical destinations on different trains or by alternate routes. The comedy reached its highest level when my father was visiting Russia. He wrote to my mother from St. Petersburg giving her detailed instructions for a move to Llandudno in Wales, a resort that he had chosen as the ideal place for her accouchement on the ground that it had remarkably good rail connections with Bournemouth, a seaside town on the English south coast that could easily be reached from London at any time of the day. In the end he dropped Llandudno in favour of what was, if anything, an even stranger location, Hunstanton, in Norfolk.

My birthplace was then, and is still, an almost recklessly unpretentious seaside resort with a northwestern exposure. Its principal attraction is a dwarfish pier which runs out into The Wash, a vast expanse of shallow water often spoken of as an arm of the North Sea which is more easily recognisable as an extension of the Lincolnshire and Camridgeshire fens. Its recommendation to my father can only have been that it was so far off the socially beaten track, so desperately without conventional allure, that nobody having any claim to be anybody—in the Edwardian sense of that term—was likely to be encountered there in conceivable circumstances. Once my mother was safely installed in Hunstanton she was very unlikely to be seen by any friend or acquaintance who might read the outward signs of her condition and start rumours. My father pushed his caution to extreme lengths. With an anticipated delivery date no closer than the end of July, he had completed my mother's disappearance from her usual haunts and got her into covert at Hunstanton by the last week in February. She spent March, April, May, June, and July there, making herself as comfortable as she could in the rawly ugly and somewhat poky late-Victorian villa called Brig-y-Don, in which a Mrs. Crown let furnished rooms. While my mother made what she could of her exile my father got on with his life and visited her when his other engagements permitted.

My father had been elated when my mother's long vigil beside The Wash had come to an end. Things had gone very well. No one had found them out. There had been no talk. And it was unlikely that there would be any. The outbreak of the war had given people other things to think about. This time everything was going to be all right, and he wasn't in danger of being forced to give up his young mistress and his child. His jubilation found an outlet in cheerful letters to the few friends in the know. He told one of them that he was overjoyed to have "a manchild" from my mother, and he said the same thing to her, in letters in which he addressed her as his "dear little mate."

But my father's enthusiasm for his paternity was apt to be greater when he was parted from my mother than when he was with her. There are not many things in nature whose interests and energies are more completely pre-empted than those of a nursing mother, and there are possibly even fewer with a greater capacity for making their presence felt than a very young baby. Every time that my father came to see my mother after that coincidentally fateful day in August he was given further cause to realise that he no longer had an exclusive claim on the person and the attention of the high-spirited and fiercely independent loner who had so determinedly set out to become his mistress.

My mother had, as a matter of fact, ceased to exist in that character. Her life style had changed, and my father could never find her alone. She had become the mistress of an establishment, and there were always people about her. There was a nurse, there was a maid, and sometimes a second maid. There was a cook, and there was, as often as not, a companion or friend in the role of chaperon. There had to be, even at that late date, to save her from a further fatal loss of respectability: a woman living on her own, without a husband, and with a young child in the house, would have been assumed to be disreputable unless there was another woman of her own class in the ménage. My mother had been brought up in Edinburgh, the town that is to the middle classes of Scotland what Rome is to the devout Roman Catholic, and she had been educated at one of its most rigidly orthodox schools, George Watson's Academy for Young Ladies. After her delivery had taken place, the values of upbringing had reasserted their authority. It occurred to her, as it had not in the absence of a baby, that her gesture of rebellion might be misunderstood, and that it might not be clear to the world at large that she was, although an unmarried mother, still every inch a George Watson's girl and respectability itself. It was to make this point that she kept herself in such state.

AT THE END

Henry Ward Beecher

PROVERBS FROM PLYMOUTH PULPIT

What the mother sings to the cradle goes all the way down to the coffin.

Albert Camus

THE STRANGER

Mother died today. Or, maybe, yesterday: I can't be sure.

EPITAPH NEAR CHICHESTER, ENGLAND

Here lies the mother of children seven,
Four on earth and three in Heaven,
The three in Heaven preferring rather
To be with Mother than stay with Father.

G. J. Scrimgeour

A WOMAN OF HER TIMES

When Elizabeth left Drury Lane she had no plan in mind. She ordered the taxi to take her home, but she was too restless to spend the shank of the evening with Mabel. She would visit her mother. She sank back to enjoy the luxury of the ride to Wimbledon and thought about how grown-up her daughter was becoming, how bossy. The lights still shone in the windows of the Wimbledon bungalow, clearer because of the autumn's trees. She paid the driver, watched the taxi swoosh away over the fallen leaves, shivering in a small breeze, walked up the wet path to the sound of her clicking heels, and pushed the doorbell. The door opened quickly and wide. Mabel stood there.

"What on earth are you doing here?" said Elizabeth. "What's wrong?"

"Thank God they reached you!" said Mabel simultaneously. "The news isn't good."

It was very late, and Elizabeth sat motionless by the bed. The figure under the coverlet hung on to life. Its breath rasped through nostrils and throat. Long, slow, embarrassing snores, fraying like old rope. Elizabeth's breath tried to keep time. Slowly, deeply in. A long, long pause. Then silently, slowly out. Then the long, slow inward rasp to tired lungs. In hope of dawn Elizabeth had drawn back the curtains and raised the blinds, but the window spaces stayed black. The night light behind marbled glass made shadows flicker. She could feel the slow thud of her heart so strongly that her crossed leg pumped to its beat and her ears heard its whir. She listened for any sound other than that breath. For the creak of old timber. For a cough or stir from Mabel, whom she had sent to bed hours ago. For the bark of morning's dog, the roar of the first lorry or the clang of the first tram.

A dozen, a score, a hundred Henriettes moved in this room. There was this slight figure on the bed, the body lumping the coverings Elizabeth had smoothed a dozen times, giving to the room a sweet-sour odour. The room gathered around it, the giant wardrobe gleaming, the glass bell filled with dried flowers catching a line of light with its curve.

Bernard's photograph on the nightstand glinting with the movements of the candle flame. She had stilled the mantelpiece clock that had tick-tocked in her parents' bedroom since their wedding night, the clock which Henriette wound with a key on each of hundreds of Friday evenings before she unpinned her hair and turned to Bernard, the clock which Elizabeth had heard when in long fever she lay in her parents' bed, the clock which had stayed when she had left, the clock which knew them better than did she.

"There's nothing more we can do," the doctor had said. She had sat there, quiet, hands in her lap, listening to that breath draw slowly in, waiting for the clasp to loosen.

A dozen, a score, a hundred Henriettes moved in her mind. That staunch little woman had become a faery feint, laughing as she changed shape from girl to wife to mother to anger to love to old age and illness, a will-o'-the-wisp fleeing just ahead to remind of a shoelace tied, a dress sewed, a greeting given, always with some quick phrase, some gesture sharp as a bite to memory. Elizabeth's shoulders ached for the need of holding, her chest hollow with the melt of things not said. Oh, my mother . . . They had been so easy all the years that life was full: the anger, the indifference, the busyness. This stubborn little woman, poking her cane into the carpet as she fought her way alone along the corridor to see her daughter out of the door, this fierce little woman who had her own life and never thought as well of her daughter as her daughter would have liked. In mind's eye Elizabeth saw her mother look away, chin up, head gesturing dismissal. Oh, my mother . . . my mother . . .

"Hail Mary, full of grace," she heard herself mumble. "The Lord is with thee. Blessed art thou among women."

She saw her mother as she had never seen her, as a bride, her eyes brilliant, laughing up at Bernard, full of future.

"And blessed is the fruit of thy womb, Jesus."

And me, Mother, and me! Almost aloud she cried it, as though there ought never have been anyone but her with her mother, with this figure quiet beneath the counterpane, strong in leaving her, object of her craving. Suddenly she saw her mother as she had stood that day she had left Dublin for the world, so clearly that it seemed not memory but fact, standing at the front door of the great rain-wet house draped with laburnum, one hand on the oval metal knob. She had been haloed by the door's coloured glass, at the top of the steps leading to the path and the street, resolute in face of her daughter's farewell desire to weep.

"'*Allons!*" she had said brusquely. "Get on with you now!" urging her down the rest of the steps to where Bernard waited with the hansom cab laden with her future, as though she would get this foolishness over and go about her business. Elizabeth had thought her unfeeling, but Henriette had written that night, "I filled your bedroom with flowers that I might not think you gone." Now the daughter would have reached up to the stern figure at the top of those steps and said, "I forgive you, I understand, I forgive you for being my mother."

"Holy Mary, mother of God. Holy Mary, mother of God. Holy Mary, mother of God." It ran inside her head as though threaded to the loops of the breath that shuddered from the dry lips of the figure on the bed where she would not look any more. Still on the chair in the darkened room, she waited once more for change. "Holy Mary, mother of God." Childish whimper against pain, incantation to ward off things evil, things inevitable. Stuck between ages, jammed as a river by blocks of ice, she could not remember what came next, the grief rising slowly through her body and spreading into limbs that began to tremble with the force of her life against that dying.

"Holy Mary, mother of God."

Life of its own, her body betraying her, suddenly her hands shot out in front of her, raised, rigid, their backs presented, their fingers spread. Though the candlelight softened their ageing, she could see them still—that network of a thousand tiny creases, the brown spots and smears, the blemishes brought by living and dying, the veins like worms. They were not her hands—not mine, please, O Lord!—straining away from her, stranger hands betraying her, making her draw breath with disgust, the tension making the right hand set up a rhythmic spasming that made it seem a live and separate beast. "Mother, Mother." Not me, O Lord, not me, and not my mother, not me, her whole body starting to shake with the fear and mourning of it, and the hundred Henriettes and she fusing, crying for escape.

"*Pray* for us sinners!" exploded the words from her, as her hands let the fear loose. "*Now* and at the hour of our death, amen! *Pray* for us sinners."

And the tide of terror swept through her and from her, and her hands fell back into her lap and the tears welled yet once more, pushed by the hollow ache in her chest, and she sat at the bedside in the room with the long, slow rasp of breaths in the night's silence.

The priest had gone before she arrived, hastening to some other death with holy but no human consolation, the provisions for this mother's journey neatly made, the paraphernalia of crucifix and oil, the talismans of lemon and cotton wool placed in their proper compartments and carried on to the next needer in the cassock's falling folds.

She sat alone at the hour of her mother's death, no companion, no shelter. Mother's mother she had been in her mother's ageing, she the grown, she the strong. Now mother alone would she be, she the next generation, she now rising to her generation's destiny unguarded, the forefront now, bared by this falling, she to sit alone forever now as she now sat alone in this room of her memories, none to remember her as she was and is, a girl inside this woman, a child, the youngest fears, the grandest triumphs, the rulings, the choices, the cherishings from which grows love. She did not like her mother; she loved her.

She found herself rocking lightly backward and forward at the edge of her chair—this comfort to herself now all the comfort she would have, oh, my mother . . .

D. H. Lawrence

LETTER

In August 1910 Mrs. Lawrence became ill, and it soon became obvious that she was dying of cancer. Lawrence was under a terrible strain. It was a time when all his relationships seemed particularly tangled and hopeless. And now his mother, the stable centre of his life, was being taken from him. And he must watch her dying by degrees. On 3 December he went by train to Leicester and met Louie Burrows. On the return journey he proposed to her. Three days later he wrote to her:

It is morning again, and she is still here. She has had the "thrush" rather badly: they say one must have it, either on coming or going. Many have it when they are little babies: and others when they're dying. Mother's is nearly better. But she looks so grievous, pitiful this morning, still and grey and deathly, like a hieroglyph of woe. One mustn't be bathetic: but there, one is vitiated by sitting up: Ada and I share the night.

I look at my mother and think "Oh Heaven—is this what life brings us to?" You see mother has had a devilish married life, for nearly forty years—and this is the conclusion—no relief. What ever I wrote, it could not be so awful as to write a biography of my mother. But after this—which is enough—I am going to write romance—when I have finished Paul Morel, which belongs to this.

This anxiety divides me from you. My heart winces to the echo of my mother's pulse. There is only one drop of life to be squeezed from her, and that hangs trembling, so you'd think it must fall and be gone, but it never will—it will evaporate away, slowly. And while she dies, we seem not to be able to live.

So if I do not seem happy with the thought of you—you will understand. I must feel my mother's hand slip out of mine before I can really take yours. She is my first, great love. She was a wonderful, rare woman—you do not know; as strong, and steadfast, and generous as the sun. She could be as swift as a white whip-lash, and as kind and gentle as warm rain, and as steadfast as the irreducible earth beneath us.

But I think of you a great deal—of how happy we shall be. This surcharge of grief makes me determine to be happy. The more I think of you, the more I am glad that I have discovered the right thing to do. I have been very blind, and a fool. But sorrow opens the eyes. When I think of you, it is like thinking of life. You will be the first woman to make the earth glad for me: mother, J—all the rest, have been gates to a very sad world. But you are strong & rosy as the gates of Eden. We do not all of us, not many, perhaps, set out from a sunny paradise of childhood. We are born with our parents in the desert, and yearn for a Canaan. You are like Canaan—you are rich & fruitful & glad, and I love you.

Lawrence and his sister could not bear to watch the pointless suffering of their mother. They put morphine in her milk. Three days later she died.

Osbert Sitwell

LAUGHTER IN THE NEXT ROOM

In the summer of 1937 my mother died in London after a short illness at the age of sixty-eight. To her last days, she remained in part child, with a child's impetuosity and humour, and in part older than her years, though she did not look more than fifty-five, and was as straight as though she had been a young woman, retaining her particular carriage of the head, so distinctive to her. She always told me that she entertained a great horror of old age. Indeed, as I drove round in a taxi-cab at six o'clock on a July morning to break to my father in his hotel—she had been removed to a nursing home—the news of her death, there came back to me, unbidden, but perhaps with a certain cruel relevance typical of the way the human mind works on very mournful occasions such as this, a fragment of conversation from many years before. It had taken place in the dining-room at Renishaw, at luncheon, on a fine August day. Only my mother, my father and myself had been present. My mother, who had been silent, suddenly observed:

"How much I should hate to live to be old!"

This remark, harmless as it seemed, pierced my father's armour, and he replied, but addressing his words to me, and in that unnaturally placid voice which in his case sometimes heralded a storm:

"I think all intelligent people would like to live to be old, wouldn't they, Osbert?"

My mother then interposed, "But I should hate to feel I was being a trouble to anyone."

And I, answering her, said, "But really intelligent people don't mind that, Mother!"

My father had glowered at me, and had fallen back on one of his favourite rebukes:

"Rude without being funny!"

That had been fifteen years ago, and now I was on my way to tell him she was dead.

Thomas Hardy

THE RETURN OF THE NATIVE

Mrs. Yeobright, mother of Clym, makes the long journey to her son and daughter-in-law's house on foot. Clym is out, and she is turned away by Eustacia, her daughter-in-law. She sets out on the return journey.

"Is the water clear?"

"Yes, middling—except where the heath-croppers walk into it."

"Then, take this, and go as fast as you can, and dip me up the clearest you can find. I am very faint."

She drew from the small willow reticule that she carried in her hand an old-fashioned china teacup without a handle; it was one of half a dozen of the same sort lying in the reticule, which she had preserved ever since her childhood, and had brought with her today as a small present for Clym and Eustacia.

The boy started on his errand, and soon came back with the water, such as it was. Mrs. Yeobright attempted to drink, but it was so warm as to give her nausea, and she threw it away. Afterwards she still remained sitting, with her eyes closed.

The boy waited, played near her, caught several of the little brown butterflies which abounded, and then said as he waited again, "I like going on better than biding still. Will you soon start again?"

"I don't know."

"I wish I might go on by myself," he resumed, fearing, apparently, that he was to be pressed into some unpleasant service. "Do you want me any more, please?"

Mrs. Yeobright made no rely.

"What shall I tell mother?" the boy continued.

"Tell her you have seen a broken-hearted woman cast off by her son."

Mrs. Yeobright's exertions, physical and emotional, had well-nigh prostrated her; but she continued to creep along in short stages with long breaks between. The sun had now got far to the west of south and stood directly in her face, like some merciless incendiary, brand in hand, waiting to consume her. With the departure of the boy all visible animation disappeared from the landscape, though the intermittent husky notes of the male grasshoppers from every tuft of furze were enough to show that amid the prostration of the larger animal species an unseen insect world was busy in all the fulness of life.

In two hours she reached a slope about three-fourths the whole distance from Alderworth to her own home, where a little patch of shepherd's-thyme intruded upon the path; and she sat down upon the perfumed mat it formed there.

Being a mother, it was inevitable that she should soon cease to ruminate upon her own condition. Had the track of her next thought been marked by a streak in the air, like the path of a meteor, it would have . . . descended to the eastward upon the roof of Clym's house.

He in the meantime had aroused himself from sleep, sat up, and looked around. Eustacia was sitting in a chair hard by him, and though she held a book in her hand she had not looked into it for some time.

"Well, indeed!" said Clym, brushing his eyes with his hands. "How soundly I have slept! I have had such a tremendous dream, too: one I shall never forget."

"I thought you had been dreaming," said she.

"Yes. It was about my mother. I dreamt that I took you to her house to make up differences, and when we got there we couldn't get in, though she kept on crying to us for help. However, dreams are dreams."

"I must certainly go to Blooms-End soon," he continued, "and I think I had better go alone."

In the evening he set out on the journey. Although the heat of summer was yet intense the days had considerably shortened, and before he had advanced a mile on his way all the heath purples, browns, and greens had merged in a uniform dress without airiness or gradation, and broken only by touches of white where the little heaps of clean quartz sand showed the entrance to a rabbit-burrow, or where the white flints of a footpath lay like a thread over the slopes. In almost every one of the isolated and stunted thorns which grew here and there a night-hawk revealed his presence by whirring like the clack of a mill as long as he could hold his breath, then stopping, flapping his wings, wheeling round the bush, alighting, and after a silent interval of listening beginning to whirr again. At each brushing of Clym's feet white miller-moths flew into the air just high enough to catch upon their dusty wings the mellowed light from the west, which now shone across the depressions and levels of the ground without falling thereon to light them up.

Yeobright walked on amid this quiet scene with a hope that all would soon be well. Three miles on he came to a spot where a soft perfume was wafted across his path, and he stood still for a moment to inhale the familiar scent. It was the place at which, four hours earlier, his mother had sat down exhausted on the knoll covered with shepherd's-thyme. While he stood a sound between a breathing and a moan suddenly reached his ears.

He looked to where the sound came from; but nothing appeared there save the verge of the hillock stretching against the sky in an unbroken line. He moved a few steps in that direction, and now he perceived a recumbent figure almost lost at his feet.

Among the different possibilities as to the person's individuality there did not for a moment occur to Yeobright that it might be one of his own family. Sometimes furze-cutters had been known to sleep out of doors at these times, to save a long journey homeward and back again; but Clym remembered the moan and looked closer, and saw that the form was feminine; and a distress came over him like cold air from a cave. But he was not absolutely certain that the woman was his mother till he stooped and beheld her face, pallid, and with closed eyes.

His breath went, as it were, out of his body and the cry of anguish which would have escaped him died upon his lips. During the momentary interval that elapsed before he became conscious that something must be done all sense of time and place left him, and it seemed as if he and his mother were as when he was a child with her many years ago on this heath at hours similar to the present. Then he awoke to activity; and bending yet lower he found that she still breathed, and that her breath though feeble was regular, except when disturbed by an occasional gasp.

"Oh, what is it! Mother, are you very ill—you are not dying?" he cried, pressing his lips to her face. "I am your Clym. How did you come here? What does it all mean?"

At that moment the chasm in their lives which his love for Eustacia had caused was not remembered by Yeobright, and to him that present joined continuously with that friendly past that had been their experience before the division.

She moved her lips, appeared to know him, but could not speak; and then Clym strove to consider how best to move her, as it would be necessary to get her away from the spot before the dews were intense. He was able-bodied, and his mother was thin. He clasped his arms round her, lifted her a little, and said, "Does that hurt you?"

She shook her head, and he lifted her up; then, at a slow pace, went onward with his load. The air was now completely cool; but whenever he passed over a sandy patch of ground uncarpeted with vegetation there was reflected from its surface into his face the heat which it had imbibed during the day. At the beginning of his undertaking he had thought but little of the distance which yet would have to be traversed before Blooms-End could be reached; but though he had slept that afternoon he soon began to feel the weight of his burden. Thus he proceeded, like Aeneas with his father; the bats circling round his head, nightjars flapping their wings within a yard of his face, and not a human being within call.

While he was yet nearly a mile from the house his mother exhibited signs of restlessness under the constraint of being borne along, as if his arms were irksome to her. He lowered her upon his knees and looked around. The point they had now reached, though far from any road, was not more than a mile from the Blooms-End cottages occupied by Fairway, Sam, Humphrey, and the Cantles. Moreover, fifty yards off stood a hut, built of clods and covered with thin turves, but now entirely disused. The simple outline of the lonely shed was visible, and thither he determined to direct his steps. As soon as he arrived he laid her down carefully by the entrance, and then ran and cut with his pocket-knife an armful of the dryest fern. Spreading this within the shed, which was entirely open on one side, he placed his mother thereon: then he ran with all his might towards the dwelling of Fairway.

Nearly a quarter of an hour had passed, disturbed only by the broken breathing of the sufferer, when moving figures began to animate the line between heath and sky. In a few moments Clym arrived with Fairway, Humphrey, and Susan Nunsuch; Olly Dowden, who had chanced to be at Fairway's, Christian and Grandfer Cantle following helter-skelter behind. They had brought a lantern and matches, water, a pillow, and a few other articles which had occurred to their minds in the hurry of the moment. Sam had been despatched back again for brandy, and a boy brought Fairway's pony, upon which he rode off to the nearest medical man, with directions to call at Wildeve's on his way, and inform Thomasin that her aunt was unwell.

"I cannot think where she could have been going," said Clym to some one. "She had evidently walked a long way, but even when she was able to speak just now she would not tell me where. What do you really think of her?"

"There is a great deal to fear," was gravely answered, in a voice which Eustacia recognized as that of the only surgeon in the district. . . . It is exhaustion which has overpowered her. My impression is that her walk must have been exceptionally long."

"I used to tell her not to overwalk herself in this weather," said Clym, with distress.

"Come here, come here!" was then rapidly said in anxious female tones and Clym and the doctor could be heard rushing forward from the back part of the shed to where Mrs. Yeobright lay.

For a long time there was utter silence among the group within; and it was broken at last by Clym saying, in an agonized voice, "O doctor, what does it mean?"

The doctor did not reply at once; ultimately he said, "She is sinking fast. Her heart was previously affected, and physical exhaustion has dealt the finishing blow."

Then there was a weeping of women, then waiting, then hushed exclamations, then a strange gasping sound, then a painful stillness.

"It is all over," said the doctor.

Further back in the hut the cotters whispered, "Mrs. Yeobright is dead."

Almost at the same moment the two watchers observed the form of a small old-fashioned child entering at the open side of the shed. Susan Nunsuch, whose boy it was, went forward to the opening and silently beckoned to him to go back.

"I've got something to tell 'ee, mother," he cried in a shrill tone. "That woman asleep there walked along with me today; and she said I was to say that I had seed her, and she was a broken-hearted woman and cast off by her son, and then I came on home."

ON ELEANOR ROOSEVELT

Mother was laid to rest in the rose garden in accord with Father's wish, set down a quarter of a century ago: "I hope that my dear wife will be buried there also and that the monument contain no device or inscription except the following on the south side ———." The stonecutter had done his work. ANNA ELEANOR ROOSEVELT 1884–1962. David Gurewitsch, camera in hand, heard Truman's comment: "I told her she was the First Lady of the World."

When the last guest had left, we returned for a while to Johnny's cottage to talk over plans for two memorial services. Anna and John would concern themselves with the first, in New York's Cathedral of St. John the Divine; Jimmy and Franklin with the second, in Washington Cathedral.

Adlai Stevenson, who mounted the pulpit in scarlet robes to address a congregation of ten thousand in the Cathedral of St. John the Divine, said of Mother, "She would rather light a candle than curse the darkness." Which was as true as something Aunt Polly sniffed at the funeral: "What *nonsense*! Eleanor would have hated all this fuss."

Ten years passed. On another day of drenching rain, I went back to Hyde Park. With my brothers and sister, I was invited to witness the fulfillment of seven lines in Mother's will: "During my lifetime I have given away from time to time part of my manuscripts and other works of mine, files, documents, correspondence, papers and memoranda of every kind. All the rest of such property which may belong to me at the time of my death I give and bequeath to the Franklin D. Roosevelt Library. . . ."

The Eleanor Roosevelt wing of matching gray fieldstone was about to be declared open. A soddened marquee sheltered the guests as they sat on little chairs unfolded on the grass. Governor Rockefeller, coming in by helicopter, was late, and time dragged. Some familiar faces were in the crowd, Joe Lash in a black beard and Marion Dickerman among them.

When courtesies had been exchanged and little speeches delivered, the rain turned to drizzle, and the children of Franklin and Eleanor Roosevelt posed together outside for the photographers.

Here we were on parade together again: Johnny, fifth-six years old, the epitome of a successful stockbroker in his gray business suit with oblong square of pocket handkerchief; Franklin, soon to be fifty-eight, assuming a head-of-the-family air; Jimmy, sixty-four, flashing his version of Father's smile; Anna, white-haired and hollow cheeked at sixty-six, guardian of the more revealing documents stored inside these walls and carrying on some of Mother's work in philanthropy. I would be sixty-two in September, and I felt a stranger. More mountains remained to be climbed, but with Patty to accompany me, I didn't doubt they could be conquered.

We five not-so-young Roosevelts had continued to walk our separate ways, heedless of Mother's yearning to unite us as a family worthy of our name. There was no trace of kinship. We had broken with each other as we had with her. We had lived in a reflection of our parents' glory. I knew that we should never meet as a family again.

Simone de Beauvoir

A VERY EASY DEATH

Her vitality filled me with wonder, and I respected her courage. Why, as soon she could speak again, did she utter words that froze me? Telling me of her night at the Boucicault she said, "You know what the women of the lower classes are like: they moan. These hospital nurses, they are only there for the money. So . . ." There were ready-made phrases, as automatic as drawing breath; but it was still her consciousness that gave them life and it was impossible to hear them without distress. The contrast between the truth of her suffering body and the nonsense that her head was stuffed with saddened me.

The physiotherapist came to Maman's bed, turned down the sheet and took hold of her left leg: Maman had an open hospital nightdress on and she did not mind that her wrinkled belly, criscrossed with tiny lines, and her bald pubis showed. "I no longer have any sort of shame," she observed in a surprised voice.

"You are perfectly right not to have any," I said. But I turned away and gazed fixedly into the garden. The sight of my mother's nakedness had jarred me. No body existed less for me: none existed more. As a child I had loved it dearly; as an adolescent it had filled me with an uneasy repulsion: all this was perfectly in the ordinary course of things and it seemed reasonable to me that her body should retain its dual nature, that it should be both repugnant and holy—a taboo. But for all that, I was astonished at the violence of my distress. My mother's indifferent acquiescence made it worse: she was abandoning the exigencies and prohibitions that had oppressed her all her life long and I approved of her doing so. Only this body, suddenly reduced by her capitulation to being a body and nothing more, hardly differed at all from a corpse —a poor defenseless carcass turned and manipulated by professional hands, one in which life seemed to carry on only because of its own stupid momentum. For me, my mother had always been there, and I had never seriously thought that some day, that soon I should see her go. Her death, like her birth, had its place in some legendary time. When I said to myself "She is of an age to die" the words were devoid of meaning, as too many words are. For the first time I saw her as a dead body under suspended sentence.

I do not blame my father. It is tolerably well known that in men habit kills desire. Maman had lost her first freshness and he his ardor. In order to arouse it he turned to the professionals of the café de Versailles, or the young ladies of the Sphinx. More than once, between the age of fifteen and twenty, I saw him coming home at eight in the morning, smelling of drink, and telling confused tales of bridge or poker. Maman made no scenes: perhaps she believed him, so trained was she at running away from awkward truths. But she could not happily adapt herself to his indifference. Her case alone would be enough to convince me that bourgeois marriage is an unnatural institution. The wedding ring on her finger had authorized her to become acquainted with pleasure; her senses had grown demanding; at thirty-five, in the prime of her life, she was no longer allowed to satisfy them. She went on sleeping beside the man whom she loved, and who almost never made love to her any more: she hoped, she waited and she pined, in vain. Complete abstinence would have been less of a trial for her pride than this promiscuity. I am not surprised that her temper should have deteriorated: slaps, nagging, scenes, not only in privacy, but even when guests were there. "Françoise has a disgusting character," my father used to say. She admitted that she flew off the handle easily. But she was bitterly hurt when she heard that people said "Françoise is so pessimistic!" or "Françoise is becoming neurotic."

When she was a young woman she loved clothes. Her face would light up when people told her that she looked like my elder sister. One of my father's cousins, who played the cello and whom she accompanied on the piano, paid her respectful attentions: when he married she loathed his wife. When her sexual and her social life dwindled away Maman stopped taking care of her appearance, except on grand occasions when "dressing up" was essential. I remember coming back from the holidays once: she met us at the station, and she was wearing a pretty velvet hat with a little veil, and she had put on some powder. My sister was delighted and she cried, "Maman, you look just like a fashionable lady!" She laughed unreservedly, for she no longer prided herself on elegance. Both for her daughters and for herself, she pushed the contempt for the body that she had been taught at the convent to the point of uncleanliness. Yet—and this was another of her contradictions—she replied to them coquettishly. She was filled with pride when one of my father's friends dedicated a book (published at the author's expense) to her—*To Françoise de Beauvoir, whose life I so admire*. An ambiguous tribute: she earned admiration by a self-effacement that deprived her of admirers.

. . . "You look splendid. The doctors are very pleased with you," I asserted.

"No. Dr. N is not pleased: he wants me to break wind for him." She smiled to herself. "When I get out of here I shall send him a box of those chocolate dog-messes."

I dared not, all by myself. I was not worried by her nakedness any more: it was no longer my mother, but a poor tormented body. Yet I was frightened by the horrible mystery that I sensed, without in any way visualizing anything, under the dressings, and I was afraid of hurting her. That morning she had had to have another enema and Mademoiselle Leblon had needed my help. I took hold of that skeleton clothed in damp blue skin, holding her under the armpits. When Maman was laid over on her side, her face screwed up, her eyes turned back and she cried, "I am going to fall." She was remembering the time she had fallen down. Standing by the side of her bed I held her and comforted her.

The next day I learned that the afternoon had gone well. A young male nurse had taken Mademoiselle Leblon's place and Poupette said to Maman, "How lucky you are to have such a young, kind nurse."

"Yes," said Maman, "he's a good-looking fellow."

"And you are a judge of men!"

"Oh, not much of a judge,' said Maman, with nostalgia in her voice.

"You have regrets?"

Maman laughed and said, "I always say to my grandnieces, 'My dears, make the most of your life.' "

"Now I understand why they love you so much. But you would never have said that to your daughters?"

"To my daughters?" said Maman, with sudden severity. "Certainly not!"

"She shall not suffer"? A race had begun between death and torture. I asked myself how one manages to go on living when someone you love has called out to you "Have pity on me" in vain.

And even if death were to win, all this odious deception! Maman thought that we were with her, next to her; but we were already placing ourselves on the far side of her history. An evil all-knowing spirit, I could see behind the scenes, while she was struggling, far, far away, in human loneliness. Her desperate eagerness to get well, her patience, her courage—it was all deceived. She would not be paid for any of her sufferings at all. I saw her face again: "Since it is good for me." Despairingly, I suffered a transgression that was mine without my being responsible for it and one that I could never expiate.

Maman had dreaded cancer all her life, and perhaps she was still afraid of it at the nursing-home, when they X-rayed her. After the operation she never thought of it for a single moment. There were some days when she was afraid that at her age, the shock might have been too great for her to survive it. But doubt never even touched her mind: she had been operated on for peritonitis—a grave condition, but curable.

What surprised us even more was that she never asked for a priest, not even on the day when she was so weakened and she said, "I shall not see Simone again!" Marthe had brought her a missal, a crucifix and a rosary: she did not take them out of her drawer. One morning Jeanne said, "It's Sunday today, Aunt Françoise: wouldn't you like to take Communion?" "Oh, my dear, I am too tired to pray: God is kind!" Madame Tardieu asked her more pressingly, when Poupette was there, whether she would not like to see her confessor: Maman's expression hardened—"Too tired," and she closed her eyes to put an end to the conversation. After the visit of another old friend she said to Jeanne, "Poor dear Louise, she asks me such foolish questions: she wanted to know whether there was a chaplain in the nursing-home. Much I care whether there is or not!"

Madame de Saint-Ange harried us. "Since she is in such a state of anxiety, she must surely want the comforts of religion."

"But she doesn't."

"She made me and some other friends promise to help her make a good end."

"What she wants just now is to be helped to make a good recovery."

We were blamed. To be sure, we did not prevent Maman from receiving the last sacraments; but we did not oblige her to take them. We ought to have told her, "You have cancer. You are going to die." Some devout women would have done so, I am sure, if we had left them alone with her. (In their place I should have been afraid of provoking the sin of rebellion in Maman, which would have earned her centuries of purgatory.) Maman did not want these intimate conversations. What she wanted to see round her bed was young smiling faces. "I shall have plenty of time to see other old women like me when I am in a rest-home," she said to her grandnieces. She felt herself safe with Jeanne, Marthe and two or three religious but understanding friends who approved of our deception. She mistrusted the others and she spoke of some of them with a certain amount of ill-feeling—it was as though a surprising instinct enabled her to detect those people whose presence might disturb her peace of mind. "As for those women at the club, I shall not go to see them again. I shall not go back there."

People may think "Her faith was only on the surface, a matter of words, since it did not hold up in the face of suffering and death." I do not know what faith is. But her whole life turned upon religion; religion was its very substance: papers that we found in her desk confirm this. If she had looked upon prayer as nothing but a mechanical droning, telling her beads would not have tired her anymore than doing the crossword. The fact that she did not pray convinces me that on the contrary she found it an exercise that called for concentration, thought and a certain condition of soul. She knew what she ought to have said to God—"Heal me. But Thy will be done: I acquiesce in death." She did not acquiesce. In this moment of truth she did not choose to utter insincere words. But at the same time she did not grant herself the right to rebel. She remained silent: "God is kind."

"I can't understand," said the bewildered Mademoiselle Vauthier. "Your mother is so religious and so pious, and yet she is so afraid of death!" Did she not know that saints have died convulsed and shrieking?

Besides, Maman was not afraid of either God or the Devil: only of leaving this earth. My grandmother had known perfectly well that she was dying. Contentedly she said, "I am going to eat one last little boiled egg, and then I am going to join Gustave again." She had never put much passion into living; at eighty-four she was gloomily vegetating; dying did not disturb or vex her. My father showed no less courage. "Ask your mother not to get a priest to come," he said to me. "I don't want to act a part." And he gave instructions on certain practical matters. Ruined, embittered, he accepted the void with the same serenity that Grandmama accepted Paradise. Maman loved life as I love it and in the face of death she had the same feeling of rebellion that I have. During her last days I received many letters with remarks on my most recent book: "If you had not lost your faith death would not terrify you so," wrote the devout, with rancorous commiseration. Well-intentioned readers urged, "Disappearing is not of the least importance: your works will remain." And inwardly I told them all that they were wrong. Religion could do no more for my mother than the hope of posthumous success could do for me. Whether you think of it as heavenly or as earthly, if you love life immortality is no consolation for death.

John Mortimer

CLINGING TO THE WRECKAGE

A neighbour, walking along the common, kept an eye on my mother's house. Once she didn't answer to a ring and the police were sent for. They drove out through the snow, climbed a ladder and peered through her bedroom window to see her sitting up in bed reading Italian short stories. Usually quiet and courteous she rebuked them severely. One evening in that November, however, my mother was trying, as she had so often done with my father, to finish the crossword. Her blood pressure had been high in her last years and she had a stroke and fell on to the carpet in front of the dying logs of her modest and economical fire.

When I saw her in hospital my mother smiled. She seemed distressed but, with her immense courage, amused at her helplessness. We held hands but, as it had been so often with us, she couldn't speak.

As I say, the play [*Voyage Around My Father*] was to open on 27 November. On the 26th we worked all night, the lighting was difficult, the stage machinery didn't work, the overworked Greenwich technicians were exhausted and no one had any particular faith in a play that had no story and was more about blindness than sex. The next day part of my life, which had been, and perhaps should have stayed, my own private and particular concern, was to be revealed. I sat in the deserted stalls of the theatre, watching an endless lighting rehearsal, drinking cooling instant coffee, and became filled with gloom and apprehension. Far away from the theatre she wouldn't visit, in a small country hospital, my mother died without regaining her speech. The next night her part was taken by an actress.

ON SIR RICHARD BURTON

His anecdotes about his mother were written lightly, with little apparent feeling. The first, and probably the most significant, is a story of betrayal. We do not know who told him the story, or how many times in his childhood he heard it repeated. But at age fifty-five, when Burton came to write about his mother, the first fact he recorded was that she was responsible for his being cheated out of 80,000 pounds.

Burton's final reference to his mother, describing the parting when he left her in Italy at nineteen and went off to Oxford, is bitter. "The break-up took place about the middle of the summer. It was comparatively tame. Italians marveled at the Spartan nature of the British mother, who, after the habits of fifteen years, can so easily part with her children at the cost of a lachrymose last embrace, and watering her prandial beefsteak with tears. Amongst Italian families, nothing is more common than for all the brothers and sisters to swear that they will not marry if they are to be separated from one another." If, after all these years of proximity he found her grief in parting thin, one can well believe that his mother over the years had been seductive as well as denying. He vowed on numerous occasions—as his niece reported—that he would never marry at all.

Then in 1853 Burton went off to explore what he called "the mother city of Islam," forbidden to all non-Moslems. Before he returned his mother was dead. He did not marry for another seven years—by then he was almost forty.

In Aden Burton found letters from England with news that his mother was dead. We do not know the cause; Georgiana Stisted tells us only that in moving to the new house in Bath, where her "harmless and amiable" life ended, she had said grimly upon entering it, "I smell death here." Richard still had the present he had purchased for her in Mecca; it was a curious, symbolic gift, "a red, sausage-shaped cushion strung with turquoise rings." Turquoise, he wrote later, if worn in a ring, was thought to "increase the milk of nursing mothers: hence the blue beads hung as necklaces to cattle." Eventually he gave the cushion to his sister.

Instead of returning to London to grieve even briefly with his father and sister, he chose to remain instead in the grim desert port revising his journal entries speedily for a new book. One can only guess whether he paused over his diary entry for that date which also marked his mother's death, December 18, 1854. His niece wrote sentimentally and incorrectly that he had been desperately ill with fever on that day, but a careful reading of his narrative makes it clear that though he had in fact been ill he had fully recovered by that date and was arriving in Agjogsi in excellent spirits. "The inhabitants flocked out to stare at us," he wrote, "and the women uttered cries of wonder. I advanced towards the prettiest, and fired my rifle by way of salute over her head."

Still, in recounting in his book the events of December 18, he did write a brief and sombre tale of death. "The cowherds bade us beware of lions: but a day before a girl had been dragged out of her tent, and Moslem burial could be given to only one of her legs." Then he went on in a discussion of native lion lore to say, "The people have a superstition that the king of beasts will not attack a single traveller, because such a person, they say, slew the mother of all the lions." So he did write of a death, and in fact of the killing of a mother, which was as close as he would ever come, in print, to mentioning the death of his own mother. It will be seen that in the same context he had also mentioned "a single traveller," like himself, as being somehow responsible.

J. R. Ackerley

MY FATHER AND MYSELF

Among the things that confronted my sister and me for disposal in my mother's sacred and filthy bedroom, with the great piles of ancient newspapers she had hoarded and the empty whisky bottles, was her personal luggage, her trunks and suitcases and those large cardboard boxes she had so carefully preserved. It was necessary to find out what they contained before deciding whether to store them or to take them along to her new flat—though, her memory going, if not gone, she asked for nothing and seemed hardly aware of what was happening in the world outside. I was personally curious too; I might find some useful information, letters, etc., about her early life with my father. I opened the cardboard boxes first. They were full of wastepaper. The wastepaper consisted of old receipts, letters, envelopes, Christmas cards, bits of Christmas crackers, newspaper cuttings about dressmaking or cooking recipes, household lists and memoranda, old theatre programmes, visiting cards, blank pieces of paper, and literary compositions of her own— rambling verses and *pensées* in her large quill-pen writing; all these had been torn up into small fragments and put back into the boxes, which had then been secured with string. I opened her three square leather hat-boxes. They were full of wastepaper. There were two large cabin trunks. They were crammed with wastepaper. The drawers of her dressing table also contained wastepaper, excepting for two or three bundles of letters, tied with ribbon, from Harold Armstrong, my brother and myself. In the midst of this sea of torn-up paper various other objects were discovered: a few old and ragged small articles of clothing, some aged feathers and other trimmings for hats, empty jewel-cases, empty boxes, empty tins, old cosmetic and powder containers, buttons, hairpins, desiccated suppositories, decayed De Reszke and Melachrino cigarettes, old and used sanitary towels done up in tissue paper, stumps of pencils, orange-wood sticks, Red Lavender lozenges. An occasional gold or silver trinket, of no value, was found, an occasional undestroyed treasury note (£3 10s 0p in all). Suddenly, for a time excitingly, bundles would appear like presents in a bran pie, done up in tissue paper and tied with ribbon or string, or large plain envelopes, bulging and sealed. They all contained wastepaper, torn into small fragments. To this mass of rubbish clung my mother's odour of "Jicky" and Red Lavender lozenge. The last thing to be opened was an ancient battered black bag such as doctors used to carry. It was locked. No key could be found, but the leather had rotted, the bag was easily torn open. The first thing that met my eye was a page of pencilled writing in my mother's hand: "Private. Burn without reading." At last! Beneath were sundry packages tied up in ribbon. They were full of wastepaper. There was nothing else in the bag.

ACKNOWLEDGMENTS

The Publishers gratefully acknowledge the contributions of the originators of the works and sayings quoted in the book. Every effort has been made to trace the ownership of copyright in the extracts included in this anthology. Any omission is purely inadvertent and will be corrected in subsequent editions, provided written notification is given to the book's creators: The Watermark Press, 29a King Street, Sydney, NSW, 2000, Australia.

Works are listed in the order in which they first appear in the book. Extracts from the following are reprinted by kind permission of:

My Mother/My Self, by Nancy Friday/Collins/A. D. Peters
Brother of the More Famous Jack, by Barbara Trapido/Viking/Victor/Gollancz
Crazy Salad, by Nora Ephron/Bantam
Dorothy L. Sayers, by James Brabazon/Victor Gollanz/David Higham
Men and Women: How Different Are They? by John Nicholson/Oxford University Press
The French, by Theodore Zeldin/Collins
The Women's Room, by Marilyn French/André Deutsch
I, Claudius, by Robert Graves/Arthur Barker
Songs of Education: III. For the Crèche, by G. K. Chesterson/Methuen/Dodd Mead
George Bernard Shaw, by St. John Ervine/Constable/Society of Authors
The Memoirs of Sarah Bernhardt, edited and introduced by Sandy Lesberg/Peebles Press
Woman to Woman, by Gloria Vanderbilt/Garden City/Doubleday
Macbeth, by William Shakespeare
Rosemary's Baby, by Ira Levin/Michael Joseph/Hughes Massie
The Rules of the Game, by Nicholas Mosley/Secker & Warburg/A. D. Peters
Peter Finch: A Biography by Trader Faulkner/Angus & Robertson
The Pursuit of Love, by Nancy Mitford/Hamish Hamilton/ A. D. Peters
Present Indicative, by Noël Coward/William Heinemann/Methuen
My Family and Other Animals, by Gerald Durrell/Curtis Brown
Tolstoy, by Henri Troyat/trans. by Nancy Amphoux. © 1967 by Doubleday, a division of
    Bantam, Doubleday, Dell Pub. Group Inc.
When We Were Very Young, by A. A. Milne/Methuen Children's Books/McClelland &
    Stewart, Toronto
Monty: A Biography of Montgomery Clift, by Robert La Guardia/Arbor House
Confessions of an Actor, by Laurence Olivier/Weidenfeld & Nicolson
Growing Up, by Russell Baker/Congdon & Weed
A Portrait of Jane Austen, by David Cecil/Constable/Hill & Wang
A Confederacy of Dunces, by John Kennedy Toole/Penguin/Louisiana State University
    Press/© 1980 by Thelma D. Toole
Noël Coward and His Friends, by Cole Lesley, Graham Payn & Sheridan Morley/Weidenfeld
    & Nicholson
The Life of D. H. Lawrence, by Keith Sagar/Eyre-Methuen/Pantheon
R. Brooke, by Timothy Rogers/Routledge & Kegan Paul
The Kelly Hunters, by Frank Clune/Angus & Robertson
The Enchanted Places, by Christopher Milne/Eyre Methuen/E. P. Dutton
The Complete Works of Saki, by H. H. Munro/The Bodley Head/Viking Press reprinted by
    permission of Viking Penguin

Mother and Son: A Japanese Correspondence, by Isoko and Ichiro Hatano/Chatto & Windus/ Houghton Mifflin

Chaplin: His Life and Art, by David Robinson/Collins

Percy Grainger, by John Bird/Grafton Books

Lautrec, by Lautrec/Macmillan/London & Basingstoke

The Works of Oscar Wilde, edited, with an introduction, by G. F. Maine/Collins

The Godfather, by Mario Puzo/William Heinemann/Putnam Publishing Group

Mothers and Daughters, compiled by Ingeborg Day, June 1975/Ms. Magazine Corp.

God on the Rocks, by Jane Gardham/Hamish Hamilton/Willliam Morrow

The Devil Drives: A Life of Sir Richard Burton, by Fawn M. Brodie/Eyre & Spottiswode/ W. W. Norton

The Bell Jar, by Sylvia Plath/Faber & Faber/Harper & Row

Journal of a Wife, by Anaïs Nin/Quartet Books

Hotel Du Lac, by Anita Brookner/Jonathan Cape

Love in a Cold Climate, by Nancy Mitford/A. D. Peters

Nancy Cunard, by Anne Chisholm/Alfred A. Knopf Inc./Sidgwick & Jackson

The Eye of the Storm, by Patrick White/Jonathan Cape/Viking Press

Lady Into Woman, by Vera Brittain/Vera Brittain's letter of dedication to her daughter, Shirley Williams, from *Lady Into Woman,* Andrew Dakers 1953, is incl. with permission of her literary executors.

Lady Sings the Blues, by Billie Holiday with William Dufty/Barrie & Jenkins, Ltd./Sphere Books

Mothers and Daughters, by Edith G. Neisser/Harper & Row

Diane Arbus, by Patricia Bosworth/William Heinemann

Imperial Mother, Royal Daughter, by Oliver Bernier/Sidgwick & Jackson

The Book of Laughter and Forgetting, by Milan Kundera (trans. by Heim)/Alfred A. Knopf Inc.

Franny & Zooey by J. D. Salinger/William Heinemann

Low Life, by Jeffrey Bernard in *The Spectator*

Dearest Mama: Letters to the Crown Princess of Russia, by Queen Victoria/Unwin Hyman

The Making of an Assassin: The Life of James Earl Ray, by George McMillan/Little, Brown & Co.

Women of Ideas and What Men Have Done to Them, by Dale Spender/Routledge & Kegan Paul

The Home of Today, Daily Express Publications

George Orwell: A Life by Bernard Crick/Martin Secker & Warburg

Victorian Outsider: A Biography of J. A. M. Whistler by Roy McMullen/Lescher & Lescher

Portnoy's Complaint by Philip Roth/Jonathan Cape/Deborah Rogers

Queen of the Head Hunters, by Sylvia, Lady Brooke/Sidgwick & Jackson/Willliam Morrow

The Secret Diary of Adrian Mole by Sue Townsend/Methuen, London

Out of This Century: Confessions of an Art Addict, by Peggy Guggenheim/Universe Books/ NY 1979 © 1979 P. Guggenheim

My Father and Myself, by J. R. Ackerley/David Higham

Clinging to the Wreckage, by John Mortimer/Weidenfeld and Nicolson/© Advanpress

Nostalgia Isn't What It Used to Be, by Simone Signoret/Weidenfeld & Nicolson

The Watcher on the Cast-Iron Balcony, by Hal Porter/Faber & Faber

The Tin Drum, by Günter Grass trans. by Ralph Manheim/Martin Secker & Warburg/ Pantheon Books

My Life and My Films, by Jean Renoir/Collins/Little, Brown & Co.

Collected Poems by George Barker/Faber & Faber

Laughter in the Next Room by Osbert Sitwell/Macmillan/David Higham

Whistler, by Frances Spalding/Phaidon Press, Oxford 1979

Salvador Dali: The Surrealist Jester, by Meryle Secrest/Weidenfeld & Nicolson/Murray Pollinger

Indiscretions of Archie, by P. G. Wodehouse/Herbert Jenkins/Penguin

Words, by Jean-Paul Sartre/Hamish Hamilton/Editions Gallimard

Father and Son, by Edmund Gosse/William Heinemann/Scribner's

Memoirs of a Dutiful Daughter, by Simone de Beauvoir/André Deutsch/Weidenfeld & Nicolson

Queen Victoria's Early Letters, ed. by J. Raymond/Batsford
Young Samuel Johnson, by James L. Clifford/William Heinemann/McGraw-Hill
Beardsley: A Biography, by Stanley Weintraub/W. H. Allen/A. D. Peters
American Caesar: Douglas MacArthur, by William Manchester/Hutchinson
Lake Wobegon Days, by Garrison Keillor/Faber & Faber/Viking Penguin
Life of Charles Dickens, by F. T. Marzials/John G. Murdoch & Co.
Letters Home, by Sylvia Plath, ed. by Aurelia S. Plath/Faber & Faber/Harper & Row
Woman to Child from *Collected Poems 1942–70*, by Judith Wright/© Judith Wright 1971/
    Angus & Robertson
Collected Poems, by Sylvia Plath, ed. by Ted Hughes/Faber & Faber
Passages, by Gail Sheehy/E. P. Dutton/Bantam
H. G. Wells: Aspects of a Life, by Anthony West/Hutchinson/Anthony Sheil
A Woman of Her Times, by G. J. Scrimgeour/Michael Joseph/Ed Victor
The Return of the Native, by Thomas Hardy/Penguin
Mother R.: Eleanor Roosevelt's Untold Story, by Elliot Roosevelt and James Brough/G. P.
    Putnam's Sons
Anne Deveson's Memories of Jonathon, by Rosemary Munday in *The Australian Women's
    Weekly*/Australian Consolidated Press
A Very Easy Death, by Simone de Beauvoir/André Deutsch/Weidenfeld & Nicolson/G. P.
    Putnam's Sons

*The editor gratefully acknowledges the work of the compilers and publishers of the following books,
which frequently provoked recall and proved to be invaluable sources of reference.*

The Penguin Dictionary of Modern Quotations, by J. M. and M. J. Cohen
The Oxford Book of Aphorisms, chosen by John Gross/Oxford University Press

The editor would also like to thank the following for their invaluable help: Simon Blackall,
Elizabeth Blackall, Kate Foord, Gwen Ormiston, and Diane Wallis. Special thanks to
Claude Parsons and James Somerled for access to their extensive libraries.

PICTURE CREDITS

INDEX